Nadezhda Durova
THE CAVALRY MAID

The Memoirs of a Woman Soldier of 1812
Translated by John Mersereau, Jr. & David Lapeza

Ardis, Ann Arbor

Nadezhda Durova, *The Cavalry Maid*
Copyright © 1988 by Ardis Publishers
All rights reserved under International and Pan-American Copyright Conventions.
Printed in the United States of America

Ardis Publishers
2901 Heatherway
Ann Arbor, Michigan 48104

Library of Congress Cataloging in Publication Data

Durova, N. A. (Nadezhda Andreevna), 1783-1866.
The cavalry maid.

Translation of: Zapiski kavalerist-devitsy.
Bibliography: p.
1. Durova, N. A. (Nadezhda Andreevna), 1783-1866.
2. Russia. Armiia. Kavaleriia—Biography. 3. Soldiers—
Soviet Union—Biography. 4. Napoleonic Wars, 1800-1814—
—Personal narratives, Russian. 5. Authors, Russian—
Biography. 1. Title.
DK190.6.D8D87 1987 940.2'7 87-17563
ISBN 0-87501-032-6 (alk. paper)

Introduction

Nadezhda Durova (1783-1866) is surely one of the most unusual figures in the history of Russian literature and in the history of Russia as well. At a time and in a country where careers in the military and, with few exceptions, in literature were open exclusively to men, Durova found a vocation in both. Masquerading as a young man, she joined a cavalry regiment in 1806 and served with valor in the Napoleonic Wars. Some twenty years after her retirement from active service, with the encouragement of Alexander Pushkin, she wrote her memoirs, whose publication in 1836 initiated a brief but productive period as a writer of society tales and ethnic sketches.

Durova was the daughter of a Russian officer and a woman from the Ukrainian gentry, whose parents adamantly opposed the match. The young couple later eloped, provoking a parental curse. Durova's parents had counted on the birth of a son to appease the intransigent maternal grandfather, but their hopes were dashed when their first-born, Nadezhda, was a girl. The mother did not get over her disappointment. She was constantly irritated by this child, whose poor health added to the difficulties of the family's itinerant life in the military. On one occasion when the child would not stop crying the exasperated mother threw the infant from the window of her carriage. From that time on, her father arranged for his wife and daughter to be kept apart as much as possible, and the little girl was entrusted almost exclusively to the care of a hussar, Astakhov. Her earliest interests were horses, arms, and military drills, which further estranged her from her mother. When the child was almost five, her father retired from the military and became mayor of Sarapul, a provincial town on the Kama River about 250 kilometers east of Kazan. For the next several years Durova's mother waged her own educational campaign in needlework and housekeeping to counteract Astakhov's training, but in vain and to her increasing chagrin. Young Nadezhda took every opportunity to exercise her freedom, constantly dreaming of a military career. At twelve she used to sneak out of the house at night to ride her Circassian stallion, Alcides, an animal which repaid her affection with unwavering obedience.

Unable to control her daughter, Mme. Durova sent her off to relatives in the Ukraine, where she enjoyed considerably greater freedom and happiness than before, and gradually became reconciled to the life of a young lady. A budding love affair with the son of a neighbor was summarily broken off when the suitor's mother learned that Nadezhda had virtually no dowry. At sixteen she was summoned home to Sarapul, since her mother thought that Nadezhda's presence might curb her husband's philandering. The plan was unsuccessful, and Mme. Durova increasingly sought seclusion. Nadezhda now spent many hours learning equestrian skills from her father, and at this time her dream of a military career was reborn.

While tormenting Nadezhda with her futile attempts to make her conform to the behavior expected of a young lady, her mother constantly railed against the lot of women, bitterly decrying the doleful role to which fate had condemned the weaker sex. Determined to escape her lot, Nadezhda did not seek emancipation or the social success by which women of the period might hope to achieve a certain equality with men; rather, she simply refused to accept her role as a woman. Writing about her feelings, she declared:

> My mother, burdened with grief, now painted the fate of women in even more terrible colors. With incredible force, martial fever blazed in my soul, dreams swarmed in my mind, and I began to seek the means to realize my previous intention—to be a soldier, to be a son to my father, and to separate myself forever from the sex whose fate and eternal dependence had begun to frighten me.

Acceding to the wishes of her parents, in October, 1801, she married a petty civil servant, Vasily Chernov. A son, Ivan, was born in January, 1803, but Nadezhda soon returned to her parents' home, leaving her child with its father. Not a word about this marriage is found in her autobiography.

At home the conflict with her mother resumed, and when a Cossack regiment arrived in Sarapul, she saw an opportunity to realize her dream. In 1806, when the regiment departed, she cut off her hair, dressed herself as a Cossack youth, and with her beloved stallion, Alcides, overtook the troops at their next bivouac. She was able to persuade the colonel that she was a Russian nobleman, Alexander Durov, who had left home for family reasons and wished to join the army. The colonel took her under his protection, and she traveled with the regiment on its lengthy trek to the Don basin. She stayed there with the Colonel's family and then accompanied the regiment to Grodno, on the Polish-Lithuanian border. There she was able to enlist in the Konnopolsk Uhlan Regiment as a cavalry soldier. Her training was particularly arduous—exhausting drills with sabre and lance, and cavalry exercises requiring her to jump her horse over obstacles—but she accepted all this as necessary to fulfill her dream. What she complained about the most were the torments of the heavy government issue boots, with their huge rattling spurs, which seemed to chain her to the ground.

When she completed her training, Durova was assigned to a combat squadron, and in May, 1807, she first saw action in the Battle of Guttstadt. The experience provided a satisfyingly exhilarating spectacle, posed personal danger to the young cavalryman, and confirmed that she had made a correct choice of vocation. For the rest of the month she was engaged in skirmishes and battles, and at the end of May she witnessed the carnage at the Battle of Heilsberg. Despite her ardor, she made a number of mistakes which might easily have caused her death or capture, including twice losing her horse, falling asleep despite orders, and valiantly rescuing a wounded soldier. In June, 1807, after the Battle of Friedland in which more than half her regiment was lost, she was ordered to the baggage train by General Kakhovsky, who was exasperated with her reckless bravery and undisciplined conduct.

After Alexander I and Napoleon signed the treaty of Tilsit on June 25, Durova's regiment was quartered in Poland, where she engaged in the menial tasks of garrison life. This is the most poignant section of her memoirs, for here she describes the accidental death of her beloved Alcides. While returning from watering at the river, the horse broke loose from his mistress and impaled himself on a post while jumping a fence. In the midst of her grief, orders arrived for her to report to staff headquarters. Thus began her journey to St. Petersburg, where Alexander awarded her the St. George's Cross for valor and promoted her to the officer's rank of cornet. Having received Durova's confession that she was not a man, the tsar gave her official permission to use the name Alexandrov, which she did for the rest of her life.

Durova returned to Sarapul and her father soon afterward, and lived there for more than two years. In 1811, she rejoined the army enlisting in the Lithuanian Uhlan Regiment.

When Napoleon attacked Russia in May of 1812, Durova served with the Russian rear guard, which was constantly under attack, until the battle of Borodino, where she was wounded. The famous hussar poet, Denis Davydov, noted, in a letter to Pushkin in 1836, that he had seen her briefly during the retreat and that one of her fellow officers had casually mentioned to him it was said that Alexandrov was a woman. Davydov later saw her at the front. After Borodino, Durova's wound resisted treatment, and, following a brief period as orderly to General Kutuzov, she was ordered home to recuperate. Her father was in ecstasy about his daughter's exploits and her association with the hero Kutuzov, but he so constantly embarrassed her by reading to visitors and friends a letter to her from the General that she burned it.

Durova's original memoir ends at this point. Subsequently she took part in the Prussian campaign of 1813, seeing action in several important encounters. She retired permanently in 1816 only at the repeated requests of her father. She held the rank of captain of cavalry.

In 1835 Durova's brother proposed that Pushkin, whom he knew slightly, edit his sister's memoirs. The poet responded favorably, admonishing the memoirist to avoid "ornamentation": "As far as style is concerned, the simpler the better. The chief thing: truth, sincerity. The subject itself is so engaging that no ornamentation is needed. It would even spoil it." (June 16, 1835)

Durova sent her manuscript to Pushkin for publication in April, 1835, but by a series of accidents, both the original notebooks and her only copy (sent under separate cover) were mislaid by the post for nearly a year. Durova was in despair. When the original was recovered in the spring of 1836, Durova arrived in Petersburg from Sarapul, to deliver her manuscript personally, after a journey of over six weeks by carriage. She was hospitably received by Pushkin, who printed a selection of her work in *The Contemporary* entitled *Notes of a Cavalry-Maiden* (2:1836, pp.53-132). The entire memoir shortly appeared in book form with the title *Cavalry-Maiden. An Event in Russia,* but without the author's name. Pushkin had taken the liberty of changing Durova's original title, *Autobiographical Notes of a Russian Amazon, generally known as Alexandrov,* which he declared "reminiscent of German novels." (June 10, 1836)

In Petersburg Durova created something of a sensation, not only because of her extraordinary past, but because she continued her male disguise, keeping her hair short, wearing a man's frock coat and trousers, and even smoking a pipe. She referred to herself in the male gender and was irritated when others did not. She preferred to be addressed as "Alexander Alexeyevich." Curiously, Durova apparently wrote her memoirs largely for a female audience, urging Pushkin to buy rights to her manuscript because it might be "highly entertaining for our fellow-countrywomen" (August 5, 1835).

Durova did not enjoy her stay in the capital. In *A Year of Life in Petersburg, or The Disadvantages of a Third Visit* (1838), she recounted her reception in society, noting that on the first visit she was the object of general interest and lionized, on the second no special attention was paid to her, and on the third visit she was ignored or rebuffed. Despite a favorable review of her memoirs by the influential critic Vissarion Belinsky, who even suggested that the work was so masterful that it may have been a "mystification" by Pushkin himself, Durova found herself with several hundred unsold copies, and nearly penniless. She finally found a purchaser, and the proceeds of the sale allowed her to return home.

For the next four years Durova was very active as an author. Soon after the appearance of her *Notes, The Library for Reading* carried her tale, *The Beauty from T., or The Game of Fate,* a story protesting the treatment of women, which doubtless had strong autobiographical relevance to her brief but unhappy marriage. Perhaps her most successful tale, *The Pavilion,* was published in *Notes of the Fatherland* and merited a lengthy review by Belinsky. In 1839 her *Notes of Alexandrov. By Durova. Addendum to The Cavalry Maid,* a collection of anecdotes primarily about her adventures and encounters while serving as an officer in peacetime, was published in Moscow by N. Stepanov's printing house. Durova produced several more works in 1839, including *Gudishki,* a novel in four parts, and in 1840, three more tales. So prolific was she that Belinsky noted "Mr. Alexandrov has apparently decided to give us a tale every month." However, 1840 marked the last year of her literary career, and she published nothing at all after that. Durova seems simply to have exhausted the store of personal experiences from which she crafted her tales.

The last years of Durova's life were spent in Yelabuga, a small town east of Kazan which, like Sarapul, was close to the Kama River. Her very modest military pension permitted only a life of extreme frugality, a circumstance made worse by her efforts to help stray animals and intercessions on behalf of the poor. She died at the age of 83 in 1866 and was buried with military honors in Yelabuga. In 1901 a monument was erected on her grave with the epitaph:

> Nadezhda Andreyevna Durova, by order of the Emperor Alexander—cornet Alexandrov, Knight of military order. Moved by love of her motherland, she entered the ranks of the Lithuanian Uhlan Regiment. She rescued an officer and was awarded the George Cross. She served 10 years in the regiment, was promoted to cornet and achieved the rank of captain of cavalry. Born 1783. Died 1866. Peace to her ashes! May her valorous spirit serve eternally as an exemplar to posterity!

John Mersereau, Jr.
David Lapeza

The Cavalry Maid

FROM THE PUBLISHER

The authoress of the *Memoirs* presented here, my cousin, has charged me to publish them absolutely unchanged. I willingly comply with her desire, supposing that an event, flattering to our national pride, and one which took place in such a famous epoch—during our conflict with Napoleon, is worthy of preservation for the curiosity of our contemporaries and in the memory of posterity.

Ivan Butovsky

Part One

My Childhood Years

My mother, daughter of the landowner Alexandrov, was one of the most beautiful young women in Little Russia. At the end of her fifteenth year a crowd of eligible young men appeared seeking her hand. From this multitude my mother's heart gave preference to a hussar lieutenant named Durov. Unfortunately, however, this choice was not the choice of her father, a proud, autocratic Little Russian *pan*. He told my mother to cast from her mind the chimerical idea of marrying a damned Muscovite, and particularly a military man. My grandfather was a great despot in family matters. If he ordered something, one had to obey blindly, and there was no way to move him or to change his mind once he had made it up. The result of this unrestrained strictness was that one stormy night my mother, who slept in a separate room with an older sister, quietly got out of bed and, having taken her cape and hood, wearing only her socks and holding her breath, crept by her sister's bed, quietly opened the door into the salon, quickly ran through it, opened the door to the garden, flew like an arrow down the long chestnut-lined alley, ending up at the garden gate. My mother quickly unlocked the small door and threw herself into the embrace of the lieutenant, who had been awaiting her with a carriage and four strong horses, which, like the blustering wind, carried them off along the Kiev road.

They were married at the first village, and then drove straight to Kiev, where Durov's regiment was stationed. My mother's action might have been excused owing to her youth, her love, and the merits of my father, who was a most handsome man possessing a gentle nature and captivating manner, but he was so alien to the patriarchal customs of the Little Russian region that my grandfather, in his initial fit of anger, cursed his daughter.

In the course of two years my mother never stopped writing to her father and begging his forgiveness, but in vain. He would listen to nothing, and his anger increased as efforts were made to mollify him. My parents, having lost all hope of touching a man who considered stubbornness a sign of character, were about to accept their fate and ceased writing to the intractable father. But my mother's pregnancy revived her faltering courage, and she began to hope that the birth of a child would regain her father's blessing.

My mother passionately wanted a son, and through the whole course of her pregnancy was occupied with the most seductive dreams. She would say, "A son will be born to me as handsome as Cupid! I will name him Modest, I myself will nourish, educate and teach him, and my son, my dear

Modest, will be the solace of my life." So did my mother dream, but her time approached and the pains preceding my birth surprised my mother in the most unpleasant way. They had no place in her dreams and produced her first negative impression of me. An obstetrician had to be called, and he found it necessary to let her blood. My mother was extremely frightened by this, but there was no alternative, so she had to submit to necessity. The blood was let, and shortly afterward I appeared on earth, a miserable being whose appearance destroyed all the dreams and overturned all of my mother's hopes.

"Give me my child!" said my mother, as soon as she had somewhat recovered from her pain and fear. The child was brought and put on her knee. But alas! This was not a son as handsome as Cupid! This was a daughter, and an Amazon! I was unusually large, had thick black hair, and was crying loudly. My mother pushed me from her knees and turned to the wall.

After several days my mama recovered and, acceding to the advice of the ladies of the regiment, her friends, decided to feed me herself. They told her that a mother who breastfeeds her child will begin to love it. They brought me to her, my mother took me from the arms of the women, placed me on her bosom to let me nurse. Clearly, however, I felt that it was not maternal love which was feeding me, and therefore, despite all the efforts to force me to nurse, I would not. Mama thought to overcome my stubbornness with patience and continued to hold me at her breast. But becoming bored when I continued to refuse, she stopped looking at me and began to speak with the lady who was her guest. At that moment, apparently directed by the fate which had destined me for a soldier's greatcoat, I suddenly grabbed my mother's breast and with all my strength pinched it with my gums. My mother let out a piercing cry, shoved me from her breast, and throwing me into the hands of the woman, fell face down on a pillow.

"Get this worthless child out of my sight and don't ever show her to me again," my mother said, waving her hand and covering her head with her pillow.

I was four months old when the regiment in which my father served was ordered to Kherson. Since this was a local move, my father took his family with him. I was entrusted to the supervision and care of my mother's housemaid, who was the same age as she. During the day this young woman would sit in the carriage with my mother, holding me on her knees. She fed me cow's milk from a horn and swaddled me so tightly that my face turned blue and my eyes filled with blood. I was able to rest at night, because they would give me to a peasant woman brought in from the village. She would take off the swaddling clothes, place me on her bosom, and sleep with me the whole night. Thus at each stopover, I had a new wet nurse.

My health didn't suffer either from the changing of the wet nurses or the painful swaddling. I was very strong and bold, but unbelievably noisy. One day my mother was in a very bad mood. I had not let her sleep all night, and the troops had set off at dawn. Mama prepared herself to sleep in the carriage, but I began to cry again, and despite all the efforts of the nurse to quiet me, I cried louder by the hour. My mother's anger boiled over, she became beside herself, and grabbing me from the hands of the maid, threw me out the window! The hussars cried out in terror, jumped from their horses, and picked me up. I was all covered with blood and gave no sign of life. They were about to take me back to the carriage, but my father galloped up, took me from their arms, and streaming with tears, put me next to him on the saddle. He was shaking and crying and pale as death. He rode without saying a word and without turning his head toward where my mother was riding. To everyone's astonishment I returned to life and was not disfigured, as they had expected; only my nose and mouth bled from the heavy impact. Father raised his eyes to heaven. With joyous feelings of gratitude, he pressed me to his breast, and approaching the carriage, said to my mother, "Thank God that you are not a murderess! Our daughter is alive, but I will not let you care for her any longer—I will watch over her myself." Having said this, he rode off, and until we bivouacked he carried me with him, without looking at my mother or saying a word to her.

From that memorable day in my life my father entrusted me to God's providence and the supervision of flank hussar Astakhov, who was inseparable from father both in quarters and on campaign. Only at night was I in my mother's room, but as soon as father would get up and leave, he would take me with him. My mentor Astakhov carried me in his arms for days at a time, he would walk with me to the squadron stables, sit me on horses, let me play with his pistol, would wave his sabre, and I would clap my hands and laugh at the sight of the showering sparks and flashing steel. In the evening he would take me to the musicians, who played various pieces before sunset. I would listen and finally fall asleep. Only when asleep could I be taken to the bedroom, for at the very sight of my mother's room I became paralyzed with fear, and with a wail would throw my arms around Astakhov's neck. From the time of my flight through the air from the carriage my mother had nothing to do with me and consoled herself with her other daughter, who was absolutely as beautiful as Cupid and on whom, as they say, she doted.

Soon after my birth my grandfather forgave my mother, and he did this in a quite ceremonious manner. He traveled to Kiev, begged the bishop to absolve him from his thoughtless vow never to forgive his daughter, and, having received the priest's dispensation, also wrote my mother that he forgave her, blessed her marriage and the child born of it, and asked her to come to him in person to accept her father's blessing and receive her share of a dowry. My mother had no opportunity to make use of this invitation until the time came for father to retire.

I was four and a half when my father found it necessary to leave the service. In his room, in addition to my little bed, were two other cribs. A life of campaigns with such a family was out of the question. He went to Moscow to seek a place in the civil service. My mother, along with me and the two other children, set forth to her father's, where we were to live until the return of her husband. Having removed me from Astakhov's care, my mother couldn't for a minute be calm or cheerful. Every day I angered her with my strange antics and chivalrous spirit. I knew all the military commands perfectly, I was insanely in love with horses, and when my mother tried to force me to crochet, I would tearfully beg her to give me a pistol, as I would say, "to crack." In a word, I couldn't have made better use of the education which Astakhov had given me! With every day my military instincts increased, and with every day my mother loved me less. I never forgot anything that I had learned all the time I had been with the hussars. I ran and jumped about the bedroom in all directions, I cried out at the top of my voice, "Squadron, Right Turn!, Ready, March!" My aunts laughed, but mama, who was in despair at all this, knew no limits to her chagrin. She would take me into her bedroom, stand me in a corner, and make me cry bitterly with her scolding and threats.

My father received a position as mayor of one of the district towns and set off for there with the entire family. My mother, who disliked me from the bottom of her heart, deliberately did everything, it seemed, that would strengthen and intensify my unbounded passion for freedom and a military life. She wouldn't let me walk in the garden. She wouldn't let me be away from her for even half an hour: I had to sit in her bedroom and make lace. She herself taught me to sew, to knit, and seeing that I had neither the desire nor the ability for this sort of work, that in my hands everything tore or broke, she became angry, lost control of herself, and beat me very painfully on the hands.

I reached the age of ten. Mama was careless enough to tell my father in my presence that she lacked the strength to handle Astakhov's pupil, that his hussar training had put down deep roots, that she was afraid of the fire in my eyes, and that she would rather see me dead than with such inclinations. Father responded that I was still a child, that it wasn't necessary for her to watch out for me, that as I grew older I would develop other inclinations, and all this would pass. "Don't put so much importance on this childishness, my friend," father said. It was fated that my mother neither believed nor followed the good advice of her husband. She continued to keep me locked up and didn't allow me a single childish pleasure. I kept silent and obeyed, but the oppression led me to think in a mature way. I developed the firm intention of throwing off this heavy yoke, and I began to work out a plan to succeed when I became an adult. I determined to use every means to learn how to ride, to fire a gun, and then, wearing different clothes, to leave my father's home. In order to put into action the proposed change in my life, I didn't let slip a single opportunity to escape my mother's supervision. These chances came every time mama had guests. She would be busy with them and, out of my mind with joy, I would run into the garden to my arsenal, that is, to the dark corner beyond the shrubbery where I kept my arrows, a bow, a sabre and a broken musket. Occupied with my weapons, I would forget the whole world, and only the piercing cries of the maids who were looking for me would make me run fearfully to them. They would lead me to the bedroom where punishment always awaited me.

In this way two years passed, and I was already twelve. At this time father bought a riding horse, a Circassian stallion, almost unbreakable. Being an excellent horseman, my father trained this beautiful animal and named him Alcides. Now all my plans, hopes and desires focused on this horse. I decided to do everything I could to accustom him to me, and I succeeded. I gave him bread, sugar, salt, I secretly took oats from the coachman and sprinkled them in his manger. I would pet him and caress him and talk to him as if he were able to understand me, and finally it got to the point that this intractable horse would follow me around like a tame lamb.

Almost every day I arose at dawn, quietly left my room, and ran to the stable. Alcides would meet me with a neigh, I would give him bread and sugar and take him into the courtyard. Then I would lead him to the staircase and mount him from the stairs. His rapid movements, his leaping about, and his snorting didn't frighten me. Holding onto his mane, I would let him gallop all over the broad courtyard, without being afraid that I might be carried outside the gates, because they were still locked. It happened once that this entertainment was interrupted by the arrival of the stableman, who, crying out in alarm and surprise, made haste to stop the galloping Alcides. The horse turned his head, reared up, and began to gallop around the courtyard, jumping and kicking. Fortunately for me, Yefim, who was frozen from fear, lost the use of his voice, for otherwise his cry would have aroused the whole house and brought a terrible punishment upon me. I easily quieted Alcides, soothing him with my voice, tousling his mane and stroking him. He went at a walk, and when I embraced his neck and leaned my face toward it, he completely stopped, because that was the way I always dismounted or, to put it correctly, slid off him. At that point Yefim approached to take hold of him, muttering through his teeth that he would tell my mother, but I promised to give him all my pocket money if he would say nothing and let me lead Alcides to the stable. At this promise Yefim's visage cleared, he laughed, stroked his beard, and said, "Well, have it your way if this scamp obeys you better than me!" In triumph I led Alcides to the stable, and, to Yefim's astonishment, the wild horse followed me quietly and, arching his neck and bending over my head, lightly pulled at my hair or shoulder with his lips.

Every day I became more daring and audacious, and, except for my mother's wrath, was afraid of absolutely nothing. It was quite strange to me that my siblings were afraid of being alone in the dark while I, on the contrary, was ready at midnight itself to go to the cemetery, the forest, into an empty house, into a cave, or a vault. In a word, there was no place where I would not go as confidently at night as during the day, although I, like the other children, had been regaled with tales of ghosts, corpses, forest spirits, bandits, and water nymphs who tickled people to death. Although I totally believed all this nonsense, I was in no way frightened by it. On the contrary, I thirsted for danger, I wanted to be surrounded by it, and I would have sought it out if I had been given the slightest freedom. But the tireless eye of my mother followed my every step, my every movement.

One day mama went with some ladies for a walk in the deep woods beyond the Kama River, and she took me with her, according to her, so that I wouldn't break my skull if left alone at home. This was the first time in my life that I had been taken out in the open, where I saw a dense forest, open fields, and a broad river. I almost choked from joy, and no sooner had we entered the forest when I, unable to control myself from excitement, instantly ran off and continued running until the voices of my companions could no longer be heard. At that moment my joy was complete and overflowing. I ran, I jumped, I picked flowers, I climbed to the top of tall trees in order to see as far as possible, I climbed up delicate birches and, grasping their tops with my hands, jumped away, and the young tree would deposit me lightly on the ground. Two hours passed like two minutes! Meanwhile, they were looking for me, and several voices were calling. I heard them, but how could I part with such captivating freedom? Finally, having become completely worn out, I returned to the group. I had no difficulty finding them, because the voices calling me never ceased. I found my mother and all the ladies in great distress. Catching sight of me, they cried out from joy, but mama, guessing from my satisfied expression that I had not become lost but had deliberately gone off, became very angry. She hit me on the back and called me a damned wench, pledged to anger her always and everywhere!

We returned home. Mama dragged me by the ear from the living room to her bedroom. Having set me down at the lace frame, she ordered me to get to work, and not to straighten up or turn my head. "So now, you good-for-nothing, I'll tie you with a rope and feed you only bread!" Having said this, she went to father to tell him about my, as she put it, monstrous behavior, and I was left to arrange the bobbins, set pins, and think about the beautiful nature which I had seen in all its majesty and splendor for the first time in my life. Although my mother's surveillance and severity became even more untiring, from that day they could not frighten me or hold me back.

From morning to night I sat over the work which, I have to admit, was nastier for me than anything else in the world, because unlike others I could not do it, I didn't know how to do it, and I didn't want to learn how to do it. I tore it, spoiled it, messed it up, and there in front of me was the linen sphere on which the strip of repulsive spiderweb was stretched—my lace, and I sat over it patiently all day, patiently because my plan was ready and my decision was made. As soon as night fell, the house became quiet, the doors were locked, the light was put out in mama's room. I would get up, dress quietly, stealthily go out the back porch, and run straight to the stable. There I took Alcides, led him through the garden to the cattle yard, mounted him at that point and rode through the narrow alley straight to the river bank and then to Startsov mountain. Here I would dismount and lead the horse by his halter, since, not knowing how to bridle Alcides, I could not make him willingly climb the mountain, which at that point was precipitous. So I would lead him by the halter, and when we had reached a level place I looked for a stump or a mound, from which I again mounted him. Then I would slap him on the neck and cluck with my tongue until the good horse started to canter, to jump, and even to gallop. At the first sign of dawn I returned home, put the horse in the stable, and lay down to sleep without undressing. And that was how my nocturnal excursions were finally discovered. The maid who looked after me, having found me every morning in bed completely dressed, told my mother, who undertook to find out how and why this was happening. My mother herself saw me go out in the middle of the night completely dressed and, to her inexpressible horror, lead the vicious stallion from the stable! She didn't dare stop me, thinking I was walking in my sleep, and she didn't dare to cry out for fear of frightening me, but having ordered the porter and Yefim to look after me, went to father, awakened him, and related all that had happened. My father was very surprised and got up as fast as possible to see this oddity with his own eyes. But everything ended sooner than they expected. Alcides and I were led back in triumph, each to his own place. The porter, whom mama had ordered to follow me, seeing that I wanted to get on the horse and not thinking, as my mother had, that I was sleepwalking, came out of his hiding place and asked, "Where are you going, young lady?"

After this occurrence my mother desired, whatever it cost, to be freed of my presence, and therefore decided to pack me off to my grandmother in Little Russia, old Alexandrovicheva. I was already fourteen, tall, thin, and well built. The military spirit was imprinted on the features of my face, and, although I had white skin, good color, flashing eyes and black eyebrows, still my mirror and my mama told me every day that I was quite ugly. My face had been pitted by smallpox, my features were irregular, the constant suppression of my freedom, the severity of my mother's behavior and her occasional cruelty had imprinted on my physiognomy an expression of fear and sadness. Maybe I could have forgotten all of my hussar antics and become a typical young girl like everyone else if my mother had not represented the fate of woman in such a repulsive form. In my presence she used to voice the most insulting ideas about the fate of her sex. It was her opinion that a woman must be born, live and die in slavery, that eternal slavery, oppressive dependency, and every kind of oppression is her fate from cradle to grave, that she is full of faults, deprived of all perfection, and suited for nothing. In one word, that a woman is the most miserable, most insignificant, and the most despised creature on earth.

My head swam from such a description. I determined, although it might cost me my life, to isolate myself from this sex which found itself, I thought, cursed by God. My father often used to say, "If I had a son instead of Nadezhda, I wouldn't have to think about what will happen to me in my old age. He would be my support in the evening of my days." I was on the verge of tears at the words of my father, whom I loved very deeply. Two feelings, so contradictory—love for my father and revulsion for my own sex—affected my young soul with equal force, and with a firmness and constancy unusual for someone my age, I worked at devising a plan to get away from the circumstances which nature and custom had destined for women.

In such a state of will and mind, at the beginning of my fourteenth year I was carted off to Little Russia to grandmother and left with her. My grandfather was no longer among the living. Our entire family consisted of my grandmother, a wise and venerable octogenarian, at one time a beauty and respected for her unusual virtue; her son, my uncle, a middle-aged man, handsome, kind, sensitive, and insufferably capricious, married to a young lady of exceptional beauty from the Lizogubov family in Chernigov; and finally an aunt of forty-five, a spinster. Most of all I liked my uncle's young and pretty wife, but I really never willingly remained in the company of my relatives: they were so solemn, so pious, such irreconcilable enemies of any martial inclinations in a young lady, that I even was afraid to think about my cherished intentions when in their presence. Although my freedom was not in any way restricted, and although I could wander wherever I wished from morning to night without fear of being upbraided, had I even so much as dared to mention horseback riding, I do believe they would have put me under some sort of church penance. That's how ingrained was my relatives' horror at the very thought of such criminal and unnatural activities for women, and especially young ladies!

Under the bright sky of Little Russia I became noticeably more healthy, although at the same time I became tanned, turned dark, and grew even uglier. Here I wasn't fettered and tormented to make lace. Passionately loving nature and freedom, I would spend whole days either running about the summer cottages on my uncle's estate or boating on the Uday River in a large rowboat, which in Little Russia is called a *doop*. Possibly they would not have permitted this latter entertainment had they known of it, but I had the foresight to undertake my navigation after the midday meal when the sharp eyes of my young aunt were closed with sleep. Uncle would leave to take care of farming or would read the papers, which his child-bride followed with such attention. That left only grandmother, who might have seen me, but she had poor eyesight, so with complete safety I was able to run right past her windows.

In the spring another aunt arrived, Znachko-Yavorskaya, who lived near the town of Luben. She fell in love with me and asked grandmother's permission to take me home with her for the whole summer. With her my activities and pleasures were quite different. This aunt was a strict woman, observing unfailing order and decorum in everything. She lived in an open-handed manner, was acquainted with the best society among the neighboring landowners, kept a good cook and often gave balls. I found myself in a different sphere. Never hearing complaints or reproach about the female sex, I somewhat became reconciled to my fate, especially when I saw the polite attention paid by men and their efforts to be gracious. My aunt dressed me very nicely and tried to remove the sunburn from my face. My martial dreams gradually were erased. A woman's destiny no longer seemed so terrible, and finally my new style of life became pleasing to me.

As reconciliation with my stormy thoughts progressed, a companion was provided. Living with my aunt was another relative, Ostrogradskaya, a year younger than I. We were inseparable. We spent the morning in our aunt's bedroom, reading, sketching, or playing. After dinner until teatime we were free to stroll about, so we immediately would go to the *levada* (that is what they call the piece of ground which usually adjoins the orchard and is divided from it only by a deep trench). I would jump across it with the ease of a wild goat, Cousin would follow my example, and for the period designated for our stroll we would flit about all the expanse of the neighboring *levadas*.

My aunt, like all Little Russians, was very pious, strictly observing and fulfilling all the rituals prescribed by her religion. Every holy day she went to the church service, morning and evening. My cousin and I had to do the same. At first I definitely did not like having to get up before dawn to go to church, but near us there lived a proprietress, Kiriyakova, and her son, with whom we always drove to church. While waiting for the service to begin, Kiriyakova would converse with my aunt, and her son, a young man of twenty-five, would be with us, or, to put it better, would be with me, because he spoke only with me. He was not at all bad-looking, had beautiful black eyes, black hair, black brows and a youthful freshness to his face. I became very fond of the divine liturgy and always was up for the morning service before my aunt. Finally my conversations with young Kiriyakov attracted my aunt's attention. She began to watch, to question Cousin, who immediately told her that Kiriyakov had held my hand and asked me to give him a ring, saying that then he would consider himself authorized to speak with aunty. Having received this explanation from my cousin, my aunt summoned me: "What does the son of our neighbor talk about with you every time we are together?" Not knowing how to dissemble, I told her right off about everything which had been said to me. Aunty shook her head. She didn't like this at all; "No," she declared, "that's not how one seeks a young lady's hand. And why explain himself to you! He should have consulted directly with your relatives!" After this they hauled me back to my grandmother. For a long time I yearned for young Kiriyakov. This was my first attachment, and I think that if they had let me marry him, I would have said goodbye forever to my martial intentions. But fate arranged otherwise, having destined me for the battlefield. Old Kiriyakova asked my aunt to inform her what sort of dowry I had, and learning that it consisted of several yards of linen, cloth and muslin, and nothing more, she forbade her son to think about me.

My fifteenth year had arrived when one day my uncle was brought a letter which caused everyone grief and consternation. The letter was from father. He had written my mother imploring her to forgive him, to return home, and he gave his oath to pardon everything. No one could understand anything in this letter. Where was my mother? Why was the letter addressed to her in Little Russia? Had she separated from her husband, and why? Uncle and grandmother were lost in conjectures.

Two weeks after this letter I was floating in the rowboat along the Uday and suddenly I heard the screeching voice of grandmother's bedroom maid: "Little lady, Little lady, go to Granny!" I became frightened hearing this summons to grandmother, turned the boat around and silently bade farewell to my beloved *doop,* assuming that now they would order it chained to the piling and my excursions on the river would end forever. How did it happen that grandmother had seen me, I asked, arriving at the shore. "Grandmother did not see you," Agafya answered, "but Stepan has come for you. Your mother sent him." Mother! Sent for me? Is that possible? Oh, beautiful land, must I really leave you! I went home quickly, and saw there the old servant who had been with father on all his campaigns. Grizzled Stepan politely gave me a letter. My father wrote that he and mother wished me to come to them immediately, that they are tired of being separated from me. This was incomprehensible to me. I knew that my mother did not love me, so it must be that Father wanted me there with him. But how did he get my mother to agree? No matter how much I thought about it and how much I regretted the need to leave Little Russia, or the lack of freedom awaiting me, or the unpleasant exchange of the beautiful climate for the cold and severe one, I had to obey. In two days all was ready. Much had been baked and roasted, a huge hamper was filled with goodies, and everything was packed. On the third day my respected grandmother pressed me to her bosom, kissed me, and said, "Set off, my child, and may God bless you on your journey. And may

He bless you on the path of life!" She placed her hand on my head and quietly summoned God's protection for me. This righteous woman's prayer was heard. In the course of my military life there where many instances when I felt the clear intervention of the Almighty.

There is no reason to describe the journey under old Stepan's supervision and with the companionship of Annushka, his twelve-year-old daughter. It began and ended as similar journeys begin and end. We traveled long distances slowly for a long time, and finally we arrived. Opening the door to the salon of my father's house, I heard my little sister Cleopatra say, "Come, Mother, some young lady has arrived!" Unexpectedly, my mother received me fondly. She liked seeing that I had acquired that modest and calm appearance so suitable for a young woman. Although in the year and a half I had grown considerably and was almost a head taller than Mother, I no longer had that military appearance which made me look like Achilles in women's clothes or those hussar traits which used to bring her to despair.

After I had been at home for several days, I found out the reason they had sent for me. My father, never indifferent to beauty, had betrayed my mother in her absence and taken under his protection a beautiful young girl, the daughter of a merchant. After her return mother knew nothing for some time, but one of her acquaintances thought to be of service by declaring the fatal secret, thus damaging her life with the most terrible poison of all—jealousy! My unhappy mother turned to stone listening to the story of her thoughtlessly solicitous friend. Having heard her out, my mother left without saying a word and went to bed. When father came home, she was about to speak to him mildly and calmly, but did she have the power to do so? From her first words her torn heart took over. Sobs choked her voice, she beat her breast, wrung her hands, cursed the day she was born and that minute when she had fallen in love. She begged my father to kill her and free her from the unendurable torture of living, having been scorned by him. Father was frightened by the state in which he saw mother, he tried to calm her, he begged her not to believe the absurd stories, but seeing that she was quite well informed about everything, swore by God and conscience to give up this criminal connection. Mother believed him, became calm, and forgave him. For some time father kept his word, gave up his mistress, and even found her a husband, but later he took up with her again, and at that point my mother, in despair, was ready to part forever with her faithless husband and set off to her mother in Little Russia, but stopped off in Kazan. Father, not knowing this, wrote to Little Russia, trying to persuade mother to forgive him and return, but at the same time he received a letter from my mother. She wrote that she did not have the strength to be separated from him, that she could not bear the thought of parting forever with her husband; although he had terribly humiliated her, he was nonetheless boundlessly loved! She pleaded with him to reconsider and return to his obligations. Father was touched, repented, and begged mother to return. At that point she sent for me, assuming that the presence of his beloved daughter would cause him to forget completely the unworthy object of his infatuation. Unhappy woman! She was destined to be deceived in all her expectations and to drink the bitter cup to the bottom! Father would move from one infatuation to another and was to abandon my mother. She anguished, grew thin, became sick, went for treatment to the famous Gral in Perm, and finally died at thirty-five, more a victim of misery than illness!... Alas, I wash these lines with my tears in vain now. Woe to me, the primary cause of my mother's unhappiness! My birth, sex, features, inclinations—all these were not what my mother wanted. My existence poisoned her life, and constant chagrin ruined her disposition, by nature sufficiently irascible in its own right, and made her cruel. At the same time, her unusual beauty did not save her. Father ceased to love her, and her untimely death was the end of love, hatred, suffering and unhappiness.

At this time, no longer finding pleasure in society, mama led a secluded life. Capitalizing upon this circumstance, I asked father for permission to ride horseback. Father ordered a Cossack's coat sewn for me and made me a gift of Alcides. From that time I was my father's constant companion on his excursions out of town. He took pleasure in teaching me to sit attractively, to be firm in the saddle, and to direct the horse with ease. I was a capable student. Father adored my lightness and absence of fear. He said I was the living image of his own youth and that I would have been the support of his old age and an honor to his name had I been born a boy! My head used to whirl, but now the whirling was constant. I was no child. I was already sixteen. The seductive pleasures of society, life in Little Russia and Kiriyakov's black eyes were erased in my memory like a dream, but my childhood, spent in military camps among hussars, was sketched out in living colors in my imagination. Everything was reborn in my soul. I could not understand now how for almost two years I had done nothing about my plan. My mother, burdened with grief, now painted the fate of women in even more terrible colors. With incredible force, martial fever blazed in my soul, dreams swarmed in my mind, and I began to seek the means to realize my previous intention—to be a soldier, to be a son to my father, and to separate myself forever from the sex whose fate and eternal dependence had begun to frighten me.

Mother was no longer going for treatment when a Cossack regiment arrived in our town. Father often invited the colonels and officers to our house to dine, and he rode with them on excursions out of town. But I had the foresight never to take part in these excursions... It was vital that I should never be seen in my Cossack's coat or that they should have any idea about how I looked in men's clothing. A ray of light had illuminated my mind when the Coassacks rode into town! Now I saw a likely means to fulfill my long intended plan. I saw the possibility of waiting until the Cossacks departed and then going with them to the place where regular regiments were stationed.

Finally the decisive time arrived to put the plan I had prepared into action. The Cossacks had received their orders to move out. They left on the 15th of September, 1806. When they reached fifty versts* from town, they were to lay over for a day. The 17th was my nameday, and the day on which fate, coincidence or irresistible urge had determined that I was to leave my parental home and begin a completely new style of life. On the 17th I awoke before dawn and sat in the window awaiting its arrival. This might be the last one I would have in my native country! What awaits me in the stormy world? Will not my mother's curse and my father's grief pursue me? Will they live through it? Will my gigantic plan be met with success? It would be terrible if its failure were to deprive me of my goal. These thoughts flocked into my head, one replacing the next. My heart contracted and tears glistened on my lashes.

At this moment dawn arrived, the sky became scarlet, and its beautiful light, pouring into my room, illuminated the objects in it: my father's sabre, which was hanging on the wall opposite the window, seemed to be afire. My thoughts became animated. I took the sabre from the wall, withdrew it from its scabbard, and, gazing at it, sank into thought. This sabre was my toy when I was still in swaddling clothes, it was a consolation and a means of exercise when I was a youth, why might it not now be my defense and my fame in my military career? "I shall wear you with honor," I said, kissing the blade and putting it back in the scabbard. The sun had risen. For my namesday mama had given me a gold chain, father had given three hundred rubles and a hussar saddle with a scarlet saddle blanket. My little brother had given me his gold watch. Accepting the gifts of my parents, I had sadly thought that they had no idea that they were equipping me for a long and dangerous road.

I spent this day with my friends. At eleven in the evening I went to say goodnight to mama, as I usually did when I went to bed. Unable to restrain my feelings, I kissed her hands several times and pressed them to my heart, which I had never done before and never dared to do. Although mama did not love me, she was touched by this unusual outpouring of childlike affection and submission. Kissing my head, she said, "Go with God!" These words meant a great deal to me, since I had never yet heard a single caressing word from my mother. I took them as a blessing, kissed her hand again, and departed.

My rooms were in the orchard. I occupied the lower floor of a small orchard cottage, and father lived upstairs. It was his habit to drop in on me every evening for half an hour. He liked to listen as I related to him where I had been, what I had been doing, and what I had read. Now, expecting my father's customary visit, behind a screen I laid out my Cossack attire on the

*A verst is equal to .66 of a mile.

bed, moved my armchair next to the stove, and began to wait for father to arrive at his quarters. I soon heard the rustle of leaves from someone going through the alley. My heart leaped. The door opened and father entered. "Why are you so pale," he asked, sitting on the armchair. "Are you ill?" With difficulty I withheld the sigh which was ready to tear my breast apart. This was the last time my father would enter my room with the assurance of finding his daughter in it. Tomorrow he would pass by with grief and shuddering. The emptiness of the grave and silence would greet him. Father looked at me fixedly. "What's wrong, are you sure you are not ill?" I replied that I was only tired and chilly. "Why don't you order your maid to heat your bedroom? It's damp and cold." Remaining silent a while, father asked, "Why didn't you order Yefim to exercise Alcides on the lounge line? One can't get near him. You haven't ridden him for a long time, and you won't let anyone else do it. He's been stood up so long that he's even rearing in his stall. He should be well ridden right away." I said that I would order this done, and again fell silent. "You are sad about something, my friend. Goodbye, go to bed," father said, getting up and kissing my forehead. He embraced me with one arm and pressed me to his chest. I kissed both of his hands, trying to restrain my tears, which were pouring from my eyes. The trembling of my entire body betrayed my inner feeling. Alas, father ascribed this to the cold. "Look how cold you have become," he said. I kissed his hands again. "You're a good daughter!" he muttered, patting my cheek, and left. I kneeled next to the armchair on which he had been sitting, and bending to the floor, kissed the spot where he had been standing and washed it with tears.

After half an hour when my grief had somewhat lessened, I arose to take off my women's clothes. I went to the miror, shaved off my braids, put them in a drawer in the table, removed my black silk capote and began to dress in my Cossack's uniform. Having bound up my middle with a black silk sash and put on my tall hat with its crimson peak, for a quarter of an hour I inspected my transformed appearance. My appearance was entirely different without hair, and I was convinced that it wouldn't occur to anyone to suspect what sex I was. A loud rustling of leaves and the snorting of a horse gave notice that Yefim was leading Alcides to the back courtyard. For the last time I stretched my arms toward the image of the Mother of God which for so many years had accepted my prayers, and then I left. Finally the door of my paternal home was closing behind me, and who knows, maybe it would never open for me again!

Having ordered Yefim to go directly to Startsov mountain with Alcides and wait for me near the forest, I ran quickly to the bank of the Kama, threw off my capote, and put it on the sand with all the appurtenances of female apparel. I did not have the barbaric intention of causing my father to believe I had drowned, and I was certain that he would not think that. I only wanted to give him an opportunity to answer

without confusion any difficult questions from our shortsighted acquaintances. Leaving my coat on the bank of the river, I went directly
upwards along a goat path. The night was bright and cold, and the moon
was shining in its fullness. I stopped to look again at the beautiful and
majestic view which opened before me from the mountain. Beyond the
Kama in the infinite distance the Perm and Orenburg districts were visible.
Extensive dark forests and mirror-like lakes were sketched out as on a
map. The town at the foot of the precipitous mountain dreamed in the
midnight silence. The rays of the moon played on and were reflected from
the gilded cupolas of the cathedral and shone on the roof of the house
where I had grown up. What are you thinking now, my father? Is his heart
telling him that tomorrow his beloved daughter will no longer come to
wish him good morning?

In the silence of the night the cry of Yefim and the constant snorting of
Alcides could be heard clearly. I ran to them, and just in time. Yefim was
shaking from the cold, and he was scolding Alcides, with whom he was not
able to get along, and me, as well, for being slow. I took my horse from
him, mounted, gave him the promised fifty rubles, begged him not to say
anything to father and, giving Alcides the reins, instantly disappeared from
Yefim's astonished sight.

Alcides galloped at the same speed for four versts, but tonight I had
to travel fifty versts to the village where I knew my Cossack regiment was
to spend its rest day, so, restraining my horse's rapid gait, I rode on at a
walk. I soon entered a dark pine forest, which stretched for thirty versts.
Wishing to conserve Alcides's strength, I continued at a walk. Surrounded
by the deathly silence of the forest and the darkness of the autumn night, I
sank into contemplation: "I have my liberty at last! I am free, I am
independent! I took what was mine, my freedom, my freedom! The
precious gift of heaven, irrevocably belonging to everyone! I was able to
seize it, to secure it for the future against all claims. From now until the
grave it will be both my fate and my reward!"

Clouds covered the entire sky. In the forest it became so dark that I
could not see three sazhens* in front of me, and finally a cold wind which
came up from the north forced me to move more quickly. My Alcides took
up a fast trot, and by dawn I arrived in the village where the Cossack
regiment was laying over.

* A sazhen is equal to 7 feet.

Memoirs

The colonel and his officers had awakened very early and all of them had gathered in the regimental quarters to have breakfast. At that moment I entered. They were conversing loudly among themselves, but seeing me they suddenly fell silent. The colonel approached me with a surprised look on his face. "Which company are you in?" he hurriedly asked. I answered that I did not yet have the honor to be in any of them, but that I had come to ask him for this favor. The colonel listened to me with astonishment: "I don't understand you. You mean you haven't enlisted somewhere?"

"Nowhere."

"Why?"

"I don't have the right to."

"What's that? What's this mean? A Cossack doesn't have the right to join a Cossack regiment! What nonsense is that?"

I told him I wasn't a Cossack.

"Well, who are you?" the colonel asked, beginning to lose his patience. "Why are you in Cossack uniform and what do you want?"

"I have already told you, Colonel, that I wish to have the honor of joining your regiment, although only until we reach the regular army."

"All the same, I must know who you are, young man, and above all how it is that you do not know that only native-born Cossacks can serve with us?"

"I do not have that intention. I only am asking for permission to go to the regular army as a Cossack in Cossack uniform with either you or your regiment. As to your question, who am I, I will say only what can be said. I am a member of the gentry, I have left my parental home, and I am going to enter the military service without the knowledge or permission of my parents. I cannot be happy in any vocation other than the military, and that is why I decided in this case to act on my own volition. If you will not take me under your protection, then I will find a means on my own to join up with the army."

While I was speaking, the colonel was looking at me sympathetically. "What am I do do?" he said quietly, turning to his *esaul*.* "I don't have the heart to refuse him!"

"And why refuse him," the *esaul* answered indifferently. "Let him go with us."

"Won't he cause us trouble?"

*an officer-adjutant.

"What sort? On the contrary, both his father and mother will be grateful to you later on that you gave him shelter. With his tenaciousness and inexperience he will get into trouble if you send him away."

In the course of this short conversation between the colonel and the *esaul,* I stood leaning on my sabre with the firm intention, were I to be refused, of mounting my foster child of the mountains and proceeding alone to my proposed destination.

"Well, young man, good," said the colonel, turning to me. "Go with us, but I forewarn you that we are now going to the Don, and there are no regular troops there. Shchegrov, give him a horse from the regimental herd!"

A tall Cossack, the colonel's signalman, was on the point of carrying out this order, but, hastening to make use of an opportunity to play the role of an obedient soldier, I said, "I have a horse, your honor! I shall ride it, if that is permitted."

The colonel burst out laughing, "So much the better, so much the better! Ride your own horse. What is your name, young man?" I said that my name was Alexander.

"And your patronymic?"

"My father's name is Vasily."

"So Alexander Vasilyevich, on the march you will always ride with the first company, you will eat and have quarters with me. Go now to the regiment. We are moving out immediately. Orderly, give the command to mount up!"

Beside myself with joy, I ran to my Alcides and flew into the saddle like a bird. The responsive horse seemed to understand my joy. It walked proudly, bending its neck in a bow and rapidly flicking its ears. The Cossack officers fell in love with my Alcides's beauty and praised me as well. They said that I had a good seat and a beautiful Circassian posture. I even began to blush and became confused by the curious glances directed at me from all directions, but such a situation could not last forever. I quickly took hold of myself and answered their questions politely, plausibly, with a firm voice, calmly, and appeared not to notice at all the general curiosity and remarks aroused by my appearance in the midst of the Don Army.

Finally the Cossacks lined up, having their fill of observing and commenting about me and my horse. The colonel came out, mounted his Circassian horse, gave the command "To the right by threes!" and the regiment moved forward. The leading division, purposely composed of those with good voices, burst into "Fine steed, my soul," a popular Cossack song. The melancholy tune put me into a thoughtful mood. Not long ago I had been at home, in a woman's dress, surrounded by friends, beloved by my father, respected by everyone as the daughter of the mayor! Now I was a Cossack, in uniform, with a sabre. The heavy lance hurt my arm, which had not yet reached its full strength. In place of my friends I was surrounded by Cossacks whose speech, jokes, rough voices and laughter touched me. A lachrymose feeling oppressed my breast. I leaned on the bowed neck of my horse, embraced it, and pressed my face to it. This horse was a gift from my father. It alone remained as a memento of those days spent in his house. Finally the conflict of feelings abated, and I again sat straight in the saddle. Occupying myself with observations of the gloomy autumn landscape, I vowed in my inner soul never to let memories weaken my spirits, but with firmness and constancy to follow the path which I had freely chosen.

The march lasted more than a month. My new circumstances delighted me. I learned how to saddle and unsaddle my horse. I myself led it to the water trough like all the others did. During the march the Cossack officers often raced their horses and proposed that I test Alcides's speed against their own, but I loved him too much to accede to this. Moreover, my dear horse was not in the first flush of youth, being already ten, and although I was certain that in the whole Cossack regiment there was not a single horse which could match Alcides's speed, just as there was none as handsome as he was, I wasn't so inhumanely vain as to torment my comrade for the simple pleasure of defeating the gaunt racehorses of the Don.

Finally the regiment arrived at the border of its territory and made camp to await inspection, after which the troops would disperse to their homes. The waiting and the inspection lasted three days, and during this time I wandered with my musket about the boundless Don steppe or went riding. At the conclusion of the inspection the Cossacks disbanded into groups. That was a picturesque sight: several hundred Cossacks scattered about the broad steppe riding away from the inspection in all directions. This picture reminded me of the scattering flight of ants when I used to shoot blanks from my pistol at their anthill.

Shchegrov called me to the colonel. "Well, young man, this is the end of our wanderings! And what are you planning to do?"

"To go to the army," I answered brightly.

"Of course you know where it is located? You know the road to follow, and you have the means to do this?" the colonel asked laughingly.

His irony forced me to blush.

"I shall enquire as to the location and the road, Colonel, and as for the means, I have money and a horse."

"Your means are satisfactory, only because you have no better ones. I am sorry for you, Alexander Vasilyevich! From your conduct, more than from your words, I am convinced of your gentry origins. I do not know the reasons which forced you to leave your parental home at such a young age, but if it was primarily just a wish to enter the military service, then your inexperience alone might conceal from you the countless difficulties which you will have to overcome before achieving your goal. Think about it."

The colonel fell silent, and I also was silent. What could I say? They are frightening me with difficulties! They advise me to think about it. Perhaps it would have been well to listen to all this at home, but now that I was two thousand versts away I had to continue, and, whatever the difficulties, to overcome them with a firm will. So I thought and still maintained silence.

The colonel began anew: "I see that you don't wish to speak openly with me. Perhaps you have your reasons for this, but I don't have the heart to let you go to certain disaster. Listen to me. Stay a while on the Don with me. You need the protection of an experienced person. For the time being I offer my home. Live in it until we set off again on campaign. You won't be bored. I have a family, our climate, as you see, is very warm, there won't be snow until December, and you can ride about as much as you like. My stable is at your service. Now let us go to my house, I will give you over into my wife's hands, for I am leaving for Cherkask to see Platov. I shall remain there until the next campaign, which won't be long. Then you can go with us to the regular army. Do you agree to follow my advice?"

I told him I would accept his proposal with sincere gratitude. One would have had to be brainless in order not to see how beneficial it would be for me to get to the regular army without attracting attention or causing suspicion.

The colonel and I got into a carriage and set off for Razdorsk Village, where his home was. His wife was exceedingly joyful at the arrival of her husband. She was a middle-aged woman, attractive, tall, full-figured, with dark eyes, brows, and hair and a swarthy face typical of the Cossack people. Her fresh lips smiled pleasantly every time she spoke. She fell in love with me, caressed me, expressing astonishment that my parents had let me wander about the earth, as she put it, at such a youthful age. "You are probably not more than fourteen and you already are alone in a strange land. My son is eighteen but I let him go into strange places only with his father, not alone! Oh, my God! What might happen to such a fledgling! Stay with us, grow up a little, become more of a man, and when our Cossacks go on campaign again, you can go with them, and my husband will be as a father to you." Saying this, the good colonel's wife set the table with various treats—honey, grapes, sour cream and freshly baked sweets, and wine.

"Drink some wine, young man," the kind-hearted hostess said, "What are you afraid of? Even we, the women, drink it by the glassful, and here three-year-olds drink it like water."

Until then I did not know the taste of wine and therefore drank the trial nectar with great pleasure. The hostess didn't take her eyes off me. "How little you resemble a Cossack. You're so pale, so thin, built like a young girl. My sewing women are thinking that very thing, and they have

already told me that you are a girl in disguise!" Talking in this manner the
colonel's wife laughed ingenuously, without at all suspecting how well her
women had outguessed her and what a chill her words, so hospitably
spoken, caused in the heart of her young guest.

From that day I found no pleasure in remaining in the colonel's
household, so from morning until evening I would walk about the fields
and vineyards. I would willingly have gone off to Cherkask, but I was
afraid of new interrogations. I could see very well that my Cossack uniform
poorly concealed the striking difference between myself and the native
Cossacks. All of them had the same sort of features, and therefore my
appearance, actions, and even my means of expression were objects of
their curiosity and gossip. Moreover, seeing myself constantly observed, I
would often become confused, start to blush, avoid conversations and go
off into the fields for the whole day, even in bad weather.

The colonel had been gone for a long time. For reasons of the service
he lived in Cherkask. The uniformity and inaction of my life became
intolerable and I decided to leave and seek out the army, although my heart
shuddered at the thought that the same questions, the same curiosity
awaited me everywhere. But at the very least, I thought, this would be to a
certain degree temporary, and not like here, where I was the constant
object of remarks and speculations.

Having decided to leave the next morning at dawn, I returned home
while it was still light in order to inform my hostess of my departure and to
get my horse and tack ready. Entering the courtyard, I noticed unusual
activity and movement among the colonel's staff, and I saw a number of
carriages and saddle horses. I entered the hall, and the first person I met
was the colonel, who had just returned. A crowd of officers surrounded
him, but there was not one of them from among those with whom I had
come to the Don.

"Hello, Alexander Vasilyevich!" the colonel said, answering my bow.
"Were you bored here? Gentlemen, let me introduce this Russian
nobleman. He will be our fellow traveler to our destination." The officers
bowed slightly and continued to talk about their campaign. "Well, how did
you spend your time, Alexander Vasilyevich? Did you fall in love with the
Don or fall in love with something on the Don?" Saying this, the colonel
smiled slyly. Catching the drift of this last question, I began to blush, but to
answer his joke politely and properly I said that I had not overly attached
myself to their beautiful countryside in order not to have to pay for this
with subsequent regrets.

"You did well," said the colonel, "because at first light tomorrow you
will have to say goodbye to our quiet Don! I have been given command of
the Ataman's regiment, and we have orders to the Grodno District. There
you will have an opportunity to enlist in any regular regiment you like—a
number of them are there."

At three in the morning I saddled Alcides and led him to the Cossack formation. As the colonel was not yet there, I tied up my horse and went into the hall where all the officers had gathered. A number of young Cossack women had accompanied their husbands. I was witness to a touching scene. Shchegrov, who had always been with the colonel on his campaigns, was also with him when on the Don. His father, mother, wife and three grown-up and pretty daughters had accompanied him to say goodbye one last time. It was moving to see a forty-year-old Cossack bending to the ground and kissing the feet of his father and mother, accepting their blessing, and then himself blessing his daughters in the same way, as they fell to his feet. This ritual of parting was completely new to me and made the saddest impression on my soul. "That's how children should part with their father and mother! But I, I ran away! Instead of a blessing, the reproaches of my distraught parents followed me and maybe..." A terrible thought!

Sunk in these sad meditations, I didn't notice that everyone had left, and the hall was empty. My attention was aroused by a shuffling behind me, which distracted me from my sad reveries in a very unpleasant manner. One of the women who served the colonel's wife was creeping up behind me.

"Why are you standing here alone, young lady? Your friends are mounted, and Alcides is running about the courtyard!" She said this with the mocking look of a true devil. My heart shuddered and contracted. I quickly left the Megaera! The Cossacks were already in formation. Near them Alcides was impatiently pawing the ground with his hoof. Hastening to catch him, I met the severe glance of the colonel. "In your situation you must always be first. That is absolutely necessary, Alexander Vasilyevich," he said, moving in front of the troop. Finally the usual "To the right by threes!" started the regiment forward. Soon there again resounded "Fine steed, my soul," again the scenes of my previous life on campaign repeated themselves. But I was no longer the same person. I was several months older, had become more confident, and no longer became confused at every question. The officers of the Ataman's regiment, being better educated, noticed in my behavior that civility which indicates a good upbringing, and showed their respect for me by seeking my company.

At the beginning of spring we arrived at the village of Druzhkopol on the bank of the Bug River. Here the Bryansk musketeer regiment of General Liders was quartered. The officers of both regiments are often together. The way they live is boring: from morning to night they sit in a stuffy room smoking pipes, playing cards, and talking rubbish. The colonel asked me if I wished to enlist in the Bryansk regiment.

"God preserve us, Colonel," I answered, "If on the whole globe there existed only infantry, I would never enter the service. I don't like the infantry."

"Well, as you wish, you'll get what you want, you're still quite young."

I love to go out alone at night into the field or the forest. Yesterday I went quite a long way from the village, and it was after midnight when I returned home. As usual I was sunk in thought, and I was walking rapidly without noticing where I was. Suddenly a deep groan, as if coming from underground, broke the silence of the night and my dreaming. I stopped, looked around, and listened. Again I hear the groan and see that I am ten paces from a cemetery. The groan is coming from there. I didn't feel the slightest trace of fear. I go to the cemetery, open the gate, enter, walk about the graves, bend down and listen. The groan carries over the whole cemetery. Going from one tomb to the next, I finally pass behind the church. With surprise I realize that the groan is being carried on the wind from the direction of a swamp located half a verst from the cemetery. Not knowing what was going on, I hasten to the colonel's quarters to find if Shchegrov is awake and to tell him what has happened.

Indeed, I found Shchegrov alert and very angry. In a certain sense I was under his direction. My prolonged absence at nighttime had caused some anxiety, and so my story made a bad impression. He told me angrily that I was behaving foolishly wandering about cemeteries at night and sniffing the graves like a jackal, and that this strange habit would get me the pleasure of falling ill with a rotten fever, from which many soldiers of the Bryansk regiment had died. And he finished his lesson with the remark that had I not come directly from under mama's roof with the milk still wet on my lips I would know that the groan which I heard comes from a bird which lived in the swamp and is called a *bugay,* that is an *ox.* The old Cossack's grumbling disinclined me to ask why this bird does not cry, or sing, or whistle, but groans, so without further words I went to bed.

The colonel's son was studying in Lyubar with the Jesuits. He invited me to come there and feast my eyes on the abnormal size and enormity of his two teachers. Our quarters were ten versts from Lyubar, and so I went there on horseback. I stopped at the same inn where the colonel always used to stop. On entering the wide room which is common to all inns, I saw a young Jewish woman reciting her prayers. She was standing before a mirror quietly whining her psalms and at the same time was darkening her eyebrows and listening with a smirk to a young infantry officer who was whispering something to her. My entrance interrupted this scene. The Jewish woman turned to me, glanced at me quickly, and came up so close that her breath poured warmly over my face.

"What do you want?" she asked almost in a whisper. I answered that I wanted her to have someone watch my horse, which I would leave at her inn.

"Will you spend the night here?" she asked with the same mysteriousness.

"I may spend the night in the Jesuits' cloister, or perhaps here. I don't know exactly."

On hearing about the Jesuits' cloister, she turned away without a word and, ordering a worker to take my horse, resumed her previous position in front of the mirror, started singing again softly, leaning towards the officer, who began to speak to her again. Leaving them, I went to see if Alcides was taken care of properly, and finding him perfectly satisfied, went straight to the cloister of the Jesuit fathers.

Indeed, the honorable fathers Jeremy and Antonio, young B***'s teachers, terrified me with their monstrous size. The huge mass of their bodies defied belief. They could hardly stand, and so sat all the time and read the whole church service while seated in their cells. Their breathing sounded like a dull roar. I sat down in a corner and watched them fixedly with astonishment and a certain fear. The young Cossack pinched his nose and squeezed his lips together to keep from laughing at me and at the strange sight of these two monsters in cassocks. Finally an invitation to supper put an end to the pious roar of the honorable fathers, the grimacing of the young scamp, and my astonishment. We went to table. That madcap B*** whispered in my ear that in accordance with the dictates of hospitality he had seated me between his two teachers, in order that I might enjoy the pleasure of their conversation. I tried to sit down next to him as quickly as possible, but without success. A huge hand seized mine, and a quietly roaring voice resounded almost from the ceiling, "Would you not like to take a place between us? I humbly beg you! Please come this way!"

The supper was a real torture for me. Not understanding Polish, I didn't know how to respond to the fearsome neighbors on my right and left. Moreover, I was afraid to eat too much of the rather dainty Polish food. I was deathly hot, blushed continuously, and sweat stood on my forehead. In a word I was uncomfortable and ludicrous in the extreme. But now the chairs thundered and the huge fathers arose. The mumbling of their prayers, like some distant rolling of thunder, resounded over my head. After all possible ceremonies were finished, I joyfully found myself beyond the walls of the monastery, and my first act, once past the gates, was to get away as fast as possible from the walls of the hospitable habitation in which it was so gloomy to live and so difficult to breathe.

The Ataman's regiment is going to Grodno. The Cossacks are sharpening their lances and sabres. There's no approaching my Alcides; he neighs, jumps about, kicks. Good steed! What will be our fate?

We arrived at Grodno. The regiment was to spend only two days here, and then leave for the border. The colonel summoned me. "Now you will have a good chance to enlist in any cavalry squadron being formed here that you like. But follow my advice, be frank with the leader of the regiment in which you decide to enlist. Although that won't make him take you on as a cadet, at least you will get into his good graces and make a positive impression. Meanwhile, without wasting time, write your parents to send you the necessary documents, for without them you certainly won't be accepted, or, at the very least, you will remain forever in the ranks." I thanked him for his advice and the solicitude which he had shown me for so long, and finally we parted. The next day the Cossacks crossed the border, and I remained in Grodno.

Grodno

I am alone, completely alone! I am living in an inn for transients. My Alcides constantly neighs and stamps his hooves: he also was abandoned. From my window I see a crowd of uhlans passing by with music and dancing. They are amicably inviting all young people to join in their merriment. I shall go find out what's happening. This is called recruitment! God save us if there is no other way to enter a regular regiment than by means of this recruitment. That would be extremely unpleasant.

While watching this dancing expedition, I was approached by the sub-ensign in charge, or, as they call him, *the deputy*. "How do you like our way of life? Is it not a happy one?" I answered that this was true and departed. The next day I learned that this was the Konnopolsk regiment, that they were recruiting to bring their regiment up to strength, since it had lost many men in battle, and that it was commanded by a captain. Having garnered this information, I sought out the quarters of the deputy with whom I had talked yesterday. He told me that if I wanted to enlist in their regiment, then I might make a request to their captain, Kazimirsky, and that there was no need at all for me to dance with the crowd of rabble which was squirming into their regiment. I was overjoyed at the possibility of entering the service without being subjected to the undesirable ritual of dancing in the streets, and I told the deputy as much. He could hardly restrain his laughter.

"Well, that's up to you, but without that we might easily miss those wanting to take part in our Bacchanalia. Would you like to go with me to Kazimirsky? He will be very pleased to get such a recruit. Moreover, I'll make him happy for the whole day when I tell him what was worrying you." Saying this, the deputy laughed heartily, and we left.

From the deputy's quarters we had to cross the large room, which I have already said is found in all inns. It was full of uhlans and enlisted recruits. Everyone was singing and dancing. Trying to get through the noisy crowd as quickly as possible, I seized the deputy's hand, but at that moment one of the uhlans, grabbing me around the waist, flew away with me into a circle of dancers, and stamping his feet, prepared to take part in a mazurka, in which several pairs had already begun, leaping and sliding about in a confused way. The deputy freed me from the arms of these spellbound dancers, his laughter doubling at this unexpected occurrence. Finally we arrived at Kazimirsky's quarters.

Captain Kazimirsky, about fifty, has a noble and at the same time a military appearance. Geniality and courage breathe in every feature of his pleasing face. When I entered, he bowed politely, evidently taking me for a Cossack officer, and asked, "What may I do for you?" I said that I desired to serve in the Konnopolsk regiment and, having learned that he had been detailed to bring the regiment up to strength, had come to ask to be accepted in the service.

"You, serve in the Konnopolsk regiment!" said the captain with surprise. "You are a Cossack. You belong to the Don Army and must serve in it."

"My dress deceives you. I am a Russian nobleman and, consequently, may choose what branch of service I wish."

"Can you prove this?"

"No! But if it pleases you to take my word alone that I am in fact a Russian nobleman, then I shall know how to value such solicitude, and at the conclusion of the campaign will be obligated to provide the regiment everything needed to establish the truthfulness of my words."

"How does it happen that you are wearing a Cossack uniform?"

"My father did not want to let me enter the service. I left secretly, joined up with a Cossack regiment, and came here with it."

"How old are you? What is your name?"

"I am in my seventeenth year, and my name is Durov."

The captain turned to an officer of his regiment. "What do you think? Shall we accept him?"

"As you wish. Why not? There's a war going on, we need people, and he promises to be a brave fellow."

"And what if he is a Cossack and for some reason or other wants to hide from his own people by entering a regular regiment?"

"That's impossible, Captain! It is written on his face that he is not lying, and at his age he wouldn't know how to make it up. Moreover, if you refuse, he will go to another regiment which won't be so unnecessarily strict, and you will have lost a good recruit..."

This whole conversation was in Polish. The captain turned to me. "I agree to accept your word, Durov! I hope that your behavior will justify my confidence." I wanted to say that he would soon see whether I was worthy of the honor of being accepted in the ranks of those having the enviable happiness of serving Tsar Alexander, but I kept silent, fearing that they might consider this indiscreet boasting. I said only that I had a horse and wished to serve on it if that were possible.

"Impossible," said the captain, "a goverment horse will be provided. However, you may keep yours until you find a chance to sell it."

"To sell it! Sell Alcides!" I cried out involuntarily. "Oh, save me from that misfortune! No, Captain, Sir, I have money, I will feed my horse at my own expense and not for anything on earth will I part from him!"

Kazimirsky had been a cavalryman from the cradle, and he was very pleased with my attachment to the best of all wartime companions. He said that my horse would have a place in his stable and be given the same food, that I might ride it abroad, and that he would take upon himself to secure permission for me to serve with it. After that he ordered that one of his uhlans be sent to him and turned me over to his care, telling him to teach me to march, fight with a sabre, shoot, use a lance, saddle, unsaddle, load saddlebags and groom a horse, and that when I had somewhat learned all this to give me a uniform and put me on active duty. The uhlan, having heard his orders, took me to the assembly—that's what they call the hut or sometimes the barn where they teach young soldiers everything about the service.

Every morning I arise at dawn and go to the assembly, from which we all go together to the stable. My uhlan mentor praises my intelligence and constant readiness to engage in drills, be they from morning to night. He says that I will be a fine fellow. However, I have to admit that I become deathly tired waving the heavy lance—especially during some purposeless exercise, such as whirling it overhead. Several times already I have hit my head. Also I am not totally relaxed when using the sabre. It always seems to me that I will cut myself with it. However, I am sooner ready to wound myself than to reveal even the slightest timidity.

Having passed the whole morning at drill, I go to Kazimirsky's to dine. He examines me with fatherly indulgence, asks if I like my present duties, and how I find the military profession. I answer that I have loved the military profession from the day I was born, that military duties were and will be my solitary occupation, that I consider the calling of soldier the noblest and the only one with which it is impossible to associate any vices, since valor is the primary and indispensible quality of a soldier, since greatness of spirit is inseparable from valor, and that within the union of these two great virtues there is no place for vices or base passions.

"Do you really think, young man," the captain asked, "that without valor it is impossible to possess qualities worthy of respect? There are many people timid from nature who have the most excellent qualities."

"I believe that strongly, Captain. But I also think that a valorous person necessarily must be virtuous."

"Perhaps you are right," responded the captain smiling. "But," he added, patting me on the shoulder and curling his moustache, "let us wait ten short years and also let us wait for your first battle—experience may change our minds about many things."

After dinner Kazimirsky would take a nap and I would go to the stable to give my horse its midday ration of oats. After that I was free to do what I wanted until six in the evening.

No matter how exhausted I was from spending the whole morning waving my heavy lance, or its sister, the sabre, marching about and jumping the horse over hurdles, after half an hour's rest my fatigue would pass, and from two until six I would walk continuously about the fields, mountains, and forests, fearlessly, without care, and tirelessly. Freedom, that priceless gift of heaven, had finally become my lot forever! My existence was infused with it and enlivened by it. Only girls of my age can understand my exhilaration. You alone can know the value of my happiness! You, whose every step is watched, who are unable to move two sazhens without supervision and protection, who from cradle to grave are in eternal dependence and under eternal protection, God knows from whom or from what! You, I repeat, you alone may understand what joyful feeling fills my heart at the sight of the broad forest, the infinite field, mountain, valleys, and streams and at the thought that I can go all these places without having to account to anyone and without fearing that anyone might forbid me to do so. I jump for joy when I consider that for my entire life I will never again hear those words, "You, girl, sit down. It is not proper for you to go walking about alone!" Alas, how many beautiful clear days began and ended when, with eyes red from crying, I could only look through the window by which my mother had ordered me to make lace! Sad memories of the oppression in which I passed my childhood years put an end to my joyous gambols. For about an hour I would be sad remembering my life at home; but happily with each day I remembered it less, and the mere thought that there was no limit to my freedom, as there was none to my gaze, caused my head to spin from joy.

The captain assigned me and one other comrade, Vyshemirsky, to the first platoon under the command of Lieutenant Boshnyakov. This platoon was quartered in the village of a poor landowner which was surrounded by swamps.

What a hungry land is this Lithuania! The inhabitants are so poor, so pale, thin and frightened that one can't look upon them without compassion. The clay soil, seeded with stones, stingily rewards the hard labor needed to improve and work it. The bread is black as coal, and moreover mixed with some sort of prickers and sand. It is impossible to eat it, or at least I can't eat even a bite of it.

We have been here more than three weeks. I have been given a uniform, a sabre, a lance so heavy that it seems more like a beam. They gave me woolen epaulets, a helmet with a plume, a white bandoleer with a cartridge belt. All of this is very clean, very pretty, and very heavy. However, I hope to become accustomed to it. But what it is impossible to become accustomed to are these tormenting government boots—they are like iron! Until now I have worn soft and properly sewed footwear, and my feet were free and light, but now! My God! I am as if chained to the ground with the weight of these boots and huge rattling spurs. I would willingly order the Jewish shoemaker to make me a pair, but I have so little money. One must endure what can't be changed.

From the day I put on government boots I have been unable to walk around as before and since I am deathly hungry every day, I spend all my free time in the truck-garden with a spade digging for potatoes which have been overlooked. By working diligently about four hours in a row, I can find enough to fill my forage-cap. Then in triumph I take my spoils to the landlady for her to boil. This grim woman grumblingly grabs the potato-laden forage-cap from my hands, grumblingly pours them into a pot, and when they are cooked and she has poured them into a wooden bowl, she shoves it toward me on the table so that several fall out onto the floor. What a spiteful old woman! It would seem that she has no reason to worry about the potatoes. The crop has already been harvested and hidden away somewhere. The fruits of my incessant labors are those potatoes that were very deep in the ground or somehow escaped the attention of the workers.

Yesterday the landlady was pouring out some milk when I entered with my forage-cap full of potatoes. The landlady became frightened, but I was overjoyed and started to beg her determinedly to add a little milk to my potatoes. It was terrible to see how her face became twisted with malice and hatred! With all kinds of curses she poured some milk into the bowl, tore the forage-cap from my hands, scattered the potatoes all over the floor, but then immediately bent down to pick them up. This last action, for which I guessed the reason, amused me.

Our platoon leader, Lieutenant Boshnyakov, has taken Vyshemirsky and myself into his quarters. Well educated, he addresses both of us as a polite, well-bred person addresses his equals. We are living in the house of the landowner. To us, that is to our superior officer, a large room has been assigned, which is separated from the master's rooms by a vestibule. Vyshemirsky and I are the complete possessors of this hall, since the lieutenant is almost never there and does not pass the night at home. He spends all his time in the neighboring village at the house of an old proprietress, a widow. She has a beautiful daughter, and our lieutenant, according to his orderly, is fatally in love with her. The wife of the owner of our quarters, a young lady of unusual beauty, is very displeased that her lodger doesn't live in his quarters. Every time she sees me or Vyshemirsky, she asks, lisping very prettily, "What is your officer doing at NN's place? He is there from morning to night and from night to morning!" From me she gets only the answer, "I don't know!" But Vyshemirsky finds it amusing to persuade her that the lieutenant fears the loss of his inner tranquility and thus flees his dangerous quarters.

I have become used to my fetters, that is my government boots, and now I fly about as easily and unconstrainedly as before. Only at drill the heavy oak lance almost breaks my arm, especially when it is necessary to twirl it above my head—an annoying drill.

We are going abroad! To battle! I am both glad and sad. If I am killed, what will happen to my old father? He loved me.

In several hours I shall leave Russia and be in a foreign country. I am writing to my father about where I am now and what I am. I am writing that I fall at his feet and embrace his knees, I implore him to forgive my flight, to give me his blessing and permit me to follow the path essential for my happiness. My tears were falling onto the paper when I was writing, and they shall speak for me to my father's heart.

Just as soon as I had taken the letter to the post office, the command was given to bring out the horses—we are setting forth this minute. I am permitted to ride, to serve and to fight on Alcides. We are going to Prussia, and as far as I can tell we are in no hurry. Our marches are limited and rest days, as usual, are after two days' and three days' march.

On the third day's march Vyshemirsky said that from the next rest stop it wasn't far to his uncle's village where his sister was living and receiving her education.

"I am going to request the captain's permission to go there for a day. Will you go with me, Durov?"

"If they let us go, I will go willingly," I answered.

We went to the captain, who, learning of our desire, immediately released us, only ordering Vyshemirsky to watch over his horse and repeating to both of us that we appear back at the squadron without fail in twenty-four hours. We set forth. The village of proprietor Kunat, Vyshemirsky's uncle, was about twenty miles from the village where our squadron was to spend its rest day. Although we rode at a trot, we arrived in the wee hours of the night. The silence was broken by the monotonous knocking on a board inside the broad courtyard of the manor, which was surrounded by a high fence. This was the watchman, who was walking around the house and pounding on his board with something. The gates were not locked, and without hindrance we entered the courtyard, smooth, broad, and covered with green grass. But once the steps of our horses were heard in the still of the night, instantly we were surrounded by a pack of loudly barking guard dogs. Despite this I was about to dismount, but catching sight of a dog which had just run up to my horse, I sat back in the saddle, determined not to get off until someone came to chase away these attacking beasts, even if it meant waiting until dawn. Finally the watchman appeared before us with his knocker in hand. He immediately recognized Vyshemirsky and was extremely pleased. At the first command the dogs went back to their quarters, servants appeared, lights were brought, our horses were taken and led to the stables, and they asked us to go to the Pan Manager's, because the masters were asleep and all the doors were locked. I don't know how news of Vyshemirsky's arrival penetrated the locked doors of the entire house, but very soon his sister, who was sleeping near her aunt's bedroom, learned of it and immediately came out to us. She was a most beautiful child of about thirteen. She curtsied solemnly before her brother, said, "Jak sie masz?" [Polish for "How are you?"] and tearfully threw herself to embrace him. I could not understand this contrast. They fed us supper and brought blankets, pillows, straw, and sheets in order to make beds for us. Miss Vyshemirska rejected this arrangement. She said that no beds were needed, that it would soon be day, and that her brother probably preferred to sit and converse with her than to sleep. The manager laughed and gave her the choice of either going to her room and not interfering with our sleep or staying to talk with her brother, while lying between us on the bed. The girl declared: "Shame on you, Pan Manager!" and left, having first kissed her brother and bowed to me.

The next day we were invited to Mr. Kunat's house to drink coffee. A Polish pan of impressive appearance was sitting with his wife and sons in an ancient hall decorated with raspberry material. The chairs and sofas were upholstered in the same material and ornamented with tassels, which one supposed were once gold but now had lost their luster and had darkened. The room had a gloomy appearance, completely opposite that of the masters, who were pleasant and congenial. They embraced their relative, politely bowed to me, and invited us to share their breakfast. The entire family fell head over heels in love with me. They asked my age, my place of birth, and when I told them that I lived not far from Siberia, Kunat's wife cried out from astonishment and looked at me with new curiosity, as if an inhabitant of Siberia were a supernatural being! Throughout Poland there is such a strange conception about Siberia! On a map Kunat located the town where my father lived and insisted, laughing, that in vain I called myself a Siberian since, on the contrary, I was an Asiatic.

Seeing paper and pencils on the table, I asked permission to sketch something. "With great pleasure," my host answered. I was so happy to have the opportunity to sketch something, since I had not engaged in this pleasant art for a long time, that I sat at my voluntary labor more than two hours. Having sketched Andromeda on the cliff, I was covered with praise from the young and old Kunats. Thanking them for their indulgence of my mediocre talent, I wanted to make a gift of my sketch to Miss Vyshemirska, but old Mme. Kunat took it from my hands, saying, "Give it to me if you have no use for it. I'll tell everyone that it was sketched by a cavalryman, a native Siberian!"

Kunat overheard this. "Excuse me, my friend, you are mistaken, Durov is an Asiatic. Here, see for yourself," he said, dragging the huge map to his wife's table.

The next day we parted with the Kunats. They accompanied us in a carriage for seven versts. "Durov, sketch the landscape around our village," said Kunat's wife. "That will remind you sometimes of the people who have begun to love you like a son." I said that even without this I would never forget them. Finally we parted. Kunat's carriage turned back, and we went on ahead at an easy gallop. Vyshemirsky was silent and gloomy. His saddlebags were filled with various provisions and stuck out like two hammocks on the sides of his horse. Finally he began to talk.

"Let's go at a walk. My kind uncle's gifts are beating on my horse's back. Why did I go there? They like strangers better than their own! They were concerned only with you, and it was as if I was not there. What can one do with such relatives!" Vyshemirsky was suffering terribly from the clear preference shown me by his relatives. I tried to calm him down.

"What do I care, Vyshemirsky, that your uncle and aunt were so busy with me, while your sister didn't look at me once and didn't say one word to me the whole time we were there. How about trading? You take your aunt and uncle's attention and give me the caresses, tears, and kisses of your sister." Vyshemirsky sighed, smiled in a melancholy way, and began to relate how his little sister complained to him about her strict supervision and regulation. Immediately I remembered my own life in father's house, mama's strictness, the terrible absence of freedom, the endless sitting over handwork, and sadness clouded my face. I sighed in turn, and we both finished our journey in silence.

Today our squadron joined the regiment. Tomorrow Captain Kazimirsky must present all of us at inspection before General-Major Kakhovsky, and tomorrow we will all be assigned to different squadrons.

The inspection has ended. Kazimirsky was kind enough not to present me in the ranks with other recruits but introduced me personally to Kakhovsky. He assigned me to the left squadron, which Captain Galer commands. My dreams are finally fulfilled! I am a soldier! A cavalryman, I bear arms, and better than that, luck has put me in one of the bravest regiments of our army!

May 22, 1807. Guttstadt

For the first time I have seen combat and taken part in it. How much nonsense have I been told about one's first battle, about fear, courage, and, finally, about heedless valor. What rubbish! Our regiment went on the attack several times, not all together but by squadrons. I was dressed down for having attacked along with each squadron. But, to tell the truth, this was not from excessive bravery but simply from ignorance. I thought I was supposed to do so, and was very surprised when the sergeant of a different squadron, next to whom I was riding like the wind, cried out to me, "Get out of here! Why are you galloping here?" Having returned to my squadron, I did not take my place in formation but rode about the vicinity. The novelty of the spectacle absorbed my entire attention. The awesome and magnificent rumbling of cannon fire, the roar or sort of thundering of the flying shells, the galloping cavalry, the glistening bayonets of the infantry, the beating of drums, and the firm step and calm look with which our infantry regiments went against the enemy, all this filled my soul with sensations that no words can express.

I almost lost my priceless Alcides. Riding about, as I have said, near our squadron and observing the interesting scene of battle, I caught sight of several enemy dragoons, who, having surrounded a Russian officer, had knocked him off his horse with a pistol shot. He had fallen, and they were about to slash him as he lay there. At that moment I flew up to them, holding my lance at the ready. I suppose that this insane daring frightened them, for at that moment they left the officer and scattered. I galloped up to the wounded man and halted over him. For about two minutes I silently observed him. He lay with closed eyes, giving no signs of life. Clearly he thought one of the enemy was standing over him. Finally he decided to take a look, and I immediately asked if he wanted to mount my horse. "Oh, be so kind, my friend!" he said in a barely audible voice. I immediately dismounted and with difficulty raised the wounded man, but then I couldn't help him any more. He fell with his chest against my arm, and I, scarcely able to remain standing, did not know what to do or how to put him on Alcides, whom I was holding by the bridle with my other hand. This situation would have ended badly for us both, that is, for the officer and myself, but fortunately a soldier of his regiment rode up to us and helped me seat the wounded man on my horse. I told the soldier to return the horse to soldier Durov in the Konnopolsk regiment. The dragoon told me that the officer I had saved was Lieutenant Panin of the Finland Dragoon Regiment, and that they would send my horse back immediately. They carried the officer off to his regiment, and I walked toward mine. I felt I was in a very unpleasant situation on foot among leaping horses, volleys, sabre attacks. Seeing that everyone either flew by like lightning or, confident of the quality of his horse, quietly galloped in various directions,

I cried out, "Alas, my Alcides, where is he now?!" I greatly regretted having given up my horse so thoughtlessly, and even more so when my captain asked me at first sympathetically, "Was your horse killed, Durov? Are you wounded?" but, having learned how it was that I was on foot, angrily cried out: "Get behind the front, you daredevil!" Sadly but quickly I went to the place where I could see the banners of the Konnopolsk regiment. Those people I encountered met me compassionately, saying, "Oh, my God, look at what a young boy has been wounded!" It was impossible to think otherwise, seeing an uhlan on foot with his uniform covered with blood. I have already said that the wounded officer lay with his chest on my arm, and I suppose he was wounded in the chest, because my entire sleeve was bloody.

To my inexpressible joy, Alcides was returned to me, not as I had hoped, but nonetheless returned. I was walking sunk in thought along the field toward our regiment when suddenly I saw Lieutenant Podvyshansky riding from the front on my horse. Beside myself with happiness and not caring how my horse ended up under Podvyshansky, I ran up to pet and caress Alcides, who also expressed his happiness by jumping about and neighing loudly. "This horse isn't yours, is it?" the surprised Podvyshansky asked. I told him of my adventure. He also did not praise my recklessness and said that he had bought my horse from some Cossacks for ten gold rubles. I begged him to give the animal back and take from me the amount he had paid. "Good, but for today leave him with me. My horse was killed, and I have nothing on which to take part in the battle!" Having said this, he gave Alcides the spurs and galloped away, while I, almost crying, seeing my comrade-in-arms in someone else's possession, swore in my soul never again in my whole life to give up my horse! Finally this tormenting day ended. Podvyshansky returned Alcides to me, and our army is pursuing the retreating enemy.

May 24. The Bank of the Passarge

A strange thing! We were so slow in pursuing the enemy that he was able to ford this little river on whose banks we now stand, and now they have met us with gunfire! Perhaps I don't understand anything about this, but it seems to me that we should have kept on the heels of the enemy and destroyed him at the ford.

The Same Place, on the Bank of the Passarge

This is the second day we have been here and have done nothing, and there is nothing to do. In front of us the chasseurs are exchanging fire with enemy sharpshooters across the little river. Our regiment is positioned directly behind the chasseurs. But since there is absolutely nothing for us to do, we have been ordered to dismount. I am deathly hungry! I don't have a single piece of hardtack. The Cossacks who took Alcides removed the saddlebags with my hardtack, my cloak, and my case. I got the horse back with only the saddle, and everything else was lost. I am trying to sleep to forget that I am hungry, but even that doesn't help. Finally the uhlan under whose supervision I have been put, and who still has the power of mentor, noticed that there were no bags on my saddle and that my face was pale, and offered me three large moldy pieces of hardtack. I accepted them joyously and put them in a hole filled with rain water to moisten them up a bit. Although I had not eaten for over thirty-six hours, they were so large, bitter and green that I couldn't eat more than one of them. We continued to remain in one place. The sharpshooters exchanged fire, the uhlans lay on the grass. Bored, I went to take a walk around the hills where the Cossack sentries were stationed. Descending a hillock, I came upon a terrible scene. Two chasseurs, who apparently had hoped to take cover or simply to drink their spirits, were lying there dead. Death had found them in this sanctuary. Both had been killed by the same shell, which, having torn away the whole front of the one sitting higher up, had passed through the side of his comrade sitting somewhat lower, torn out his intestines, and was lying there with them. Immediately next to them was a canteen with vodka. Shuddering, I left the ghastly sight of these two bodies.

Having returned to the regiment, I lay down in the bushes and was about to fall asleep when I was summarily and unpleasantly aroused—a shell fell near me, and several others flew after it. I jumped up and ran about ten steps away, but my forage-cap remained behind, and I was unable to grab it. It was lying on the grass and against the dark green it resembled a huge flower because of its bright raspberry color. The sergeant told me to go get it, and I went, although not entirely willingly, since shells were falling rapidly and heavily in this garden. The cause of this unexpected barrage was our banners: we had stuck our lances in the ground near the horses. The variegated banners playing with the wind and flapping in the air had attracted the attention of the enemy. From this they guessed our presence in the copse and directed their cannons our way. Now we have been withdrawn further and the order has been given to place the lances on the ground.

In the evening our regiment was ordered to mount up. Until the wee hours we sat on our steeds and waited for the command to move off. We have been assigned the rear guard and will cover the withdrawal of the army. That's what the captain says. Having become deathly tired from sitting so long on my horse, I asked Vyshemirsky if he didn't want to get off. He said that he would have dismounted long ago had he not been expecting the regiment to move at any moment. "We'll hear when that happens and can mount up in a moment," I said, "so let's lead the horses across this ditch and lie there on the grass." Vyshemirsky followed my advice. We led our horses across the ditch and lay down in the bushes.

I hear my name repeated twice. I feel Alcides pushing me with his head, snorting and stamping his hoof. I feel the earth shaking under me, and then everything becomes quiet. My heart chilled, I felt danger, tried to wake up, but could not do so. Although he remained alone and could hear his comrades in the distance, my Alcides, priceless steed, was free, because his bridle was loosened and had fallen from my hands. However, he had not run off but was continually striking his hoof against the ground and snorting, poking his muzzle at me. With difficulty I finally opened my eyes. I see that Vyshemirsky is gone. I look toward the place where the regiment had been and it is gone! I am surrounded by the darkness and silence of night, so terrible in such a situation. The heavy echo of hoofbeats means the regiment is moving away at the trot. I hastened to mount Alcides, but truth demands I admit that my foot didn't find the stirrup immediately. Once seated, I gave him his head, and my steed, a loyal, magnificent steed, jumped the ditch and with a light and quick gallop carried me across the bushes directly to the regiment. I caught up to it in a quarter of an hour and joined my formation. Vyshemirsky said that he thought I had perished. He told me that he himself had become very frightened when he heard the regiment departing and, therefore, having called me twice, left my fate to God's will.

May 29 and 30. Heilsberg

The French fought furiously here. Oh, man is terrible in his frenzy! All qualities of a wild beast are united in him then. No! This is not valor. I don't know how to name this wild, beast-like daring, but it is not worthy of being called valor. In this battle our regiment was scarcely able to play an active part; rather, the artillery thundered and the victorious bayonettes of our infantry did the cutting. However, we got some action. We covered the artillery, which is quite unpleasant, because in this situation you receive punishment without being able to respond. That is, you must stand your ground at whatever cost. Up until now I still had not seen anything terrible in battle, but now I see many people, pale as sheets, I see how they bend low when a shell flies by, as if it were possible to bend away from it. Clearly fear is stronger than judgment in these people. I had already seen many killed and badly wounded. It is pitiful to look at the latter, as they groan and crawl about the so-called field of honor! What can compensate the simple soldier for the terror of this circumstance? Or a recruit? It is quite another matter for an educated person: an exalted feeling of honor, heroism, allegiance to the Emperor, and sacred duty to the fatherland force him to meet death fearlessly, to overcome pain manfully, and to part with life calmly.

Now for the first time danger was so close to me that it couldn't have been closer. A shell fell under my horse's belly, immediately exploded, and whistling splinters flew in all directions. Deafened, showered with earth, I was scarcely able to keep my seat on Alcides, who gave such a jump sidewards that I thought he had been possessed by the devil. Poor Vyshemirsky, who grimaces at every shot, told me that he could not have kept his seat during such a frenzied leap. But what is more amazing is that not one splinter hit either myself or Alcides! This is so extraordinary that my comrades cannot get over it. Oh, truly the prayers of my father and the blessing of my old grandmother preserve my life amidst these terrible, bloody scenes.

It has been raining since dawn. I am shaking, since nothing on me is dry. Rainwater pours onto my helmet, through the helmet onto my head, along my face and down my neck, over my whole body, into my boots, fills them up and flows in several rivulets to the ground. Every limb is shaking like an autumn leaf. Finally, we are ordered to move back, and another cavalry regiment is put in our place. And it's high time, high time! We have been here almost all morning, soaked to the bone, stiff. We have seen no one advancing against us, but despite all this have lost a lot of men.

When our regiment was at a safe distance from the enemy fire, I asked the captain for permission to ride to Heilsberg, which was located about a verst away. I had to shoe Alcides. He had lost a shoe, and besides I wanted to buy something to eat. I was so hungry that I had even gazed with envy at a hunk of bread in the hands of one of our officers. The captain gave me permission to go, but ordered me to return quickly, because night was coming and the regiment might change location. Alcides and I, both shaking from cold and hunger, flew like a whirlwind to Heilsberg. I put up my horse at the first inn which met my eye, and, seeing blacksmiths there shoeing Cossack horses, I asked them to shoe mine as well and went inside. There was a large fire on some sort of hearth or stone of special construction. Next to it stood leather armchairs, on one of which I immediately sat down. I was scarcely able to give some money to a Jewish woman to buy me some bread before I sank into the deepest sleep. Fatigue, cold from my wet clothes, hunger and the pain in every limb from constantly sitting on the horse, my youth, unaccustomed to experiencing so many problems all together, all this at once, having deprived me of strength, delivered me defenselessly into the power of sleep, as untimely as it was dangerous. I was awakened by my shoulder being vigorously shaken. Opening my eyes, I looked about with surprise, unable to understand where I was. Why was I in this place? And in fact what was I? Although my eyes were open, my mental faculties were still fettered by sleep. Finally I regained my senses and became extremely alarmed. Night had already arrived and covered everything with darkness. On the hearth there was hardly enough fire to illuminate the hall. By the light of the now flaring, now guttering flames I saw that the person who was shaking me by the shoulder was a chasseur. Taking me for an officer because of my luxuriant white epaulets, he was saying, "Wake up, wake up, your honor! The bombardment is getting heavier! Shells are falling in the town!"

I rushed to where I had left my horse. I saw that he was standing in the same place. I looked at his hoof—unshod! Not a soul in the tavern, the Jew and his wife had fled. There was no point in even thinking about getting bread! I led Alcides out and saw that it was not yet so late as I had thought. The sun had just set, and it was a beautiful evening. The rain had stopped and the heavens had cleared. I mounted my poor, hungry, and unshod Alcides. Approaching the city gates, I was horror-stricken at the number of wounded who crowded together there—they had to be left behind! There was no way to push oneself through this crowd of infantry, cavalry, women and children. Damaged guns and pontoons had been dragged here, and everything was so crowded together, so packed against the gates, that I completely despaired. Time was flying, and I was unable even to wiggle, surrounded on all sides by the crowd that constantly moved towards me, not thinning out in the least. Finally it became totally dark. The cannonade stopped, and everything around became quiet, except the place where I found myself. Here moans, squeals, screeches, curses, and cries almost drove me and my horse out of our minds. He would have reared up had there been enough room, but as there was not, he snorted and kicked whomever he could. God, how can I get myself out of here? Where can I find my regiment now? The night was becoming black, not just dark. What shall I do? To my great good fortune, I saw several Cossacks somehow beating their way through this thick mass of people, horses and cannons. Seeing them deftly galloping through the gates, I instantly joined them and also galloped through, only I injured my knee painfully and almost broke my shoulder. Having torn myself free at some distance, I stroked Alcides's bowed neck. I am sorry for you, my true comrade, but there is nothing for it, gallop on! From the light pressure of my legs, my steed set off at a gallop. I entrusted myself to Alcides's instinct. There was nothing by which I could find my way: the night was so dark that it was impossible to see anything well at twenty paces. I gave him the reins. Alcides soon stopped galloping and went at a walk, constantly snorting and rapidly flicking his ears. I guessed that he saw or smelled something frightening, but since it was pitch dark, as they say, I could not have avoided trouble even if it were imminent. It was clear that the army had left its position and that I was wandering alone among strange fields surrounded by darkness and deathly stillness.

Finally Alcides began to ascend some incline that was so steep I had to hold onto his mane as tightly as possible to keep from falling from the saddle. The darkness was so thick that I could see absolutely nothing in front of me, could not understand where I was going, and what sort of end awaited such a journey. While I was thinking and mulling over what to do, Alcides suddenly began to descend the same sort of terrible incline that we had climbed. There was no time to think. To save my skull I quickly sprang from my horse and led him by hand, bending almost to the ground in order to see where to put my feet and taking every precaution needed for such a dangerous descent. When Alcides and I finally stood on level ground, I saw a terrible and lamentable spectacle: innumerable corpses covered the field. One could see them, because, being either completely naked or just in their shirts, they lay like white shadows on the black earth. A number of fires were visible at a great distance, and right next to me there was a highway. Behind me was the redoubt, which Alcides had climbed onto and from which I had so fearfully descended. Learning, finally, where I was and guessing correctly that the fires I saw were those of our army, I remounted and directed my way along the road toward the fires straight ahead, but Alcides swerved to the left and took up a gallop. The path he chose was horrible for me: he leaped among the dead, now jumping over them, now approaching them and jumping to the side, now stopping and lowering his muzzle, he would smell the corpses and snort over them. I could bear it no longer and turned him again to the road. My steed obeyed with obvious reluctance and proceeded at a walk, still trying, however, to bear to the right. After several minutes I heard the hoofbeats of numerous horses and people's voices, and finally caught sight of a group of cavalry coming straight for me. They were talking about something and often repeating "Your Excellency." I was overjoyed, supposing that doubtless "His Excellency" would know where the fires of the Konnopolsk regiment were, or, if not, would permit me to join his suite. When they had come close to me, the one riding in front, presumably the general himself, asked me, "Who goes there?"

I replied, "One of the Konnopolsk regiment."

"Where are you going?"

"To my regiment!"

"Your regiment is over there," said the general, indicating with his arm the direction towards which my trusty Alcides had so urgently tried to turn, "but you are riding towards the enemy!"

The general and his suite galloped towards Heilsberg, while I, having kissed my priceless Alcides's little ear several times, gave him the reins to seek his own way. Feeling himself free, in an expression of joy my trusty steed reared up, neighed, and galloped straight towards the fires which were showing to the left side of the road. There were no corpses on my path, and, thanks to Alcides's speed, within a quarter of an hour I was home, that is, at the regiment. The Konnopolsk men were already mounted. My Alcides took his place in his rank, with quiet, friendly nickering, and he had just time to get set when the command resounded, "To the right by threes, march!" The regiment moved out.

Vyshemirsky and the other comrades of my division were overjoyed by my return, but the sergeant felt it his duty to reprimand me: "You do stupid things, Durov! You don't look out for yourself! At Guttstadt, in the very heat of battle, you figured to give your horse to some wounded person! Didn't you have sense enough to know that a cavalryman on foot in the middle of a battle is the worst sort of lost creature? At the Passarge River you dismounted and lay down to sleep in the bushes while the whole regiment momentarily awaited the order to move out at a trot. What would have happened to you if you had not had a horse which, and I say this without anger, is far more intelligent than you! You were allowed to go to Heilsberg for half an hour, and you succeeded in falling asleep on the hearth, while even to think of sleep was forbidden. A soldier must be more than a man! Age does not matter in this calling. Duty must be fulfilled the same at seventeen, at thirty, and at eighty. I advise you to die on your horse at your station, for otherwise, I prophesy to you that you will either dishonorably become a prisoner or will be killed by stragglers, or, worst of all, be considered a coward!" The sergeant ceased speaking, but his last words stung me. Blood rushed to my face.

There are, however, limits beyond which a person cannot go! Notwithstanding the philosophizing of our sergeant about the duties of a soldier, I was falling down from lack of sleep and fatigue. My clothes were soaking, for forty-eight hours I had not slept or eaten, been continuously on the march, or if not moving, then still on horseback, wearing only my uniform, subjected to the cold wind and rain without any protection. I felt that my strength was lessening by the hour. We moved by threes, but, if we encountered a small bridge or any other obstacle, it was impossible to advance as units, so we went two side by side or sometimes alone. In such a case the fourth platoon had to stand for several minutes in one place without moving. I was in the fourth platoon, and at each fortuitous stop immediately dismounted, lay down on the ground, and in a second fell asleep. The platoon would move from its position, my comrades would cry out and call me, and since sleep which is often interrupted cannot be sound, I would immediately awaken, get up, and scramble onto Alcides, dragging my heavy oak lance behind. This scene was repeated at each stop. I exhausted my corporal's patience and angered my comrades. All of them told me that they would abandon me on the road if I dismounted even one more time. "Surely you see that we are drowsy, but we don't dismount and lie on the ground. You do as we do!" The sergeant growled under his breath, "Why do such puppies crawl into the service! They should stay at home!"

For the remainder of the night I stayed on my horse, drowsing, falling asleep, bending right down to Alcides's mane and rising up with fear. I thought I was falling! I seemed to have gone crazy! My eyes were open, but things moved around like in a dream. The uhlans seemed to be a forest, the forest seemed to be uhlans. My head burns, but I am shaking, I am very cold. Everthing on me is soaked to the skin!

It has grown light. We have stopped. We have been allowed to light a fire and cook gruel. Oh, praise God, now I can lie down to sleep in front of a fire, get warm and dry out!

"Impossible," says the sergeant, seeing me sitting near the fire and rolling some grass into a ball under my head, "Impossible! The captain has ordered the horses to be grazed. Take the bit out of your horse's mouth and lead it to the grass."

I went with Alcides to walk about the field like the others. He ate the dewey grass and I stood sadly next to him.

"You're as pale as a corpse," said Vyshemirsky, approaching me with his horse. What's the matter? Are you ill?"

"No, I'm fine, but really frozen to the marrow. The rain soaked me to the skin, all my blood is like ice and now I've got to walk about the damp grass!"

"It seems that the rain sprinkled all of us equally, so why are we dry?"

"You all have your overcoats."

"And where is yours?"

"The Cossacks took it along with my saddlebags and case."

"What sort of wonder made that happen?"

"You haven't forgotten that I put a wounded dragoon officer on my horse to be carried to his regiment?"

"I remember. So what?"

"This is what. I found my horse in Podvyshansky's hands. He had bought it from the Cossacks with just its saddle—everything else was lost!"

"That's bad, comrade. You are younger than any of us. On a cold night you won't last long without an overcoat! Tell the sergeant to give you an overcoat from one of the dead. They are sending a pile of them to the supply train."

We talked for some time. Finally the sun rose high in the sky, the day became warm, my uniform dried out, fatigue left me, and I would have been quite happy if I had any hope of eating something. But I couldn't even consider that. I had no share in the gruel which was being boiled. And so I started to search diligently in the grass for some sort of berries. The captain, who was riding by the uhlans walking their horses about the field, noticed my effort.

"What are you looking for, Durov?" he asked, having ridden up to me.

I answered that I was looking for berries. Apparently the captain guessed the reason, because he turned to the squadron corporal and said to him quietly, "See that Durov and Vyshemirsky are filled up." He rode on, but the veterans exclaimed, "When we are filled up, then they can be! They think more about these puppies than about us veterans."

"What fools you are, you veterans!" said the sergeant, coming up to us. "About whom should we worry, if not about children! I imagine you can see for yourselves that both these soldiers were children not very long ago."

"Come with me, children," said the sergeant jokingly, taking us both by the hand, "The captain gave orders to feed you." They gave us soup, roast meat and white bread.

Seeing that our horses were quietly grazing and that the uhlans were sleeping on the meadow, I found no need to keep watch alone. It was already past noon, the heat had become intolerable. I went down to the bank of the river which flowed past our camp and lay down in the high grass to sleep. Alcides was walking about nearby. My deep sleep was broken by the cry, "Bridle your animals! Mount up!" by the footsteps of the uhlans running for their horses, and by the sound of horses headed for the front. I jumped up abruptly. The sergeant was already mounted and urging the uhlans to fall into formation. I looked around for Alcides and to my horror I saw him swimming across the river to the other bank. At that moment the sergeant galloped up to me.

"Why are you standing here without a horse?" This was no time to be indecisive. I threw myself after Alcides and we climbed out onto the opposite bank together. In an instant I had put on his bridle, mounted, swum back and was in my place before the squadron had fully formed up. "Well, at least you put things right in a determined way," said the sergeant with a satisfied look.

Schoeppenbel

Great God, what terror! The village is almost totally burned down! So many people are badly burned! Oh, miserable people!

June 1807. Friedland

More than half of our brave regiment was lost in this fearsome and final battle. We attacked several times, several times routed the enemy, and in turn were routed ourselves more than once. We were sprinkled with grapeshot, shelled until we ached, and the penetrating whistle of the hellish bullets completely deafened me. Oh, I can't bear them! A shell is a different matter. At least it roars magnificently, and there's always a short interval between them. After several hours of heated battle the remainder of the regiment was ordered to retreat a bit in order to rest. Taking advantage of this, I went to see how our artillery was going, not at all concerned that my head might be taken off totally gratuitously. Bullets sprinkled about myself and my horse, but what are bullets compared to this wild, unceasing roar of cannons?

Some uhlan from our regiment, all bloody, with a bandaged head and blood-streaked face, is riding aimlessly about the field, now in one direction, now in another. Poor fellow, he doesn't know where he is going, and he can scarcely stay in the saddle! I rode up to him and asked him which squadron he was in. He muttered something and lurched so badly that I had to hold him to keep him from falling. Seeing that he did not recognize anything, I tied his reins to Alcides's neck and, supporting the wounded man with one arm, rode to the river to refresh him with some water. Near the river he somehow came to, slid off his horse, and collapsed at my feet from weakness. What could I do? It was impossible to abandon him, for he would perish. There was no way to take him to a safe place. And just where was there a safe place hereabouts? Everywhere was firing, cannonading, shells bouncing in all directions, mortar shells exploding in the air and on the ground, waves of cavalry advancing and retreating, and in this terrible confusion I could no longer see the banners of our regiment. However, there was no time to be lost. I dipped up some water in my helmet and poured it over the wounded man's head and face. He opened his eyes. "For God's sake, don't leave me here," he said, raising himself with difficulty. "Somehow I'll mount my horse. Lead me at a walk to the rear of our army. God will reward your humanity." I helped him mount his horse, got on Alcides, again took the reins of the wounded uhlan and rode to Friedland.

The inhabitants are fleeing, the regiments retreating. A multitude of good for nothing soldiers who have fled the battlefield without having been wounded are spreading terror among the retreating hordes, crying, "All is lost, we've been totally defeated! The enemy is on our heels! Flee! Save yourselves!" Although I did not in the least believe these cowards, seeing whole squadrons of dragoons passing through town at a trot, I could not remain calm. I regretted with all my heart that I had been distracted by curiosity to see the cannons firing and that bad luck had sent me this wounded officer. To abandon him to the whim of chance seemed to me the highest degree of baseness and inhumanity—I could not do that! The miserable uhlan with the moribund face turned his frightened gaze upon me. I understood his fear.

"Can you travel a little faster?" I asked.

"I can't," the miserable one answered and sighed heavily.

We continued at a walk. People were running and galloping past us, crying out: "Go faster! The enemy is close!" Finally we came into a forest. I turned from the road and went into the thick part of the woods, not releasing the bridle of the wounded uhlan. The shade and coolness of the forest somewhat refreshed my comrade, but he, to his misfortune, made the worst of this: he decided to smoke his pipe. He stopped, struck a light, began to smoke his repulsive tobacco, but inside a minute his eyes began to roll, the pipe dropped from his hands, and he fell lifelessly onto the neck of his horse. I halted, dragged him down onto the ground, stretched him out, and, not having any means to restore him to consciousness, stood next to him holding both horses, waiting until he would regain his senses. After a quarter of an hour he opened his eyes, raised himself, sat up, and gazed at me with an insane look. I saw that he was confused. His head was all cut up, and the tobacco smoke had had the effect of wine on him. "Mount your horse," I said. "Otherwise we shall be late. Get up, I'll help you." He didn't answer but tried to get up. I helped him onto his feet. Holding the reins of the horses with one hand, I assisted him with the other to rise in the stirrup, but almost fell because the half-comprehending uhlan, instead of grasping the mane of his horse, leaned the whole weight of his arm on my shoulder.

We were off again. The crowds were still fleeing with their same cry of "Save yourselves!" Finally I caught sight of some guns that were being hauled past us. I asked my protégé if he didn't want to stay with them, since it would be easier to lie on a gun-carriage than to sit on his horse. He was visibly pleased with my proposal, and so right off I asked the artillery corporal if he would look after the wounded uhlan and his horse. He willingly took charge and immediately ordered my comrade taken from his horse, several horse blankets to be laid on the gun-carriage and the wounded uhlan put onto them. I shook from happiness, seeing myself free, and at that point set off in search of my regiment, if only I could find out from someone where it was. I rode about alone until night asking all those that passed me whether they knew where the Konnopolsk uhlan regiment was. Some said that it was up ahead, that one part of the army had gone off in a certain direction, and that my regiment was in that division. I was in despair. Night fell and I had to rest Alcides. I saw a group of Cossacks making a fire and cooking themselves some supper. Dismounting, I approached them:

"Hello, brothers! You are probably going to spend the night here?"

"We shall," they answered.

"And what about the horses? Will you let them graze?"

They looked at me with astonishment. "What else? Of course they'll graze."

"And they won't go away?"

"And what's that to you?" asked an old Cossack, looking me steadily in the eye.

"I should like to let my horse loose with yours to pasture, only I am afraid he might go away."

"Well, take care of it. Tie it with a lasso, wrap it around your hand, and then the horse cannot go off without waking you. We let ours out on lassoes."

Having said this, the old Cossack invited me to eat gruel with them. After that, they turned their horses loose and, having tied each with the ends of lassoes wrapped around their hands, they lay down to sleep. I walked off with Alcides, not knowing what to do. I also wanted to sleep, but how was I to leave my horse free all night? I had no lasso. Finally I decided to tie Alcides's front feet with my handkerchief. It was a thin cotton handkerchief, one of a dozen given me by my grandmother while I was still in Little Russia. Only one of this dozen was still left, and I kept it with me everywhere. I liked it very much, and I washed it myself every day in a creek or a river or lake or pond, wherever I could. I bound Alcides's legs with this handkerchief and let him graze, and I lay down to sleep not far from the Cossacks.

It was already dawn when I awoke. The Cossacks and their horses were gone, and so was my Alcides. Frightened to death and inexpressibly depressed, I arose from the grass on which I had slept so quietly. Dragoons' saddled horses were walking all over the entire field. With bitter regret in my soul I walked aimlessly among them looking for Alcides. Having gone in one direction and another for half an hour, I caught sight of a piece of my handkerchief showing white in the distance. I ran in that direction, and to my indescribable joy, Alcides ran up to me, bucking. He nickered and put his head on my shoulder. Only an end of the white handkerchief was still wrapped around his right leg, but the rest of it was torn to shreds and spread about the field. The snaffle bit and the bridle and reins had been taken. It was useless to ask the dragoons about them. Who would order them to tell me what had happened to them, or, more important, to give them back. A dreadful situation! How could I show up at the regiment looking like this? This was a wonderful example to teach one to be selfish— to intend steadfastly forever and in all circumstances to think more about oneself than about others. Twice I had given way to a feeling of compassion, and both times I had been very badly rewarded. Moreover, the first time the captain had called me a madcap, but now what would he think of me? The battle had been going on when I had decided to go to our cannons, and suddenly what had become of me? A frightening thought! I was afraid to linger on it. The dragoons, learning the cause of my agitation, gave me a long strap with which to fashion a bridle and told me that my regiment could not be very far ahead, since it had also spent the night in the same place as they had, and that I might find it still in that place. Tying the nasty strap to the headband, which had remained on Alcides, I felt terribly angry with myself. "Oh, my beautiful steed," I said thoughtfully, "what a silly ninny you have for a mistress!"

But neither remorse, nor pity, nor anger could save me from misfortune. I arrived at the regiment, but now it was not the captain but Kakhovsky himself, our general, who told me that my valor was mad, my compassion mindless, that I threw myself into the thick of battle when it was not necessary, that I went on attack with squadrons other than my own, that in battle during the most vigorous skirmishes I save the first comer and give him my horse and myself remain on foot, that he has totally lost patience with my antics and was ordering me to the supply train. Me, to the supply train! Every drop of blood left my face. The most ghastly nightmare could not have included a punishment more terrible than this. Kazimirsky, who had a fatherly affection for me, looked sympathetically at the change in my face. He said something quietly to the chief, but the latter answered, "No! No! We must preserve him." Turning to me, he began to speak much more kindly:

"I am sending you to the supply train in order to preserve a brave officer for the future of the fatherland. In several years you will be better able to use that daring which now will cost you your life without accomplishing anything."

Oh, what do I care about such empty consolations? They are mere words, and the essence of the matter is that I am going to the supply train. I went to Alcides to prepare him for this shameful situation. Embracing the trusty companion of my military life, I cried from shame and sorrow! My hot tears, falling on his black mane, rolled and flowed along the pommel. Vyshemirsky is also being sent to the supply train. But why he? He is always where he should be, and one can't blame him for thoughtless daring or for misplaced pity. He has the presence of mind and judiciousness of an adult.

Everything is ready. Thus began our funeral procession: wounded horses, wounded people, and the two of us, in the blush of youth, completely healthy, slowly moving one foot after the other to that place of tranquillity, the damned supply train. There is nothing I regret more than Kakhovsky's decision, which kept me from taking part in any battle again before the campaign ended.

Tilsit

We joined our regiment here. Everyone who is able to bear arms is in formation. They say we shall go from here to Russia. So, the campaign is over! And my hopes and dreams have ended. Instead of brilliant exploits, I acted like a fool. Will I ever have a chance to erase this record? Napoleon's impatient spirit and the shakiness of the crown on his head guarantees me this possibility. He will force Russia once more to lift its mighty weapon, but will this happen soon? And what shall I do until then? Will I still be just a common soldier? Will they make me an officer without proof of gentry birth? And how am I to obtain it? My papers are at my uncle's place. Would that he would send them! But no, he won't do that. On the contrary. Oh God, God! Why do I remain alive? I was so sunk in these lachrymose thoughts that I didn't see the captain gallop up to where I was standing.

"What's this, Durov!" he said, lightly adjusting my sabre. "Is this the time to hang your head and brood? Sit up smartly and look happy, the Emperor is coming!"

Having said this, he galloped on. Commands resounded, the regiments lined up, trumpets blared, and we lowered our lances to our beloved Tsar, who flew towards us on a beautiful horse accompanied by a large suite.

The Return of the Armies to Russia

Having entered our homeland, the army dispersed to various places by corps, by divisions, and even regiments. Our regiment, the Pskov Dragoons, and the Orden Cuirassiers are staying in camp. We have tents as big as dancehalls. Each houses a platoon. The captain sent for Vyshemirsky and me. He told us that wartime, when we all might sleep together on straw, had ended, and that now it was necessary to observe strictly the decorum and duties of the service, that we had to stand at attention for officers, present arms when on guard duty, and at roll call answer with a loud and clear voice. Like the others I must stand guard over our hay at night, use a spade to clean the *platz,* that is, the place for parade in front of the main guard house, and stand guard at the church and over the powder supply. Every morning and evening we water our horses at the river, which is about a verst away. Sometimes I get to lead two and ride the third. In that case I ride decorously to the river, but on the way back to camp I fly like a whirlwind with my three horses, and in flight I hear the curses showered after me by the uhlans, dragoons and cuirassiers. They are all unable to handle their own horses, which have been led astray by the bad example of mine, which, knowing that they will be given oats at the tethering area, carry me at full speed, and at a gallop, jump, kick, and pull away; every minute I expect to be torn from Alcides's back. Each time I get a reprimand from the sergeant and duty officer for failing to restrain the playful horses.

Finally we are in quarters. My life passes in the monotonous occupations of a soldier. At dawn I go to my horse, groom him, feed him, and, having covered him with a sheet, leave him in care of the soldier on duty. Then I go to the apartment where, to my delight, I am quartered alone. My hostess here is a good woman. She gives me milk, butter, and good bread. Late autumn makes my excursions not so pleasant. How happy I would be if I could have some books! The captain has lots of them. I suppose he might not think it strange if I were to ask him to let me read them; however, I am afraid to take that risk. If, contrary to expectation, he were to say that a soldier has other things to do besides reading books, then I would be very ashamed. I will wait, there will be time to read. Certainly I won't be a simple soldier all my life. Vyshemirsky has already been promoted to corporal. True, he has a patroness, Countess Poniatowska. At the beginning of the campaign she took him to Bennigsen and got his promise to be the protector of her foster-child. But I, I am alone in this wide world. Who should worry about me? Everything must come with time and from my own effort! It would be strange if my superiors were unable to distinguish me from soldiers recruited from the plough.

Kresses—that is what the Konnopolsk men call the assignment to distribute orders from the staff to the squadron quarters. "To be on *kresses,*" means to be sent with this sort of order. Today is my turn. Gachevsky, my platoon corporal, assigned me: "You are on kresses, Durov."

"I'm very glad!"

Indeed, I am happy for anything new. In camp I have been very pleased when assigned to clean the *platz.* I have worked willingly, scraping the grass from the ground with a spade, sweeping it into a pile with a broom, and I have done all this as if I had done nothing else all my life. My previous mentor has been present at almost all these labors. He claps me on the shoulder and says, "You will work yourself to death, child. Take it easy."

In the evening an order was brought from the staff, and Gachevsky ordered me to set off immediately with it to the captain, who was quartered five versts from our village.

"I shall go on foot," I told Gachevsky, "I don't want to bother Alcides."

"Bother him! It's only five versts. However, if you have more concern for Alcides's legs than for your own, go on foot."

I set off. The sun had already set, and the evening was beautiful. The road lay across fields sown with rye, and in some places wound between coppices. The weather in Poland is captivating. In any case, I find it better than our northern weather. In Russia one cannot forget about the winter cold even in summer, because it is always nearby. Our winter is a real winter, frightening, annihilating! But here it is so brief, so indulgent.

Here the winter snow permits the eye the pleasure of seeing tips of grass, and the sight of this not entirely hidden greenery provides the heart a consoling prospect that with the first spring wind the ground shall appear, and there will be grass and even the springtime will be warm. As I walked and dreamed, the sky became covered with clouds and a fine drizzle began. I increased my pace, and, since the settlement was in sight, I was able to reach it before a heavier rain had begun. The captain read the order, asked me if my quarters were nice, and then said: "Well, it's already night. You can go back to the platoon tomorrow, so spend the night in the stables."

I had certainly not expected this, and I became ashamed for Galer:

had he lost his mind? True, even dreaming, he could not imagine that I was... However, why send me to the stables? That's a charming bedroom!

The rain has entirely stopped, it was sprinkling only occasionally. I walked back. But in order to get home more quickly, I decided to go on a bee-line, that is straight in the direction in which I know our village was located. To do this I had to leave the road and cross the grain fields, which I did without a moment's thought. But might not this direct route be longer than the regular road? While I was walking along the edge of a rye field, everything was quite tolerable. The night was bright, and I could distinguish objects clearly. The rye had been dampened by the rain and wound itself around me, but my clothes were still not soaked through. Finally the path began to go deep into the middle of the field, and I entered rye which was tall and thick, and I was only a head taller than it. Burning with impatience to come to a clear area as soon as possible. I walked rapidly, not concerning myself that the thick rye was transferring all its rain drops onto my uniform. No matter how I hastened, I could not see the end of that infinite plain of rye ears, which undulated like the ocean. I became tired, water was flowing off me in streams, and my rapid pace had made me unendurably hot. Now I went somewhat more quietly and took comfort in the fact that the night would end sometime and that when daylight came I would finally see our village. Mentally submitting to the sad destiny of having to wander all night about the damp field in the high rye, I proceeded calmly but unhappily. And why should I have been amused, having to walk in rye up to my ears and with nothing more before my eyes but heads of grain?

After half an hour of patient walking, and when I least of all expected to see anything resembling a village or a fence, suddenly I found myself at the very gates of the village. Oh, how happy I was! In an instant I opened the gates and in a flash arrived at my quarters. There everyone was sleeping, the fire had gone out, and so for a long time I had to crawl about in the dark until I found my locker, took undergarments from it, undressed, dressed again, wrapped myself in my cloak, lay down and instantly fell asleep.

Alcides! O fatal heartache, when will you be stilled? Alcides, my invaluable Alcides! Once so strong, so unruly, whom no one could break and who permitted my youthful hand to guide you. You, who so dutifully bore me on your back in my childhood, who passed with me through the bloody field of honor, glory and death, who shared with me hardship, danger, hunger, cold, joy and satisfaction! You, the only animal who ever loved me. You are gone. You exist no longer!

Four weeks have passed since that unhappy occurrence. I have been unable to take up my pen. A mortal anguish has oppressed my soul. I go about everywhere dejected and with hanging head. Reluctantly I fulfill the duties of my calling. Wherever I am or whatever I do, sadness is with me everywhere, and tears constantly fill my eyes. On guard duty I am overcome with grief. When relieved from duty I no longer run to Alcides.... Alas, I go slowly to his grave. The evening ration of oats is given out, I hear the contented nickering of our horses, but the voice of the one who brought joy to my soul is quiet! Oh, Alcides, Alcides, I buried my happiness with you! I do not know if I will have the strength to describe the tragic death of that unforgettable comrade of both my youth and my military life! My pen shakes in my hand, and tears cloud my vision. However, I shall write. Someday father will read my memoirs and will pity my Alcides.

Our horses were all together in a large squadron stable, and as in camp we would take the whole squadron together to water them. Bad weather, which did not permit any drill or riding, was the reason that our horses stood inactive so long, and there was no way to control them during their return from watering. On that most unfortunate day of my life, I decided, to my eternal regret, to take Alcides on a halter. Previously I had always ridden him and led the other horses on halters, but now to my misfortune I did the opposite. As we were going toward the river, Alcides jumped about lightly, now pulling on the halter, now pushing my knee with his nose, now taking my epaulet into his lips. But as we returned, all the horses began to jump, rear up, snort, kick, and several, having pulled away, began to play and squeal. My unfortunate Alcides, distracted by this example, reared up on his hind legs, jumped to the side, pulled the halter from my hand, and borne by his evil fate, flew like an arrow, leaping over the low fences and hedges at a gallop. Oh miserable, miserable me, the unhappy witness of my most terrible misfortune! Watching Alcides's rapid gallop, I see him leap... and a mortal chill runs through my body... Alcides is leaping across a fence from which sharpened stakes an arshin in length are pointing upwards. The powerful steed was able to leap that high, but alas, he was unable to jump far enough. The weight of his body brought him down right into the fence. One of the stakes pierced his innards and broke off. With a cry of despair I flew headlong after my unfortunate friend. I found him in his stall, his whole body trembling, and sweat was pouring from him in streams. The ruinous splinter remained in his innards and a quarter of it was visible outside. Death was inescapable. Running up to him, I embraced his neck and burst into tears. The good steed put his head on my shoulder, sighed heavily, and in five minutes fell and stretched out convulsively. Alcides, Alcides! Why didn't I die right then. The duty officer, seeing that I was embracing and covering the still body of my horse with kisses and tears, said that I was being childishly silly, and gave the order to drag his body into the field. I ran to the captain to beg him to order the body of my Alcides be left in peace and to permit me to bury him myself.

"What? Your poor Alcides has died?" the captain asked sympathetically, seeing my red eyes and pale face. "That's a pity, a pity! You loved him so. Well, what's to be done, stop crying. I'll order them to give you any horse in the squadron. Go now, bury your comrade."

He sent his orderly with me, and the duty officer no longer hindered me from the sad work of burying my Alcides. My comrades, touched by the extremity of my grief, dug a deep pit, lowered Alcides into it, sprinkled him with dirt, and having cut sod with their sabres, made a border for the high mound under which the single being who loved me sleeps the sleep from which he will never awaken.

My comrades, having finished their work, went back to the squadron, and I stayed and cried on the grave of my Alcides until the middle of the night. The compassionate captain ordered that I be allowed to mourn for two days and not be given any duties. For almost all this time I did not leave the grave of my steed. Despite the cold wind and rain, I remained at the grave until midnight. Having returned to my apartment, I ate nothing and cried until morning. On the third day the platoon commander, having summoned me, said that I should choose a horse for myself, and that the captain had ordered him to give me any I wanted.

"I thank you for the kindness," I answered, "but now all horses are the same to me. I will take whichever one you care to give me."

When I used to have to tack up Alcides, I did it willingly, but now this task is very unpleasant for me. With a deep sigh I led my new horse into the stall where my Alcides had died and covered it with the blanket with which I had covered him three days before. I am not crying any longer, but I wander joylessly about the yellowing fields. I see the cold autumn rain sprinkle the grave of my Alcides and dampen the turf on which he used to leap so happily.

Every morning my first steps are to Alcides's grave. I lie down on it, pressing my face to the cold earth, and my hot tears sink into it along with the raindrops. Returning in thought to my childhood years, I recall how many joyful hours were provided me by the rare attachment and obedience of this beautiful horse. I recall those gorgeous summer nights when, leading Alcides behind me, I ascended Startsov Mountain along that path on which only goats had clambered. It was not difficult for me to go along it, my small feet could step on it as conveniently as goat hooves, but my good steed risked falling off and being smashed to pieces. Nonetheless, he followed me obediently, although he shook from fear seeing himself at a terrible height above the precipice. Alas, my Alcides! How many misfortunes, how many dangers passed you by without causing you harm! But my thoughtlessness, my fatal thoughtlessness, finally put you into the grave. This thought rends and tears my soul. Nothing makes me happy any more, the very shadow of a smile has disappeared from my face. Everything that I do, I do mechanically, by habit. With lifeless indifference

I ride on maneuvers, silently return when they are finished, unsaddle my horse and put it away, not looking at it, and I leave, without saying a word to anyone.

A corporal came for me from the chief. I am wanted at staff headquarters. Why? It seems I have been ordered to turn over to the squadron my horse, saddle, lance, sabre and pistols, so apparently I will not be returning. I go to say good-bye to Alcides. I cry on his grave as unconsolably as on the day of his death, and having bade him farewell for ever, for the last time I kiss the earth covering him.

Polotsk

Some sort of important change is occurring in my life. Kakhovsky asked me if my parents were agreeable to my serving in the military and whether I had done so against their wishes. I immediately told the truth, that my father and mother would never have let me enter the military, but that having had an insurmountable attraction to arms, I had secretly departed from home with a Cossack regiment. Although I am only seventeen, I am already sufficiently experienced to guess immediately that Kakhovsky knows more about me that he indicates, because after hearing my answer, he showed no surprise at the strange mentality of parents who didn't want their son in the military, when all the gentry prefer to choose a military calling for their children. He only said that I had to go with Mr. Neidgardt, his adjutant, to Vitebsk, to see Buksgevden. Neidgardt was also there. When Kakhovsky gave me that order, Neidgardt immediately bowed and went with me to his own house. He left me in the hall and joined his family in the inner rooms. After a quarter of an hour first one, then a second head began to peek out at me from the partly open doors, Neidgardt did not come out. He dined there, drank coffee, and sat for a long time, and all the while I was alone in the hall. What strange people! Why didn't they invite me to dine with them?

We left Polotsk toward evening. At the posting stations Neidgardt drank coffee, whereas I had always to stand by the carriage while they changed horses.

Now I am in Vitebsk, and I live in Neidgardt's apartment. He has become a different person. He converses with me in a friendly manner, and, like a polite host, he regales me with tea, coffee, breakfast. In a word, he acts like he should have acted from the beginning. He says that he brought me to Vitebsk by the order of the commander-in-chief, and that I must appear before him.

I am still living at Neidgardt's. In the morning we breakfast together, and afterwards he goes to the commander-in-chief while I stay in the apartment or go for a walk. But now it is late autumn and along with that the mud is deep. Not finding any place where I might walk as people should, I go to the tavern in which Neidgardt always dines. There I await him, and we have dinner together. After dinner he leaves, and I stay behind in the room of the tavern's proprietress. I am very happy there. The tavern keeper is a good, jocular woman. She calls me the *ulan-panna* [uhlan-miss] and says that if I let myself be girdled, she would bet her entire tavern and its income against gold that there was not one maiden in Vitebsk with such a narrow and pretty waist as mine. With these words she goes and brings her girdle. Her daughters laugh, because it would be possible to put all of them and myself inside her girdle.

Five days have passed since I have been living in Vitebsk. Finally this evening Neidgardt told me that tomorrow I must be at the commander-in-chief's, that he had been ordered to bring me at ten in the morning.

The next day I went with Neidgardt to Count Buksgevden. The former led me into the Count's study and immediately left. The commander-in-chief greeted me with a pleasant smile and asked right off: "Why have you been arrested? Where is your sabre?" I said that all my arms had been taken from me at the squadron.

"I shall order that everything be returned. A soldier must not go around without arms."

After that he asked me how old I was and continued speaking: "I have heard a great deal about your bravery, and I am very pleased that all your superiors responded about you in the most positive terms." He fell silent a minute and began again. "Do not be frightened by what I am going to tell you. I must send you to our Sovereign. He wants to meet you. But I repeat, do not be frightened. Our Sovereign is full of kindness and greatness of spirit, as you will find by experience." Nonetheless I was frightened.

"Our Sovereign will send me home, Your Excellency, I shall die from grief!" I said this with such a deep feeling of grief that the commander-in-chief was noticeably touched.

"Don't be afraid of that. In reward for your courage and excellent behavior, the Sovereign will not refuse you anything. And as I was ordered to make a report on you, I shall add my own report to those of your chief, the squadron commander, the platoon leader and Captain Kazimirsky. Believe me, they will not take away the uniform to which you have brought so much honor." Saying this, the general politely bowed to me, which was a sign that I was to leave.

Going into the hall, I saw Neidgardt conversing with Wing-Adjutant Zass. They both approached, and Neidgardt said, "The commander-in-chief ordered me to give you into the charge of Mr. Zass, the Wing-Adjutant of His Imperial Majesty. You will travel with him to Petersburg. So, permit me to wish you a pleasant journey."

Zass took me away by the hand: "Now come with me to my apartment, and from there we shall send for your things from Neidgardt's, and very early tomorrow morning we shall return to Polotsk, because Buksgevden ordered that your arms be returned immediately." Very early the next morning we left Vitebsk and quickly traveled to Polotsk.

Polotsk

Zass went to Kakhovsky and returned after an hour, saying that Kakhovsky, to his surprise, was dining at twelve o'clock and kept him there, and that he had to eat even though he didn't want to.

"Tomorrow we will leave very early. It's nothing new for you, Durov, to get up at dawn."

I told him that I never arose except at dawn. In the evening my platoon mates came to me and ordered me to report. I went. What nice people! These were the platoon corporal and my mentor, the one who had taught me everything an uhlan needs to know whether on foot or mounted.

"Goodbye, dear comrade," they said, "God grant you happiness. We have heard that you are going to Petersburg. Praise us there. We praised you here when the chief asked about you, and I especially," said my mentor, twisting his graying moustache. "I was your drillmaster by Kazimirsky's orders. The chief took me into his apartment and for a whole hour asked even the smallest things about you, and I told him everything, even how you cried and rolled on the ground when your Alcides died."

This memory caused me to sigh heavily. I said goodbye to my mates, gave my tutor my year's salary, and returned to the hall in the most depressed spirit.

Finally we set off for Petersburg. Our carriage hardly moves, we drag along rather than travel. At each station they harness up twelve horses, but together they aren't worth two decent ones. They look more like calves than horses, and often, when trying fruitlessly to pull the carriage out of the deep mud, they themselves finally lie down in the mud.

Something funny happens to us at almost every station. At one they gave us some blood-streaked sugar for our tea. "What's the meaning of this?" asked Zass, shoving the sugarbowl away.

The station master, who was in another room waiting to see what effect this sugar would have, entered at this question and with a kind of triumphal note said, "My daughter was cutting up the sugar loaf and she injured her hand. That is her blood!"

"Take your blood, you fool, and order some clean sugar for us," Zass said, turning away with disgust.

I laughed from the bottom of my heart at this new way of showing the sincerity of one's hospitality. At yet another station Zass yelled at the station master because he was drunk, spoke rudely, coarsely, and didn't want to give us horses. Hearing the loud conversation, the station master's wife jumped at Zass with her fists, hopping about from anger, and cried out in a squeaky voice, "What sort of lawless land is this where they dare to rebuke a station master!" The deafened Zass, not knowing how to escape this devil, thought to pinch her nose, and this proved effective. The Megaera ran off squealing, and the station master behind her. We waited for horses for half an hour, but seeing that we were not given any, made preparations to drink tea. Zass sent me as spokesman to the station master's wife to conduct negotiations about cream. Our enemy was happy with a truce, and I returned with a full cup of cream. After an hour horses were brought, and we parted very amiably with the station master, who had napped a bit, and with his wife, who wished me in particular a pleasant journey and covered her nose with her apron.

My First Trip to the Capital

Petersburg

Here is our bright, clean, magnificent capital, a memorial to the invincible heroism, great spirit, and heroic steadfastness of our immortal Peter!

Three days have already passed since we arrived. I am staying with Zass, and every day I go to look at the monument of Peter the Great. How worthy he is of this name! Peter would have been great in whatever status he might have been born. His magnificent appearance completely suits his broad genius, which once ruled his great spirit.

My fate has been decided. I was with the Sovereign! I saw Him, I spoke with Him! My heart is so full of such inexpressible joy, that I cannot find words to describe my feeling. The magnitude of my happiness astonishes me, enraptures me. Oh Sovereign, from this hour my life belongs to You!

When Prince V*** had opened the door for me to the Sovereign's study and closed it behind me, the Sovereign immediately approached me, gave me his hand, and approaching his table and laying a hand on it, and continuing to hold my hand with the other, he began to ask quietly and with such an expression of kindness that all my timidity disappeared and hope was reborn in my soul. "*I have heard,*" said the Sovereign, "*that you are not a man, is that so?*"

I could not immediately get up the courage to say, "Yes, Your Highness, it is true." For a minute I stood silently and with lowered eyes, my heart was beating violently, and my hand shook in the hand of the Tsar. The Sovereign waited. Finally, raising my eyes to his and answering, I noted the Sovereign was blushing. I instantly blushed myself, lowered my eyes and did not raise them until the moment when a feeling of involuntary grief cast me to the Sovereign's feet! Enquiring in detail about everything that had caused me to enter the service, the Sovereign highly praised my intrepidness, saying that this was the first example of its kind in Russia, that all my superiors had praised me most highly, calling my bravery unparalleled, that He was very pleased to believe this, and that accordingly he wished to reward me and to return me to my parental home, giv...

The Sovereign did not have time to finish. At the words "to return home" I cried out in horror, and instantly fell to the Sovereign's feet. "Don't send me home, Your Highness!" I said in a despairing voice, "Don't send me home. I shall die there, I shall certainly die. Don't force me to regret that not a single bullet found me in this campaign. Don't take my life away, Sovereign. I willingly wished to sacrifice it for You." Saying this I embraced the knees of the Sovereign and cried. The Sovereign was touched. He raised me up and asked in an altered voice, "What then do you want?"

"To be a soldier, to wear a uniform, to bear arms. That is the only reward which you can give me, Sovereign. There is no other for me. I was born in camp. The sound of the trumpet was my cradle song. From the day I was born I have loved the military. From the time I was ten years old I planned to enter it, and I achieved my goal when I was sixteen—alone and without any help! In my glorious station I was supported by my bravery alone, having neither protection nor aid. Everyone has unanimously admitted that I am worthy of bearing arms, and now Your Highness wants to send me home. If I had foreseen such an end, then nothing would have prevented me from finding a glorious death in the ranks of Your soldiers." I said this having folded my hands as before an icon and looking at the Sovereign with tear-filled eyes. The Sovereign listened to me and vainly sought to hide how touched he was. When I stopped speaking, the Sovereign remained somehow undecided for a couple of minutes. Finally his face lit up.

"If you wish," said the Emperor, "that permission to wear a uniform and to bear arms should be your only reward, then you shall have it!" At these words I trembled from joy. The Sovereign continued, "And I shall give you my name—Alexandrov! I do not doubt that you will prove worthy of this honor by the excellence of your conduct and actions. Do not forget for a minute that this name must always be unsullied, and that I will not forgive you even for a trace of a stain on it. Now tell me, to what regiment do you wish to be assigned? I am promoting you to officer's rank."

"In that case, permit me, Your Highness, to be subject to Your will," I said.

"The Mariupolsk Hussar Regiment, is one of the bravest and the corps of officers are from the best families," the Sovereign said, "I shall order you assigned there. Tomorrow you will receive from Liven what you need for the trip and for your uniforms. When you are all ready to set off for the regiment, I shall see you again. Saying this, the Sovereign bowed to me. I immediately went to the door, but not knowing how to open it, I turned the bronze knob which was in my hand in all directions. The Sovereign, seeing that I could not exit without his help, approached, opened the door for me, and watched me all the way to the next door, from which I went on by myself. On entering the hall, I immediately found myself surrounded by pages who kept asking me, "What did the Sovereign say to you? Did He make you an officer?"

I didn't know what to say to them. But Zass and an aide-de-camp approached me, and the crowd of scamps respectfully withdrew. The aide-de-camp, who had approached with Zass, asked me, "Aren't you about fifteen years old?" I answered that I was already eighteen.

"They wrote us wonders about your bravery," he said with a polite bow. Taking me by the hand, Zass interrupted this conversation.

"We must be going now, Prince," he said to his companion, and we left the palace. Descending the stairs, he asked, "Durov, would you like to be introduced to my relation, General Zass's wife?"

I answered that I would be very pleased.

"Well, then we shall go at once to dine with her. And after dinner we shall all go together to show you the Hermitage. There is much of interest there."

Mme. Zass received me very politely. After dinner we went to the Hermitage. The paintings attracted my attention most of all. I passionately love art. The general's wife said that if I would only look at pictures, I wouldn't finish in a month. "Look," she said, showing me a bouquet of gems, diamonds, and similar jewels, "Look, this is incomparably more interesting." I am not of her opinion. What do stones mean in comparison with the most beautiful products of the brush, which breathe with life? I liked very much four pictures representing two maidens full length. In the first two they were represented in childhood, and in the second in their youth, so that looking at the older ones you would recognize in them the pretty children so captivating with their youthful beauty. I looked at a depiction of Cleopatra, seeking to find in it the Tsaritsa who preferred death to humiliation, but I saw only a woman with a yellow, puffy face, in whose features there was no expression of anything, not even an expression of pain. On her bare arm a leech is crawling straight toward her shoulder. This comic asp is not worthy of the honor of poisoning the Tsaritsa. I would mortgage my head that not one person in the world would recognize the Egyptian Tsaritsa in this depiction, and I recognized it only because Zass told me so, indicating with his hand, "There's the famous Cleopatra!" Would he have had to say that if her depiction had suitably represented what she was?

Today is Sunday. I dined with the general's wife. In the evening she, her relative the spinster Yurkovskaya, Zass, and I went to the theater. From everything it was clear that they went only for my sake: on Sundays no one from the upper classes goes to the theater, and on Sundays they usually present *The Water Spirit* or some similar farce filled with absurdities. Now they also presented a certain part of *The Water Spirit*. The actress playing Lesta made every possible effort to distort her role. Not understanding in the least the character of the figure she was playing, she was dressed in the loose garment of a water spirit, grimaced, minced about, spoke haughtily, smiled, looked at the stalls, with no concern for her Vidostan. I have never spent a more boring evening. The play and the actress were anguishing. When we were seated in the carriage, the general's wife asked me how the performance had seemed to me. I answered candidly that the play seemed composed of absurdities and the leading actress did not resemble the person she was playing. My candidness, apparently, was not pleasing. They answered dryly that Petersburg actresses are considered the best.

Today a new temptation to surprise, attract, and amuse me, and again an unsuccessful one, and from a strange source. They decided to show me *Chinese Shadows*.* But as I am neither a child nor a peasant woman, after the first picture I stopped looking at these pieces. I am obliged to think that the general's wife does not suppose that I am either well educated or have good taste. Nonetheless, her good intentions deserve my gratitude.

I was at the Sovereign's again. The first words with which he greeted me were, "I am told that you saved an officer. Did you really drive the enemy away from him? Tell me the entire circumstance."

I related in detail the entire occurrence and named the officer. The Sovereign said that this was a well-known name, and that my bravery in this single case did me greater honor than the course of the whole campaign, because I had the motive of the best of virtues—compassion. "Although your action," the Sovereign continued, "serves as its own reward, however justice demands that you receive that which is owing you by statute: for saving an officer's life the Cross of St. George is awarded." With these words the Sovereign took a cross from the table and with his own hands hung it in the buttonhole of my uniform. I burned with joy, and in my confusion I seized both of the Sovereign's hands in order to kiss them, but he did not permit this. "I hope," the Sovereign said, "that this cross will remind you of Me in the most important events of your life."

Much is contained in these words. I swear that the revered Father of Russia does not err in His trust. This cross will be my guardian angel! I shall preserve to the grave the memory connected to it. I shall never forget the circumstance in which I received it, and always, always I will see the Hand which is now touching it.

Returning to Zass's quarters, where I have been living since my arrival in Petersburg, I hadn't even taken off my bandoleer when I caught sight of an old man entering behind me, who, with a quavering voice was asking

*Magic lantern slides, *trans.*

Zass, "May I see soldier Durov of the Konnopolsk Regiment? I am his uncle." Hearing these words, I guessed that I was looking at my father's younger brother, and my first thought was to run. Fortunately, I didn't have time to commit this stupidity. At uncle's question, Zass immediately indicated me with his hand, and uncle, having approached me, said quietly, "Your mother has died!" These words penetrated my heart like a sharp dagger. I shook, turned pale, and, feeling that tears were ready to burst from my eyes, lacking strength to say a word, I took my uncle by the hand and left Zass's apartment. "Let us go to my place," uncle said, when we reached the street. I sat in his sleigh, and for the whole ride I was silent, covering my eyes and face with my cloak so that passersby would not see that I was crying.

At home uncle told me that my father had received my letter from Grodno, and seeing from that letter that I had entered the Konnopolsk Regiment as a soldier, was frightened by my unusual step. Not knowing how to help and what to do, he sent my letter to mother. The result of his thoughtlessness was disastrous. I had had the lack of circumspection to write that my mother's excessive strictness had driven me from my father's house, and I asked Father in the event that I would be killed to forgive the sadness which my death would cause him. Mother was lying dangerously ill in bed when this letter was brought to her. She took it, read it through, was silent for a moment, and then with a sigh she said, "*She blames me!*", turned to the wall, and died! Hearing this account, I cried like a five-year-old child. Could I have thought that Father would show her this letter!! Uncle let me surrender to my fearsome sorrow and remorse and postponed the rest of the story until another day.

Having received the letter back, my father sent it to my uncle in Petersburg, asking him to find out if I were alive. Uncle showed this to some generals he knew, and thus it went to the Sovereign, who, having read it, was touched to tears, as they say, and immediately gave orders to find out about me in the Konnopolsk Regiment, and, if the reports were to my advantage, then to present me personally to him. All my superiors praised me beyond my accomplishments and expectations. The result of all this was the Sovereign's unheard-of kindness, permission to devote my life to Him in the capacity of a soldier.

Finally all is prepared for my departure. I have a traveling pass, orders to the regiment, and two thousand rubles for a hussar's uniform and the purchase of a horse. Uncle is very angry that I will not say where I am going. Although I tell him that I am going to Father's, he doesn't believe this and says that sooner or later he will find out where I am.

January 15, 1808

From that day, from the happiest day of my life, a new existence began for me. A glittering perspective was opened, glorious, unique, and to crown my happiness, it was at the will and under the protection of the most powerful Monarch in the world!

On the fourth day after leaving Petersburg, I arrived in Vilno, where I made arrangements for my uniforms to be tailored. A crowd of Jews came to me with propositions for all sorts of services. In half an hour I had everything: an apartment, servants, tailors, a pile of cloth, gold braids, tassels, goat skins, three-cornered hats, a shako, plumes, spurs. In a word, my room became a shop full of goods, and all I had to do was to choose. The Jews all talked at the same time and deafened me. I didn't know what to do until a very adroit Jew said quietly to me, "You won't get rid of them until you choose a factor for yourself. He will send all this rabble packing and bring a merchant, from whom you can buy whatever you need at quite reasonable prices."

"What is a factor?" I asked.

"A factor," responded the Jew, "is the kind of servant who is adroit, zealous, resourceful, indefatigable and unbelievably cheap. Do you wish such a servant?"

I said that I needed one precisely of that sort, and I asked him to select one. "Why select," the Jew said, "I shall be your factor!" He announced his status to the crowd and immediately began his duties, having dismissed all the candidates for the factorship and conspiring with the merchants, who were those same Jews, to deceive me as unconscionably as possible. I, like others, from youth and inexperience, paid the tribute which these swindlers collected.

My uniform was beautifully tailored. All my hussar clothing glittered with taste and richness. My cheap servant took only one ruble from me for his six days of service, but, on the other hand, I arrived at my regiment with only a single ruble left from the two thousand which Vilno had swallowed through the services of my zealous and cheap servant.

I arrived at Kovel. My travel pass was just this far, but the Mariupolsk Regiment was not there. It was quartered in Lutsk and thereabouts. I didn't know what to do. Lutsk is fifty versts from Kovel. I had one ruble, for which certainly no one would convey me to Lutsk, and it was impossible to live in Kovel without money until I had a chance to leave. While mulling over how to get out of my unpleasant situation, I heard the crack of a whip and, looking out the window, saw a lady in a britska coming right toward my tavern. The Jewess ran to open the door. A woman of about thirty entered, well dressed, and immediately attracted

attention to herself. She began to converse with me, and learning that I was
an officer in the regiment stationed in the neighborhood, was about to ask
me about some of her officer acquaintances. But the Jewess didn't give her
time to ask about her officer acquaintances and immediately said that I
was a new officer, and I didn't yet know anyone in the regiment, and that I
lacked the means to get to headquarters, because my travel pass was just to
Kovel while the headquarters, as she knew, were in Lutsk, and that Panna
Nowicka could do well to take the young hussar in her britska and convey
him to the village of Golob, for there he would be at home, since the
Mariupolsky squadron was stationed in Golob. She said all this with one
breath and so fluently that neither I nor Panna Nowicka were able to
collect our wits before finding ourselves obliged to travel together. This
was fine with me, but an unmarried woman might become upset when
asked to take a young hussar officer into her conveyance and travel with
him alone for thirty versts. However, to the honor of Panna Nowicka I
must say that without the slightest constraint and with the most charming
politeness she immediately offered me a place in her britska. In two hours
Panna Nowicka finished her business, which consisted in the purchase of
sugar, tea, chocolate and similar items. We left. The young lady was
disposed to converse with me and began to do so several times, but I
answered only "yes" and "no," and not always appropriately, because, not
liking the Polish language, I never tried to learn it and was terribly
embarrassed by the garrulousness of my fellow traveler. I felt that my
behavior was strange, but didn't know how to overcome this problem and
remained silent. Poor Nowicka! It pleased fate that of all hussars the most
maladroit had to be her traveling companion. Finally she fell silent, began
to yawn, leaned her head against a pillow, and—fell asleep! In this fine
manner we arrived at the village of Golob. Nowicka immediately
awakened and ordered the coachman to drive to the quarters of Captain
Ageyev. The conveyance flew leaping over the ruts and stopped in front of
a small whitewashed little house.

"There are your captain's quarters," said Nowicka, politely bowing to
me. I blushed from the stupid role which I had played with the nice young
lady. I wanted to express my gratitude in Polish, but I was afraid to mouth
rubbish and blushed even more from this misgiving. Finally I got out of the
conveyance without saying a word, bowed to the panna, also silently, and
the good horses carried off my companion to the porch of a huge manor
house.

There was no one in the captain's quarters except his batman. Ageyev
had gone to headquarters. Having given me tea, the old hussar asked,
"Your honor, are you staying here or going further?" Learning that the
captain would not return to the squadron sooner than in two days, I
decided to spend the night in his quarters. Questioning the batman, I found
out that Golob belonged to the widow of the voivoda Wilga, or Wilzyna, as

the Poles call her, that this old lady was about eighty, very hospitable and beneficent, that she had living with her a number of young and pretty but poor girls from the petty gentry, whom she married off at her own expense, and that officers of this squadron often dined at her place. But a ball had never been given at this house and never would be.

"Why is that?" I asked the garrulous hussar.

"Because, your honor," he answered, "the son of this proprietress, young Pan Wilga, lost his wife whom he passionately loved. This loss affected his health and to some extent his mind, so that he now avoids everyone in general, not excluding his mother and the children.

Very early the next morning at the porch I saw a woven basket sitting on a peasant's sledge, to which was harnessed a pair of emaciated horses. The hussar who entered and put my breakfast on the table, said, "The *kurmanka* is ready, your honor!"

In order not to display my ignorance, I didn't ask what sort of a beast a *kurmanka* was and why it was ready just for me. Having breakfasted, I said to the hussar, "Find out if there will soon be horses for me."

"They are ready now! The *kurmanka* is in front of the porch," the hussar answered, pointing out the window. Finally the riddle was explained. This woven basket is called a *kurmanka*. However, I think that is so only when horses are harnessed to it, and without them it becomes a basket. However that might be, I had to go to headquarters in it. Luck, be kind to me! Don't make me meet any of my future fellow officers! I am entering the regiment in a far from brilliant manner!

I took a seat in my basket, which was filled with straw. The horses, which did not have bridles, ran at a trot, and the driver for the whole trip waved a long switch over them, crying "Viu! viu! iss! iss!" Clearly this was the way he forced his horses to run.

Lutsk

Arriving in this town, I stopped, as is the custom of all who arrive and depart, at a tavern, dressed myself as if for formation, and went to report to the battalion superior, Major Dymchevich. I gave him the packet which Count Liven had given to me. Having read this, Dymchevich said to me, "Go to the regimental adjutant and tell him that I have given orders to place you in my squadron. Give him these papers." He then asked several questions about our Grand Prince Konstantin Pavlovich, and seeing I knew nothing about him, repeated his order that I go to the adjutant, and from him I immediately set off to the squadron.

I had to give my last ruble in order to get to Rozhishcha, where Dymchevich's squadron was quartered. The staff captain commanding this squadron received me with imperious importance, which suited neither the insignificance of his status nor his appearance. He was extremely short, snub-nosed, and with a common look to his face. His first question was, "Do you have a horse to ride?" I answered that I did not.

"You must buy one," he said.

"It seems to me that I have the right to a government one."

"You do, but a hussar officer cannot serve on just a government horse. You must have three: for yourself, for your batman and packs, and your belongings."

I said that I didn't have a batman and I had no money to buy horses.

"You shall get a batman tomorrow if you like, and whether you have or don't have money is not the question. But you must have horses at once. Now please go to the village of Berezolupy and take command of the fourth platoon until its present commander returns from leave."

Not having derived much pleasure from the company of this strange creature, I set off at once for my village. Here they had set aside for me the quarters which Dokunin had occupied, in the house of the proprietress of the village. The sub-prefect's wife received me with maternal kindness and asked that I dine with her every day, "Because," she said, "I see that you don't have your own cook." She treats me no differently from her two grandsons, boys of twelve. Like them, I am also given a glass of warm milk in the morning. We live almost in a single chamber. Only a plank partition separates my bed from theirs. They pray, study, cry, pound each other, and quarrel as if I were not there. Moreover, each morning the scamps ask as a favor to let them clean my boots, which is fine with me.

Mr. Malchenko proposed that I buy a horse from him for a hundred silver rubles, on condition that he will wait for the money until it is sent from home. I agreed. A horse was brought up. It would have been acceptable if it hadn't held its ears so strangely. Malchenko praised it excessively. I was embarrassed to tell him that his horse's ears hung down on both sides, and the purchase was completed. Following this, Malchenko asked me if I knew how to drill with a musket, and when I said I did not, he said, "You must learn. This is essential! You must know that which you are obliged to teach the soldiers. Order one of the old hussars to show you all the musket drills. In two weeks you will know them. It is not difficult."

The sub-prefect's wife has a granddaughter about eighteen, not bad looking, but with the most absurd inclinations. She is ready to fall in love with anything, a peasant, coachman, valet, cook, officer, general, priest, or monk! Now the object of her affection is her brothers' teacher, a yellowed, dry pedant, and in order to be with this Adonis she sits in our room all morning.

Every morning, the file-leader hussar of my platoon, old Grebennik, comes to me, with a musket, and for more than two hours I do order arms, shoulder arms, port arms. The exercise order arms is very difficult for me, and I do it clumsily and awkwardly. Each time that he commands, "Order arms!" he adds, "Don't spare the foot, your honor." I tried to obey him and not spare my foot, as he says, but I bruised it so badly with the butt that I felt pain for a whole month. Finally I learned the musket drills.

Emperor Alexander ordered me to write Him via Count Liven about anything I might need. So I wrote to the count, asking that I be given five hundred rubles. In two months I received them, but not via Liven. Count Arakcheyev sent them to me, and wrote that in case of need I turn to him, because he had taken Liven's place with the Sovereign. Having received the money, I paid my debt to Malchenko, and now I don't know what to do with my droop-eared horse. Besides these damned ears, she had some even stranger habits. She will not leave the other horses, she always rears and begins her gallop on her hind legs.

The Mariupolsk Regiment has been ordered to form up near Lutsk. Here Dokhturov, the corps commander, will inspect it. But first we must pass inspection before the divisional commander, Count Suvorov. So we went out onto a green plain in our white uniforms, gleaming with gold and with waving plumes on our helmets. In this camp uniform, white with gold, many of us look more like pretty girls than masculine soldiers, especially those like me, who are not over eighteen.

I am certain that my droop-eared horse was always in the ranks, because the role of leader which she should have played noticeably frightened her. She tried to turn toward the formation, moving her hind end in that direction, and when I hit her with my sharp spurs in order to make her go forward, she turned her head and reared. Judging by this beginning, I expected murderous tricks from her when maneuvers began. And so it happened. The count rode past our whole regiment at a walk, attentively inspected the whole formation, and withdrawing several steps in front of the center of the regiment, said loudly, "Officers!" The glittering horde flew to their superior with the speed of the wind. But my devil went at a melancholic gallop, waving her ears smoothly, and then not until after she had received a couple of cruel blows with the sabre and kicked out with her hind legs. Suvorov had the solicitude to wait until I had joined my companions. Then he gave us our orders, which consisted in what particular maneuvers we would perform for Dokhturov, and which ones would follow that. "Now gentlemen," the count added, "we will only do a rehearsal. Please take your places." Everyone flew to the regiment, and this time I flew like a whirlwind. I stood before the rank, straightened them out, gave the command, "By platoon! Left flank forward! March!" The whole regiment did its maneuver smoothly, in order, but my demon began to back up, jump about, snort, and shake her droop-eared head with all her might. Not foreseeing a good ending to this beginning, I commanded the platoon sergeant to take my place and, having given my horse two or three blows with the whip as hard as possible, I forced her to fly headlong with me along the road to Lutsk. Observing this scene, Suvorov said with a smile, "The young officer doesn't care to drill with us."

Our maneuvers before the corps commander concluded satisfactorily for me: the battalion commander gave me his horse. After the inspection and drill, all the officers went to dine at Suvorov's. The count is extremely captivating and amiable. The officers and soldiers love him like a father, like a friend, like a comrade of their own rank, because in their opinion he unites all these qualities in himself.

It will soon be three years since I left home. How I should like to see Father! Now we are in camp for a six weeks' drill, but when we return to quarters I shall request a leave.

Today, to my shame, I fell off my horse. I might say to my misfortune, because I fell when the entire regiment was moving on attack. Podyampolsky had given me his horse, a young and playful stallion. The maneuvers had gone well, and it remained only to move on attack as a regiment. At the command "Move off! March! March!" my horse reared, sprang forward, and from this violent movement the forward straps of my sabre scabbard broke and fell between the hind legs of my horse, which began to buck at the full gallop, and on the third jump threw me over its head onto the ground. I fell and lost consciousness at that moment. The regiment stopped instantly, which was not difficult with people and horses so well trained. At the first command, "Halt!" the regiment stopped on the spot. The officers lifted me off the ground, unbuckled my dolman, loosened my tie, and cried for a doctor to let my blood at once. But to my great joy I regained consciousness. The fuss and further undressing ended. I retied my tie, fastened on my dolman, threw off my broken sword belt, and remounted, but I didn't drill and rode quietly behind the regiment. When the drill finished, Dymchevich summoned me, and when I rode up to him, he moved away from his officers and rode off a bit with me and began to speak. "You fell off your horse today." I was about to say that the horse bucked me off. He continued in a severe voice: "You fell from your horse! A hussar may only fall with his horse, never from it. I don't want to hear anything. Tomorrow the regiment goes to quarters. Tomorrow go to the supply squadron and the riding master and learn how to ride a horse."

Turisk Village

I am living at our regimental riding master's, Lieutenant Vikhman's,
and every morning for an hour and a half I ride without a saddle on the
saddle blanket, and in the evening for an hour or so. It is very pleasant here.
Vikhman and I spend the whole day with Lieutenant Colonel Pavlishchev,
who commands the supply squadron. Pavlishchev's family love me like
one of their own. The elder daughter is as pretty as a cherub. She is a real
spring rose. Immaculate purity shines in her eyes, breathes in the features
of her innocent face. She is teaching me to play the guitar, on which she
plays excellently, and with childish joy she relates to me whatever she has
heard or seen that is amusing.

In the local church is an icon of Our Most Blessed Virgin, that is the
Virgin Mary, and at her feet the child, leaning on a globe. There is a
legend about this image, that it was painted at the request of the previous
owner of Turisk, Prince Osolinski. The Prince fell passionately in love with
a peasant's daughter, divorced his wife, who was born the Princess O***,
gave his lover an education suitable for an important lady, and married
her. In the first year of their marriage a son was born. The happy prince,
wishing to see the image of his passionately loved wife and son everywhere,
gave an order to paint an icon of the Mother of God, giving Her the
features of the young princess. I looked at this image for a long time. The
princess is charming, she has a meek and captivating physiognomy. Her
little child is the usual lovely infant. The death of both was premature and
tragic. The strong and powerful O***s, seeing that the birth of a son
strengthened the marriage of Osolinski and the peasant woman, and losing
hope that they might see the first Princess Osolinska in her previous place,
ordered the mother and child to be poisoned. The objects of Osolinski's
tender attachment died a terrible death before his eyes, and he, although he
survived the loss, began to hate society, withdrew from it and became a
monk. His estate fell into the hands of the counts Moszynski, and now one
of them, a quite old man, is the owner. I also saw a portrait of Osolinski's
first wife, Princess O***. Such touching beauty: sadness and pensiveness
are sketched in her black eyes, her thin dark brows, her rosy lips and pale
but kindly face, all the features which together express intelligence and
humility, are charming. I am surprised at Osolinski!

I continue to take riding lessons. To my chagrin, Vikhman is a
passionate hunter and willy-nilly I must ride with him on the hunt. Besides
all the discomfort and unpleasantness united in this barbaric amusement,
the piteous squeal of the tormented hare causes me to be sad all day.
Sometimes I resolutely refuse to take part in these murders, but then
Vikhman frightens me with the idea that if I don't ride on the hunt I won't
learn how to sit tightly in the saddle. The hunt, says he, is the only means
to achieve perfection in the art of riding. So I again set off galloping

headlong through some forest fringe, across islands, swamps and hillocks, and freeze from the tiny hoar-frost which ices up my cloak and gloves, finally to rest in some tumble-down shack and eat ham, whose unpleasant salty flavor forces me to throw it away as soon as I put in in my mouth and to eat just bread. These hunters are enchanted—everything seems different to them than to other people. They think this hellish ham, which I can't put in my mouth, is gourmet food, the severe autumn a pleasant time of year, a furious gallop and a somersault with the horse a useful exercise, and low swampy places where only scrubby brush grows a beautiful place. At the end of the hunt the hunters begin a conversation about it, judgment is pronounced, there are anecdotes, and terms which I don't understand a word of. Amusing scenes occur in the company of the gentlemen hunters. The most desperate among us are Dymchevich, Merlin, Soshalsky, and Vikhman. I think that even a dying man would burst out laughing at the sight of Dymchevich, who, hearing the bark of the hounds on scent, becomes deranged, cries, and wiping away his tears says, "the poor hounds." Not long ago he went on an excursion in a carriage with the Pavlishchev's elder daughter, and catching sight of a rabbit running across the field, became so excited that forgetting the presence of a lady, the absence of hounds, and the complete impossibility of pursuing this beast in a carriage, began to cry at the top of his voice, 'Attu, attu! Go, go, go!!" His sudden rapture frightened the girl, the coachman, and even the horses.

A new chief has arrived at the regiment, Miller-Zakomelsky. He immediately ordered me to headquarters. I had to leave the charming company of the supply squadron with which I had fallen in love. Miller had ordered me to appear to tell me that I had two months' leave and to find out why I had requested this not through the command but directly from the Sovereign. I answered that I had permission to do so and made use of it in order to receive my leave more quickly. Miller ordered me to go to Count Suvorov in Dubno, saying that there I would find Komburley, the Zhitomir governor, from whom I would receive my travel pass.

Dubno

The count is preparing to give a luxurious ball tomorrow, and told me that I could not receive my travel pass before the end of the celebration, and that I must dance at his house, that this was my duty. Having heard this, I went to his adjutant, Count Kakhovsky, where I found many officers of my regiment drinking tea. Suvorov came in shortly in robe and slippers, lay down on Kakhovsky's bed, saying that he was leaving the unendurable racket and dust which was being raised by the sweeping, dusting, and decoration of the entire house for tomorrow's festival. Kakhovsky gave him a glass of tea. After a couple of hours Suvorov went back to his own place, and a whole load of hay was brought into Kakhovsky's chamber, put on the floor and covered with rugs, onto which they threw several morocco pillows and thus made a wide bed for Kakhovsky's guests. Bidding my fellow officers good-night, I went to the tavern where I was staying. The daughter of the tavern owner, Panna Dobrowolska, unlocked the glass doors which lead directly from the street into the hall. "I have waited for you to sup for some time," she said, "No one is here now, so come to my chamber. I went with her to her room, where we were brought wood-cock, apples, white bread, jam and half a bottle of Malaga, which we drank up.

The Ball

The wide salons of Suvorov's house were filled with glittering society. Endless lamps cast a bright light through all the rooms. Music resounded. Beautiful Polish ladies waltzed, leaning lovingly on our graceful, well-built hussars. Suvorov was terribly spoiled by the Polish ladies. Because of his handsome appearance, they forgive him too much. He tells them anything that comes to his mind, and sometimes strange things come to his mind! Seeing that I was not dancing and had not even entered the place where the ladies were, he asked the reason for my strange behavior. Stankovich, my squadron commander, and, as they say, a dashing hussar, answered for me, "Your Excellency, he is afraid of women, they embarrass him, he doesn't like them or meet them under any circumstances."

"Indeed," said Suvorov, "Oh, that is unpardonable! Come, come young man, you must make a beginning." Saying this, he took me by the hand and led me to the young and beautiful Princess Lubomirska. He introduced me to the lady, saying "*A la vue de ses fraiches couleurs vous pouvez bien deviner qu'il n'a pas encore perdu sa virginité.*" After this unique introduction, the count released my hand. With a scarcely noticeable smile the Princess tapped him lightly on his cuff with her fan. I went back to my comrades, and after half an hour left the ball for good. It is now past midnight, and I have become accustomed to retire early. Moreover I don't like gatherings where there are so many women. Stankovich was not wrong saying that I am afraid of them. In fact, I *am* afraid of them. It is enough for a woman to stare at me to make me blush and become confused. It seems to me that her look penetrates me, that by my appearance alone she guesses my secret, and in mortal fear I hasten to hide from her eyes!

Furlough

My father had not seen me for three and a half years. I had changed greatly, grown taller and put on weight. My face, once pale and long, had become swarthy and round. My light hair had darkened. I think that my father won't immediately recognize me. I travelled alone by post-chaise, with my sabre as my only companion.

The station masters, who took me for a mere youth, created many difficulties along my path—they wouldn't give me horses for six hours on end, so that I would order something, dinner, tea or coffee. Then the horses would appear. The bill would appear accompanied by the following words: "With the fare, you owe such and such." It was usually a rather significant sum, which I paid without a word. Sometimes, they wouldn't give me horses to force me to hire sick ones at twice the fare. Oh, this journey instilled in me both fear and loathing of station masters!

I arrived home exactly at that hour of the night I had quitted my father's roof—at one in the morning. The gates were locked. I took my sabre and small suitcase from the sledge, and sent my driver back. Alone before the locked gate of the home in which I spent my childhood, oppressed, joyless, I did not experience the feelings of which so many write! On the contrary, I sorrowfully went off along the palisade to the place where I knew four stakes had come out. Often as a child I had gone out through this opening to run on the church square. Now I was going in! Could I have thought, when I would crawl out through this hole in my little white dimity dress, shyly looking about and listening for every sound, shaking from fear and the cold night, that I would someday go in through the same opening, at night, as a *hussar*!! The windows of the whole house were locked. I approached the one that had been the nursery and tried to seize the shutter to open it; but it was somehow fastened from the inside, and I did not want to knock for fear of frightening my little brother and sister. I went to the building where the nurses lived. As I crossed the courtyard, our two dogs heard me, Mars and Mustafa. They rushed at me with a loud bark that instantly changed to a happy yelp. These faithful, kind animals curled around my feet, then jumped up at my chest, then ran around the courtyard at full speed in delight, and then ran up to me again. I stroked and petted them, and then mounted the porch, and went from door to door, knocking quietly. For a quarter of an hour I had no success. Both dogs followed me, and they both scratched at the door I was knocking at. Finally, I heard someone opening the hall door, and soon a woman's voice asked, "Who's there?"

I immediately recognized that it was Natalya, the nurses' chambermaid. "It is I. Open up, Natalya!"

"Oh, my heavens, Miss!" Natalya cried joyfully, hurrying to open the door. She rattled with the bolts and locks for about a minute, until the door finally opened, and I went in, with my sabre under my arm, and accompanied by Mars and Mustafa. Natalya stepped back in amazement. "Oh, my Lord! Is that you!" She stood motionless at the door and wouldn't let me in.

"Oh stop it, Natalya. What's wrong with you? Don't you even recognize me?"

"Oh, my dear, Miss! How could I recognize you? If I hadn't known your voice, I wouldn't have recognized you in a million years!" Natalya opened the door into the chamber for me, took my overcoat, and again exclaimed in surprise when she saw the gold braid on my uniform. "My dear, what fine clothes you have, Miss! Are you a general or something?" For a quarter hour, Natalya continued talking nonsense and stroking my gold braid and the fur collar of my pelisse, until I finally reminded her that she should make up a bed for me. "This instant, this instant! Oh, my dear...." Then she added, talking to herself, "Perhaps I shouldn't call her Miss anymore! Now, how shall I get used to that..." She was about to leave, but turned round again. "Won't you have some tea? It will be ready in two minutes!"

"Yes, make some, my dear Natalya."

"Oh, my dear, Miss! You are just as kind as before!" Natalya started talking again. "I'll make tea this instant! But what should I call you now, Miss? I hear you don't talk the same as you did before."

"Call me what others call me, Natalya."

"But how will others call you, my lady?.. sir! Excuse me...."

"Enough, Natalya! Go get the tea!" The chatterbox left, but returned once again to call Mars and Mustafa. They were both lying at my feet, and ran off after Natalya when she called them.

"Send them out, Miss. They should be in the courtyard."

"Later, later Natalya! Please go get the tea, I'm dying of cold."

Natalya ran off, and I was left to contemplate the fact that similar scenes would be repeated, not only with all of the servants, but with all of my father's friends as well. Imagining all of that, I was almost sorry I had come.

A quarter of an hour later, Natalya appeared with the tea and pillows. "When does Father get up?" I asked Natalya.

"Just as before, dear Miss, at ten o'clock...." After she answered, she again mumbled to herself: "I'll never get used to this...what are you going to do...." I gave a pretzel each to Mars and Mustafa, and ordered them to go. They immediately disappeared.

At seven o'clock in the morning, I dressed in my white dolman, though our regiment's greatcoats had been changed some time ago, and blue ones were assigned us instead of white. But Stankovich's squadron, for some reason, still had to wear the white for a whole year. Not wishing to clash with the rest of the front line, Stankovich asked us to wear the white greatcoats too, to which I most readily agreed, because I really liked the combination of white and gold. While I was dressing, Natalya watched me with new surprise. "You have changed a lot, Miss. Your father won't recognize you."

I went to see my sisters. They had already risen and were waiting for me. At that very moment, my father came in! I embraced his knees and kissed his hands, without the strength to utter a single word. My father wept, pressed me to his chest and said, smiling through his tears, that there wasn't a line of my face unchanged, that I looked like a Kalmyk. Finally, my little brother came in in his Mining Service uniform. He had long deliberated with his nurse how he should address me—bow only, or kiss my hand. And when his nurse told him that he should do just as he liked, he immediately ran and threw himself in my arms. As I kissed him, I told Dad that it was a shame to leave such a fine boy in the Mining Service, and that in three years or so, he should allow me to take him with me to the hussar regiment.

"No, no. God forbid!" Dad said. "You do what you like, since you have already set off on this path, but the comfort of my old age, my Vasinka, will stay here with me." I fell silent and was sincerely sorry that I had been so careless as to distress my father with a proposal at once silly and too premature. But then my brother, hugging me, whispered in my ear, "I'm going with you."

Although I love my father dearly, the inactive life, the lack of society, the cold climate, and the constant questions from our local provincials made me so sad that it was almost with joy that I saw the dawn of the day when I had to return to the regiment. My present journey is much more difficult than the first —but not because of the horses this time; I had no problem with them, for I told every station master who started to say "No horses," that I would write in his complaint book how many hours I waited there and would hold him responsible if I were late. And so, I was given horses very quickly everywhere; but the winter road was beginning to deteriorate, and my post carriage was now incomparably more full than before, and I had a terrible time dragging all my things about by myself. I didn't take an aide with me, and I couldn't have.

Now that I have returned to my comrades and my favorite occupations, I think myself the most lucky creature on earth! My days pass happily and carefree. I always rise at dawn and immediately go to walk in the fields. I return before they finish grooming the horses, that is, by eight o'clock in the morning. At our quarters, my horse is already saddled and ready. I mount it and go back to the field, where I drill my platoon for about an hour and a half. After that, I ride off to headquarters, or to the squadron commander, where I stay until evening.

For his riding lessons, I gave Vikhman my worthless horse. He had her harnessed to a droshky, and to our surprise, made a fine horse. So the shafts were the sphere Nature intended for her. I think the same is true of

man! He is good if he finds precisely his place. I also gave Vikhman a horn
made of an elephant tusk, with fine carving. My father gave me this rare piece
for Count Suvorov; but I was somehow embarrassed to give a gift to the
count, and I gave the horn to Vikhman, and was immediately punished for
failing to fulfil my father's wishes. Vikhman accepted this curio just as
coldly and thoughtlessly as if it were a cow's horn with tobacco.

Our battallion has gone to Galicia with Miller-Zakomelsky.
Stankovich's squadron, and all its officers, remains here as reserves, and,
with the depot batallion, will be under the command of Pavlishchev. I, too,
as an officer in Stankovich's squadron, remain here. Although I would very
much like to be abroad again and in action, Stankovich says, "Wherever
they send you, don't question; wherever they send you, don't refuse! This
rule is followed by men of proven bravery." His advice, and the excellent
company of the officers who stayed behind with me, helped me see with less
regret the departure of our brave hussars across the border. Fortune had it
that even the nicest of the regimental ladies stayed here. I avoid women, but
not the wives and daughters of my cohorts in the regiment. I like them a lot.
They are the most beautiful creatures in the world!—always kind, always
obliging, lively, brave, merry, they love to ride, stroll, laugh, dance! No
whims, no caprices. Oh, regimental women are not at all like women of any
other status! I would not willingly spend a quarter hour with the others. It's
true that even my female cohorts don't miss a chance to make me blush,
calling me in jest, *"the virgin hussar*!" But since I am always with them, I am
getting used to the name, and sometimes make so bold as to ask them, "In
what way do you think I'm like a virgin?"
    "Your slim figure," they answer. "Your small feet, and a high color
that any one of us would gladly have. That's why we call you the *hussar-
maid*, and—by your leave—some even suspect that the name is not wholy
undeserved!" Since I heard such jokes almost every day, I became so used
to them that I almost never was embarrassed.

We have stopped on the border of Galicia, in the town of Kolodno.
There is no river on the border here, and it is our duty to mount patrols and
supervise the Cossack cordon. Kolodno belongs to Shveikovsky. His wife
is a great beauty, raised in Paris. A grand allée of chestnut trees, dark as
night, leads from the porch of the manor to a small white house, planted
round with lime trees. In that little house lives the steward, with his good
wife and two merry, sportive, sweet daughters. In that little house, we visit
every day. I have noticed that my comrades sit longer here than with the
proud, beautiful Mme. Shveikovsky.

Officer Vontrobka told us that on one of his rides on horseback over the border he met Baron Chekhovich, and that the baroness was a ravishing beauty, the like of which he had never even imagined. But fortunately for all of the men of her acquaintance, her limited mind and lack of modesty serve as strong antidotes to the fatal infection; and for all her charms and indescribable beauty, no one has fallen in love with her, because her words and actions destroy in a moment the impression made by her heavenly appearance.

Near our borders the damned *ruchawka* has set up—that's what the Poles call their irregulars, or more accurately, their crowd of rabble. All this ragged, barefoot, hungry throng took it in their heads to gain glory, prosperity and freedom! To the shame of the gallant men of the Mariupolsk Regiment, some of them were seduced by this nonsense, and ran off to join the disgusting *ruchawka.*—Stankovich was greatly offended by such an unheard-of action on the part of hussars, and sent Vontrobka and me with a whole platoon to find our deserters, if possible, take them by force, and bring them back to the squadron. Vontrobka undertook our mission as if our reconnaissance excursion were more like a sortie against the enemy than a simple search. We crossed the border, and a half-verst from the town of **** we halted, dismounted, and waited—for what I don't know. Vontrobka is the senior officer. He is in command and gives the orders; and why I am here, I really do not know! Stankovich does everything with such excessive triumph. We stood silent! I lay down on the grass and looked at the shining constellation of the Great Bear. It reminded me of the happy times of my night-time rides in childhood. How often, I would give free rein to my Alcides, and not worrying about what path he would take, lean with both hands on his withers, cast my head back, and gaze at these seven beautiful stars! Completely lost in reverie, I was by turns a twelve-year-old child on the back of my Alcides, then a cavalry-man, then among the dense forests of Siberia, then on the fields of Heilsberg, then on your grave, oh unforgettable steed! So long a time! So many events! So many changes since then! But here I see you again, my dear constellation! It is still the same, just as brilliant, the same seven stars, in the same place! In a word: they're still the same... but I!.... Years will pass, decades pass, and it will always be the same; but I!..My thoughts were carried off into the future, sixty years hence, and I rose in fright.... Shako! sabre! my zealous horse!... Eighty years!!... "Argenty, let's go, for God's sake, let's go! What are we waiting here for?..." I mounted my horse, and started doing vaults at a gallop. My unpleasant thoughts whirled round with me.

"Why are you worrying your horse?" asked Vontrobka.

"Why are we waiting here to no purpose!"

"What do you mean, to no purpose! I know when we must ride into the town."

"Well, it's time now.... Mount up!... Three abreast, right, march!..."
My dreams vanished, and I returned to reality. We mounted our horses and
set off toward the town. We rode in secretively, quietly, and took the
precaution of extending a line opposite the walls of some stronghold.
Vontrobka sent a non-com and four hussars into that stronghold to find
our deserters. Of course, the envoys came back with nothing, because the
stronghold was completely locked up.

At dawn, Vontrobka left the men and went with me to the mayor of
this town, Colonel N ***, who was also commander of the *ruchawka*.
Vontrobka had met the Colonel earlier, but I saw him for the first time. He
received us in confusion and haste, asked us to sit down, apologized for not
being dressed, and immediately went off into another chamber, saying that
he would return in just a minute. Such a reception seemed suspicious to
Vontrobka, and he told me that we should leave immediately. And so,
without waiting for our host, we walked out of the room, rejoined our men,
and rode off! I found Vontrobka's actions strange, and asked him why he
did that. He said that he had noticed hostile intentions in the mayor.

"But what could he have done to us? We have a whole platoon of
hussars."

"That's just wonderful! A whole platoon! And why are we here? We
couldn't have said in excuse that we had come to find some hussars who'd
deserted, and that if we found them we wanted to take them by armed force.
This was being done secretly. It's a house-keeping measure of the squadron
commander's, excusable under the circumstances. It would be unpleasant
to report that so many hussars ran across the border.

The failure of our efforts did not stop Stankovich. He sent me to
Tarnopol, to Prince Vadbolsky, with a letter and orders to bring back the
fugitive hussars, if they would deliver them to me. I had to ride through the
very same town where we had made our night-time search. At the town
gates, I was asked if I had a pass from the colonel.

"No!"

"We can't let you through. Get a pass...."

I sent a hussar to the colonel to ask for a pass. The colonel ordered him
to ask me to come for the pass myself. I went.

"You should have known your duties better, Sir," said the Pole,
frowning. "You should appear in person to a superior, not send a private."
Having said this, he quickly signed the pass. "You came with armed men,
searched the stronghold, came to see me, and when I stepped out for a
minute just to order some coffee, you rode away as if from a den of thieves!
A strange way for a Russian officer to behave!" And I had to listen to all of
that! For about two minutes I thought to invite him to a duel, but the
danger of exposing Stankovich to responsibility restrained me. I put off the
challenge until I should return to Tarnopol. Then we could meet on the
border. In the meantime, I said that for now he is free to say what he likes,

because I am alone here, surrounded by Poles, and across my country's borders. As I spoke, he handed me the pass with a polite bow, extended his hand to me, and asked if we could be friends. But I refused his hand, and answered that after all I had heard from him, I had no desire to be his friend. He bowed to me, saw me to the door, and we parted.

I set off further. Stankovich had ordered that if I did not find the hussar deserters in Tarnopol, I should go on to Brody.

The Lithuanian Uhlan Regiment is stationed in Tarnopol. Its commander, Prince Vadbolsky, sent one of his officers with me to Brody. When we arrived in the town, we immediately went to the Polish colonel's, where we found a numerous company and thunderous music. The colonel received us very kindly, asked that we stay for dinner and take part in their amusements. Strakhov, my comrade, agreed, and I was far more than willing to listen to the beautiful music and the merry conversation of the witty young Poles. However, we told the colonel why we had come, and asked him to order our fugitives given over to us. "Most willingly," answered our kind host, and immediately sent his officer cadet to deliver our hussars. He invited us, while we were waiting, to listen to his music and have a glass of champagne. In half an hour, the officer returned, and putting his hand to his fur shako, began to say respectfully to his colonel, that the hussars he'd been sent for were not in the guardroom!

"Where are they, then?" asked the colonel.

"They ran off!" answered the cadet, in the same respectful tone.

The colonel turned to me and said, "I am very sorry that I can be of no assistance in this matter. Your hussars have escaped our custody!" I wanted to say that this did no honor to their guards, but I didn't. What purpose would it have served? There was no doubt that the hussars were with them, and that the colonel had no intention of giving them over to us. The Polish officers could not stop admiring my uniform, which was excellently sewn. They said that their tailors were not capable of giving such a fine shape to a jacket. At the table, I sat next to some mustachioed gentleman, an old raider who had served in the National Cavalry. When he had drunk several glasses of champagne, he bothered me with the question why I had taken the French eagle down from Lemberg and put up the Austrian one. I didn't understand what he meant. Strakhov, seeing my perplexity, told the quick-tempered nationalist that I had not been in Lvov at the time of that event.

"What do you mean, he wasn't there?" exclaimed the old uhlan. "I remember that uniform well!" And he continued to upbraid me, asking if that was a good thing to have done. The colonel asked him to stop, but he asked in such an overbearing tone that even drunk uhlans would obey. The captain fell silent. Then Strakhov explained to me in a whisper that our regiment, under command of Miller-Zakomelsky in Lemberg, or Lvov, took down the French eagle from somewhere, and put the Austrian arms in its place. The nationalist captain, who witnessed the event, saw me in exactly the same uniform, and figured that I was one of those, as he said, wild rascals. After dinner I said farewell to the Polish colonel and, leaving him the booty of our fugitive hussars, returned to Kolodno.

Vontrobka invited me to go to Baroness Chekhovich's. "You have to have some idea of her beauty," he said. "My description does not do her justice!" We set off and, to my great good fortune, did not find her at home. The baron received us alone. In the garden, I saw various forms of amusement, all of which, Vontrobka said, were designed to break the heads of those who engaged in them. The baroness, he added, tries to get at the heads of all of her visitors by any means possible—whether by her beauty, or by her amusements. Not waiting for the arrival of our hostess, we rode back.

Vontrobka confessed to me his design in having me meet the baroness: "Her extreme impudence," he said, "encountering your own unusual shyness promised to provide me with a thousand amusing scenes." I was very displeased with his satanic plan, and I told him that he was a false friend and that I would henceforth beware of him.

"As you wish," he answered, "but you are unbearable and ridiculous with your girlish modesty. You know what? If I had a wife as modest and bashful as you, I would kiss her feet; but if my son had the same qualities, I'd flog him with a birch rod. Now judge for yourself, shouldn't you try by every possible means to wean yourself of your ridiculous modesty? It does not at all suit a hussar, and is completely worthless to him."

Stankovich prepares some not very pleasant surprises for us: at the very moment we are as far from any thought of disturbances as the sky is from the earth, he orders an alarm drill, and in a second everything is in great agitation. The hussars run headlong, lead out their horses at a run, saddle them anyhow, mount, gallop at full speed, and as they ride, straighten out what could not be done in place. The one who manages to do all this in two minutes receives an award from the captain, and the one who arrives last also gets an award, only of a completely different sort. One of these alarms cost me dearly. My knee hurt, and precisely in the spot one must press against the saddle. I couldn't sit on a horse, and was even frightened when I heard the damned alarm. But there was nothing to be done. I quickly got my platoon, and mounted myself, carefully so as not to press down on my sore knee. But we had to gallop. My horse threw its head in the air and flew off. However, I still managed to maintain the necessary position in the saddle. Unfortunately, there was a hollow in my path, and my horse jumped into it with all its might, and then all was lost. My knee was soaked with blood, and I trembled with pain which no words could express.

Suffice it to say that involuntary tears poured from my eyes like rain.

A few days later, Stankovich asked me to ride with him to Kremenets, to see Pavlishchev. I always visit that town with pleasure. Its beautiful romantic situation at the foot of a precipitous mountain, on which the ruined walls of the fortress of Queen Bona stand out so vividly, offer me charming and varied walks. I suppose that Kremenets got its name from the stony mountains which surround it.

I spend the time very pleasantly in Pavlishchev's home with his daughter and the cadet Drevich, a very well-educated young man. How strange the fate of that unhappy cadet. With all his brilliant gifts, noble actions, pleasant appearance and distinguished birth, no one liked him, and he served for nine years as a junior ensign. A year before my acquaintance with him, a terrible event occurred in which he played the primary role, and which cost him his rank, his freedom, his clear conscience, and with all that, his desire to live as well. He carelessly speared a hussar, was tried for his death, confined to the guardhouse for a whole year, and later demoted to service as a common soldier.

I learned of his misfortune by chance. Miller-Zakomelsky had not yet left for Galicia with the battalion, and the regiment was stationed in Kremenets. In my capacity as duty officer, I had to learn of and report on the prisoners. I entered the little closet where poor Drevich sat, and asked him if there was something he might need—that my current duty gave me the chance to mitigate somewhat the severity of his position.

"Oh, if you do not disdain the request of a murderer," he said sadly, "I would ask you to allow me to breathe again the air in those mountains, where I earlier spent so many happy hours!" I said that I could not do that myself, but that I would ask Gorich, and that I thought that through him I would be able to get permission from his chief for the excursion. Gorich very kindly heard out my request, and immediately went off to see Miller. A minute later, he returned, saying, "The general gives you permission to do as you please with regard to easing the lot of the prisoner. But he asks that you observe the required order." I went to Drevich and witnessed his happy, and at the same time sorrowful feelings at the sight of the beauties of Nature. Two hussars were to ride behind us, with sabres drawn, but I told them that I would be his guard myself, and that they should follow us at some distance. Drevich almost fainted several times—so much had the sedentary life weakened him!

Both of our squadrons are ordered on the march. Drevich is entrusted to Colonel Pavlishchev's supervision. This worthy officer had no need of an education to treat the prisoner in the most noble and delicate manner. He

simply followed the suggestion of highest virtue. "You are," he told
Drevich, "entrusted to my squadron for surveillance until the
determination of your case. But I cannot, I do not have the heart to see you
under arrest in the guardhouse. In place of that, I offer you my house, my
table and the care of my wife. If you decide to run away, of course, I would
then have to take your place, that is, I would be a soldier!" There is no pen,
no words, human language is too poor to express Drevich's feelings. I won't
attempt to describe it. But here is the sequel: Drevich lived in the house of
his benefactor, loved him like a father, and was about to be reconciled with
his fate. But then the judgment came: Drevich was to remain a soldier until
the expiration of his service. Pavlishchev was obliged to employ him in that
capacity on duty, and apparently his prolonged misfortune, his pangs of
conscience for the murder (even if it was not intentional, it was still a
murder), and—as I had occasion to figure out—his hopeless love for
Pavlishchev's daughter, made life hateful to the unfortunate Drevich!
About two weeks after sentencing, he shot himself. He was found in the
garden on his cloak with his head blown to pieces. Near him lay a carbine.

We arrived in Chernigov Province and took up quarters in a vast
settlement known as Novaya Basan. Here there lives the landowner
Cheadayev, an old, lonely, boring man, with a sister exactly like him. We
never visit.
There is a wedding in the neighborhood. The landowner M*** is
marrying his daughter to Captain I*** of the Alexander Hussar Regiment.
We are all invited, and tomorrow we will go. At M***'s house, all the men
were assigned a single room—soldiers and civilians, young and old,
married men and bachelors. As a hussar, I was obliged to stay with them.
Among the guests was a certain broker named Plakhuta—about three
arshins high, a most convivial and witty fellow, and a great enthusiast for
anecdotes. Among the many curious events he related, I had the pleasure of
hearing my own story.
"Imagine my surprise, gentlemen, when while dining at an inn in
Vitebsk with a young uhlan, I heard later that that same uhlan was an
Amazon, that she had been in all the battles in the Prussian campaign, and
that she was now riding to Petersburg with an aide-de-camp that our Tsar
had sent especially for her! I had not paid any attention to the young uhlan
before, but after this news, I could not stop looking at the heroine!"
"What did she look like?" the young men cried from all sides.
"Very swarthy," answered Plakhuta, "but she has a fresh complexion
and gentle glance. But for someone not forewarned, there is nothing about
her that would reveal her sex. She looks like an extremely young boy."
Although I blushed terribly hearing this story, since it was already
dark in the room, I was mischievous enough to ask Plakhuta if he would

recognize this Amazon if he saw her now. "Oh, absolutely," answered the broker. "I remember her face very well, as if I were looking at it this instant; and wherever I met her, I would immediately recognize her."

"Apparently your memory is very good," I said, wrapping myself in my greatcoat. Plakhuta started to relate some other story, but I didn't listen anymore and immediately fell asleep.

The next day, we all rode back to Basan. Miss A*** told me of a funny mistake which might, however, have important consequences. The third day after our return from the wedding feast, I went to see the lieutenant colonel. Seeing that he was busy, I went to Miss A***'s room, and found her sunk deep in thought. To my question why she was so sullen, and wasn't it perhaps exhaustion from the dance that caused it, she sighed and answered, "No, it's not exhaustion from the dance, but an event at the dance that lies heavily on my heart! I gained a victory, not willing it, not intending it, and not only not desiring it, but not even suspecting that such a disaster could befall me!"

I laughed at her sorrow and asked how such extraordinary misfortune could have happened to her, and who this god-forsaken wretch was, over whom victory caused her such bitter sorrow. "It's fine for you to joke," said A***, "I'm ready to cry. Listen to what happened: You know that I am very close friends with Katinka Alexandrovicheva. When we have occasion in a set dance to offer our hand to one another, we both always squeeze it. Forgetting myself, I didn't see that I had to offer my hand to Ch***, that young hussar officer in the Alexander Regiment. When I felt that someone had taken my hand, I immediately squeezed, imagining that it was Katinka's hand. But when I felt no response to my squeeze, I turned round and to my inexpressible embarrassment saw that it was Ch*** who held my hand, looking at me with an expression of joy and amazement! I blushed and did not know where to turn my eyes. Yesterday, Ch*** made me a proposal of marriage through Stankovich's wife, desiring, as he says, to satisfy himself of my feelings before he asks my parents for my hand! But I haven't the least inclination toward him, and I don't at all want to marry so young. It would be a real calamity if he ascribed my refusal to bashfulness and courted me openly. My father would marry me off! Ch*** is wealthy!"

"Yes, you've caused yourself an awful lot of trouble with that untimely squeeze of the hand. However, you must not be surprised at the nobility of Ch***'s feelings—a single squeeze of a young lady's hand forced him to propose marriage, while another, some rake, would squeeze your hand thirty times, and never give you any peace, not once troubling himself about proposing an indissoluble union."

Our conversation was interrupted by the arrival of Miss A***'s father, Stankovich and his wife. Miss A***'s fears were well-founded. Ch*** had made a proposal to the father, who accepted it gladly; and probably supposing that his daughter would agree, came to tell her of the proposal.

There were many surprises, tears, curses, troubles, before Miss A*** finally rid herself of the unwanted party.

Walking past the mill in the evening, I saw our hussars setting up a straw scarecrow on the other side of a ditch. When I asked what it was for, they answered that tomorrow there was a cavalry drill with small arms fire.

At six o'clock in the morning, we were already on the field. Stankovich commanded the squadron. Pavlishchev was the inspector for the review. The action began with the first platoon, under T***'s command. He was the first, and was to leap the ditch, fire his pistol at the straw scarecrow, and immediately hack it with his sabre. The men were to follow, and do likewise. T*** immediately refused to jump over the ditch, and to our general laughter gave as the reason for his refusal that he would fall off his horse.

"How dare you say that," screamed the inspector. "You're a cavalry-man! a hussar! Aren't you ashamed to tell your commander to his face that you are afraid of falling off your horse. Break your neck, Sir, but ride! Do what you are supposed to do in the cavalry service or don't serve."

T*** listened to all of this, but would not dare make an attempt at the feat, and was just an observer of his distinguished hussars. After him, P*** galloped off smoothly, phlegmatically lept over the ditch, fired on the scarecrow indifferently, hit him in the head with his sabre, and stood calmly to one side, not troubling to see whether his platoon would do the maneuver well or poorly.

Then it was my turn. I didn't have my horse this time, and I was mounted on one of the front horses. It was an ardent steed, handsome, but extremely timorous. He flew like a whirlwind towards the ditch, flew over it with me like a bird, but my pistol shot made him jump aside. For half an hour, he wandered here and there, reared and turned quickly away from the scarecrow, which I had to hew. I completely lost patience and, wishing to finish this bother as soon as possible, I hit my capricious steed with my sabre, as I thought, with the flat side. The horse threw himself at the scarecrow as fast as his legs would carry him, and even knocked it down. Not troubling myself about the cause of this sudden obedience, I turned the horse around, jumped back across the ditch, and started watching how my hussars were doing the same maneuver.

The fourth platoon came on stage. They were under command of Vontrobka—an excellent shot and horseman. I in turn became a simple observer and rode up to Stankovich and Pavlishchev to watch the brave sallies of the last platoon. "What's that blood on your horse's leg, Alexandrov?" asked Stankovich. I turned around. Blood was streaming down the hoof of my horse's rear leg and stained the turf. Surprised, I anxiously checked to see where it could be coming from, and to my deep regret, I saw on his haunch a broad wound which I had probably inflicted when I hit him so carelessly with my sabre. When Stankovich repeated his question, "What is it from?" I had to answer what from. "Go behind the lines, Sir! Go back to quarters! There's no sense your being in drill, it's useless. You wound all of my horses!"

Deafened by this salvo of rebukes, I went back to quarters, not so much vexed by the captain's reproaches as saddened by my cruel treatment of a poor horse. When I arrived at quarters, I ordered the wound washed with wine and lint put on in my presence. When the drill was over, everyone went to Pavlishchev's, including Mr. T***. To Pavlishchev's question, "Where is Alexandrov?" that coward T*** hastened to say, "He is washing his horse's wound with hot tears."

"How's that! What horse?"

"The one he was riding, the one he slashed when it wouldn't ride at the scarecrow."

"That wouldn't happen to you, Grigory Ivanovich! The scarecrow would be more likely to attack you than you would it." The scoffer fell silent in displeasure.

Official Business

Kiev, 1810

Stankovich received orders to send one officer, one non-com, and a private to the commander-in-chief of the reserves, General Miloradovich, as orderlies. My squadron commander took it into his head to send the youngest men as orderlies, and in accordance with these instructions, it fell to my lot—as Stankovich says, the youngest of all the officers. Luckily, I am no longer as young as I look. I'm twenty-one; otherwise, I can't imagine that anything good would come of Stankovich sending three raw youths, alone, under their own command, and to such a prominent post! Cadet Grava is sixteen, the hussar eighteen, and my appearance gives no promise of even sixteen. Excellent orderlies!

At dawn I set off with my company to Kiev, where our corps's quarters were located. To escape the intolerable heat and save the horses, I rode by night from Brovary to Kiev. The dense pine forest is all criss-crossed with innumerable roads, cut deep in the sand. Not knowing that they all led out to the same place, to the banks of the Dnieper and the Red Tavern, I thought that we were lost. As we continued to ride, by guess-work, on the road that fell before us, surrounded by impenetrable copses, I caught sight of something flash past from the road into the forest. Spurring my horse, I galloped up to the place where something was hiding behind the trees. To my call, "Who's there?" a peasant woman came out, breathless with fear. But when she saw the calm and friendly expressions of the three young hussars, she calmed down herself and said, laughing, "How terrible! I scared you, and you me!"

Grava thought it very funny that the Little-Russian woman could think that three armed hussars would be scared of her. "Tell us, ma'am, where are we headed? We have to get to Kiev."

"Well, you're going there," answered the woman in her Little-Russian dialect.

"How are we to guess which way to turn? There are so many roads here!"

"As for that," said the peasant woman, "they all come out at the same place, by the Red Tavern, not far from the ferry." We thanked her and set off at a trot, and soon we saw the Dnieper sparkling in the moonlight. While the ferry-men woke up and prepared the boat, the moon began to pale, a sign of the coming dawn. We boarded the ferry, and as we crossed it became quite light. I went straight to our General Yermolov. My cadet and hussar settled in to bivouac in his courtyard, and I went into the hall and lay down on a divan without undressing. I arose a half-hour before Yermolov awoke, put my uniform in order, and waited for him to wake up, so I could go into him immediately. The general's reception was extremely kind and cordial. Yermolov's manner has some sort of enchanting simplicity to it, and at the same time obligatoriness. I noticed in him a trait that made me suppose that Yermolov has an extraordinary mind: he does not presume in any of his officers lack of education, ignorance, inability to get on in the world; he speaks with each of them as an equal and does not try to simplify his speech to make himself understood; he does not have that absurd prejudice that the expressions and manner of explaining themselves of people of higher tone will be incomprehensible to men of lower rank. This great trait of intellect and virtue prejudiced me to see everything from the good side in our general. Yermolov's facial features and physiognomy show a great and unbending soul!.

Miloradovich's adjutant, K***, sent for me. I arrived and saw immediately that I was not whom he had expected. This crude, uneducated officer asked, without even asking me to sit down, "Why didn't your squadron commander send the officer I designated as orderly?"

"Probably because," I answered, "your designation was incompatible with the command at his disposal in the squadron. We have a schedule of detachments that others need not concern themselves with." I saw that my answer had offended K***. He is exceptionally proud, like all petty people. Despite my apparent youth, I had the pleasure of making an enemy of K***.

Certain days are appointed when I do nothing from morning 'til night but fly about on my horse, Almaz—either by the side of Miloradovich's carriage, or with commissions from him to various persons in Kiev. In the latter case, he sends me only when the person he must find is a general, arriving or passing through; but when he rides out himself, in his carriage or on horseback, then I alone accompany him, with my hussars, and no other orderly ever rides with him. From this I conclude that Miloradovich loves splendor and magnificence. It is pleasing to his pride to have a hussar, shining in gold braid, on a proud steed, appear at his carriage window, ready at the wave of his hand to fly off like an arrow wherever he might order.

K*** took it into his head to review whether the orderlies were dressed as they should be—not just the soldiers, but the officers as well. A crazy fantasy! Can an infantry officer know all the details of a hussar uniform, and, what is more, better than the hussars themselves? I did not obey his order, assuming that it could not apply to me. I did not go to him for inspection, nor did I send my hussars. He had the weakness to complain to Yermolov, under whose direct command we all were, as duty general. Yermolov asked me why I had not reported to K***.

"Because, your Excellency," I answered, "K*** doesn't know the first thing about our uniform. And it would be strange if a hussar officer had need of an infantry-man's instructions on how to dress in his own uniform."

Yermolov did not persist, but said simply, "Miloradovich ordered K*** to do it. Arrange it somehow."

"Believe me, General, K*** is lying! Miloradovich has enough sense not to send a hussar to a musketeer for inspection." The matter ended without further difficulties. K*** gave up his pretensions.

Today was the dedication of an invalids' home. After all the ceremonies, we all dined in tents. The day was unbearably hot. Even before the dedication of the home, Miloradovich rode round the whole fortress, accompanied by his entire suite of orderlies, a distance of about twenty versts. His small Arabian horse, galloping quite calmly, did not tire his rider in the least. The same could not be said for mine: my Almaz was unable to conform his gallop to the light and fluid pace of the child of the steppes, grew angry that I did not allow him to gallop as he wanted, and constantly jumped, reared, trotted and tore the reins from my hands. He tormented me so much that when we arrived at the tents, I thought my blood would boil, it flowed in such a hot stream through my whole body!

Immediately after the consecration, we sat down at table. I put a piece of ice in my glass. Golitsyn, who was standing next to me just then, was horrified. "What are you doing?" he asked. "You could come down with a terrible cold." As he said this, I drank the whole glass of wine with the ice at one go. "Aren't such changes from hot to cold bad for you?" I answered that I was used to it. And, indeed, my health was unparalleled. I was, as

they say, in the flower of health; and I disliked my scarlet cheeks in the
extreme. I once asked Lyubarsky, our regimental doctor, if he didn't know
some way of eliminating excessive color. "I do, indeed," he answered.
"Drink more wine, and spend your nights on cards and debauchery. After
two months of such a commendable manner of life, you will have a most
interesting pallor."

I live very happily in Kiev. I have many pleasant acquaintances here,
including the home of the mayor, Mass, and of his nephew, Shlein, an
officer in the cuirassiers, and my good friend. Mass, despite his sixty years,
is still a fine fellow, and gallops as heartily on his horse as the best of our
hussars.

Yesterday, there was a concert for the benefit of the poor.
Miloradovich gave each of his orderlies two tickets, including me. The
concert was arranged by certain noble ladies. The head of this musical
society was Princess Kh***, a beautiful young woman, whom our
Miloradovich courts indefatigably. I had occasion to notice more than
once that success in love makes our general very obliging. When I meet him
in the gardens, I can always guess how things went with the princess. If he is
in her good graces, he talks and jokes with us; if he's not, he walks by
sullenly, answers our salute coldly, and is not annoyed if we stand at
attention, whereas, if he is in a good mood, he cannot abide it.

Miloradovich gave a ball on the name day of the widowed Empress. A
spectacular, wonderful ball! The halls were filled with guests; the huge,
ancient garden was wonderfully illuminated, but you couldn't even think of
walking there. Miloradovich had taken it into his head to entertain his
Apsheronsky Regiment there, which was later the cause of an amusing
incident. In the evening the innumerable lamps, the thunderous music, and
the crowds of beautiful ladies aroused the curiosity of our brave comrades-
in-arms in the garden. They came as close as possible to the glass doors of
the hall, which were open and secured by two guards. Mass saw the crowd
of soldiers growing thicker by the hour, and pressing on the doors so that
the guards had difficulty keeping them from breaking into the hall. He
called me, since I was on duty that day. "Alexandrov, tell the guards to lock
the doors." I was about to go and follow his order, but Miloradovich had
heard what Mass had told me, and stopped me, asking, "Where are you
going?"

I answered that I was going to tell the guards.

"I know," Miloradovich interrupted impatiently. "It's not necessary to
lock the doors! Let them come in! Cadets can dance! Stay where you are!"
Saying this, he straightened his tie a few times, a sign of annoyance, and

went to tell the guards not to prevent any of the soldiers who wanted to from entering the hall.

As a result of these instructions, in less than five minutes, the hall was filled with soldiers, pouring in swarms through the doors to the garden. In a moment, they had mingled with the guests. Mass shrugged his shoulders, Yermolov grinned; the ladies retreated in amazement, seeing these coarse and corpulent creatures at their sides. With the other orderlies, I laughed whole-heartedly at the strange sight. The ladies all gathered in one chamber. The men waited, smiling, to see how the whole scene would end.

Miloradovich, who had not at all expected such a noisy and multitudinous visit from his cohorts, said that he would advise them to go back out into the garden, where they could amuse themselves more freely, adding that "fresh air is the Russian warrior's element!" The Russian warriors understood nothing of this pronouncement, except that they had to go back out into the garden, which they immediately did. This time, Miloradovich himself ordered the doors locked.

Order was restored, the music started playing, the beauties spilled into the hall and again shone their gazes on hussars, uhlans, cuirassiers, dragoons, in short, on anyone wearing a mustache and spurs. An officer of the Tatar Uhlan Regiment, a young man of exceptional beauty and exceptionally great height, Baron N***, seemed to be the king of all this glittering throng. The eyes of all the ladies and girls shone their rays upon him. One cannot calculate all the rivalries, disappointments, and acts of jealousy he provoked that evening. Fits of jealousy did not escape Miloradovich. The princess danced the quadrille with him, but constantly turned her head toward another set, where the baron was dancing.

Half an hour before supper, the dances stopped, and everything quieted down. Several young men, including the broker P***, a prankster, a gossip, and a rake, went with us, that is, the orderlies, to a room adjacent to the hall. There P*** began to tell about all the beauties of Little Russia, and where he had happened to see them. "In Piryatin," said P***, "I saw Miss Alexandrovicheva, a girl of rare beauty, and—? She has such an outlandish name that I can neither pronounce it nor hear it without irritation: *Domnika Porfirovna*! Have you ever heard anything like it?"

I shuddered at the name. Domnika Alexandrovicheva was my cousin, and I in all truth feared that by that direct tie things would get around to me. My fears were immediately justified. P*** continued, "Besides her beauty, and her ridiculous name, Domnika is notable for her close kinship to the Amazon so many people were speaking of three years ago and who later disappeared God knows where."

Everyone started discussing and talking about this phenomenon. I was silent, and while I was considering whether or not I should take part in the conversation, Davydov, one of our collegium of orderlies sitting next to me, suddenly cried out, slapping me on the knee: "What do we care about your Amazons! We have our own girl! Right? Slim as a match-stick, blushes at every word...."

"Why have we hidden away here, gentlemen?" asked Shlein, rising and taking me and the dragoon Shtein by the hand. "Let's go to the general!" Everyone rose after us and went into the hall.

What bad calculation on the part of those regimental commanders who wish to distance themselves from an officer's unacceptable behavior by sending him off on official business. In the regiment, he is hidden with all his imperfections, and whatever he might do, it is all, as they say, in the family. But once he is sent off for all the world to see, he is playing *solo,* and so abominably that all who wear his uniform are ashamed to hear him. The source of this reflection was an event at yesterday's ball. The uhlan orderly, T. A***, saw the opportunity to drink as much punch as he pleased, and drank so much that even his narrow little Kalmyk eyes were almost closed. In a complete drunken stupor, he walked among the ladies, asking each of them to dance, although the music had stopped some time ago, and preparations were being made for supper. The ladies smiled, and as the eccentric approached, retreated. He continued wandering through the company, and finally bumped into the old Mass and stepped on his foot.

The mayor's blood boiled at such impudence. He grabbed A*** by the arm, saying, "Apparently you, Sir, cannot see where you are going?"

"What am I supposed to see?" A*** objected, attempting to open his eyes a bit wider.

"The people whose feet you are trodding on!"

"Whose?" asked the drunken uhlan.

"Mine, mine, the commandant's. You stepped on my foot! said Mass, out of patience.

"We are all commandants here!" muttered A***, and with a wave of his hand, went off again to walk the hall, swaying from side to side. The next day, they sent him back to the regiment.

We were on maneuvers today—battle exercises. Yermolov, who commanded the army that was to retreat, asked Miloradovich to give him two of his orderlies. Miloradovich gave him a dragoon and an uhlan, keeping the hussar and the cuirassier. In the midst of this vanity of vanities—races, cannonades, attacks—some unfortunate rider with his feet out by a half-arshin from his horse, caught my spur and tore it off. I soon learned the inconvenience of being left with one spur.

Miloradovich sent me alone everywhere, and in the course of all the maneuvers I flew in my golden greatcoat, with my pelisse on my shoulders, like a shining meteor, flashing through the men firing, marching, shouting

"Hurrah!" and fighting at bayonet point. Finally, my horse could scarcely breathe. Miloradovich was just then standing by a deep ditch and looking over our position. On the other side of the gully, which our commander-in-chief held, were the chasseurs' riflemen. They were, unfortunately, standing, when by order, they should have been lying down. Miloradovich got angry, started pulling at his tie, and looking at me, said abruptly, pointing to the gully, "Go tell those riflemen and their slow-witted officer that they were ordered to lie down!" I touched my horse with my remaining spur; but when she saw that she would have to go into a deep ditch, she stopped short.

"What, you won't obey me!" cried Miloradovich. A blow from my spur and sabre made my horse race headlong into the ravine; and I, like Curtius, flew with my horse into the abyss!

When maneuvers were over, my poor Almaz was led to the stable and lay down as soon as he was unsaddled. The next day, I didn't recognize him, he had changed so much.

My two months' duty as an orderly for the commander-in-chief is over. Tomorrow, I return to the squadron.

My service in the squadron started very unfortunately. At dawn, the duty non-com galloped up to me with the news that Cornet Paradovsky had shot himself. I was dressed in an instant, mounted my horse with no saddle, and galloped off at full tilt to Paradovsky's quarters. Stankovich was already there. The unfortunate Paradovsky lay in the middle of the floor, face down. His blood had gathered in a big puddle by the door. His skull was broken in several pieces, which lay on the floor and the benches. The carbine he had shot himself with was near the body; two bullets were in the ceiling. Stankovich examined all the letters and some notes of the deceased, but couldn't find anything to suggest the reason for his suicide. He ordered the face and remnants of the head of the unfortunate Paradovsky wrapped up in a kerchief, and the body taken out to the crossroads, where they dug him a grave. The highway runs past it, and in the evening when I pass it, I shudder as I approach Paradovsky's green mound. Yesterday, we went together on this road! and today...

We are ordered to march! What an unstable life! You're not given a chance to get used to anything! We became so well acquainted with the local landowners, and now we've torn off into the distance again. Our current quarters will be near Rovno, on the Korvitsky estate, in the town of Mizoch (on the Volynya).

Our squadron rode through Kiev. Yermolov rode with us to the city gates. He spoke very kindly to me, asking if I didn't regret something in

Kiev. And when I said that I regretted nothing, he praised me, saying: "Conduct yourself so always, young man. I will respect you."

Mizoch

There is a large manege here, and a beautiful garden, two splendid things. The rest is like everywhere in Poland—tumble-down shacks, straw roofs, and nothing more. We have nothing to do with the manege. We ride the good horses in the field. But the garden! That's another story. I spend all my time there after dinner. So many flowers, and such beautiful ones that I jump for joy when I see them; and not for the life of me could I refrain from gathering one of the roses that grow so high that I can't even see them. These bushes are three arshins high and more, strewn with the most lovely roses, and I cannot get one but by cutting one off with the edge of my sabre. One day I was caught in the act by the arrival of the gardener. Embarrassed, and pointing to the rose I had cut off, I asked, "Is it all right to cut flowers from these rose-bushes on occasion?"

"Well, since you already have, I suppose you can," the gardener answered, laughing. "Just don't spoil the bush."

Yesterday, Stankovich had an inclination for drill at noon. The heat and dust were unbearable. The maneuvers were all done at a full gallop, something Stankovich, a dashing hussar, had got used to under Vitgenshtein, the former chief of the Mariupolsk Regiment. Yesterday this method almost cost the life of a poor Jew, the most cowardly of all creatures that inhabit the earth. Our final maneuver is the attack. On the command: *Forward! March! March!* we rushed forward like madmen. Stankovich decided to lead the attack on Mizoch, near which there was a highway with dust a half-arshin deep. As we galloped along this road, the squadron was enveloped in such a thick cloud of dust that I not only could not see where I was riding, I couldn't see the horse I was riding on. Then suddenly the command rang out, *"Halt! Right dress!"* and I heard someone's desperate wail right at my stirrup. I stopped my horse in alarm, and then the settling dust allowed me to make out at my horse's feet the prostrate Jew, who cried at the top of his lungs, "Spare me!" His pale face, his eyes full of terror, his tousled locks, and wide-open mouth made him seem like a monster. My horse started snorting, reared; and the Jew crawled away on all fours from our line, then stood and, bent almost double, ran away to the town. I later learned that he had fallen from fear. He was not injured only because by chance it was time to stop the galloping squadron.

After the drill I told my comrades about this event. "Well," asked

Vontrobka, "when you saw the Jew groveling at your horse's feet, with his gaping mug and his eyes bugged out, weren't you reminded of the passage from *Phèdre*:

> De rage et de douleur le monstre bondissant
> Vient aux pieds des chevaux tomber en mugissant,
> Se roule, et leur présente une gueule enflammée
> Qui les couvre de feu, de sang, et de fumée.*

Dombrovitsa

We parted with the Alexander Regiment and arrived at quarters in the town of Dombrovitsa, which belongs to Count Plater, who lives about three versts away. I made a pleasant acquaintance, and in a rather strange manner. Dymchevich, our battallion commander, occupies the first floor of a large stone house. We had no idea who lived on the upper floor. One day, when I was on guard duty, my responsibilities required me go to Dymchevich with a report. As I mounted the porch, I heard the sound of a pianoforte. This unusual occurrence, and the excellent playing, made me forget Dymchevich, the report, and everything related to the watch. I went toward the source of the enchanting harmony. I went up the stairs, down a corridor, and came to a door, behind which I heard the music quite distinctly. I opened the door, and to my surprise, found myself in a kitchen, in which there was not and could not be a pianoforte. I stopped in amazement and continued to listen. Someone was playing in the next room. With hussar-like enterprise, I went farther, determined to find out who so bewitched my ear.

I came to another door, opened it, and the exclamation: "Oh, my heavens!" immediately stopped the music. The lady who cried out was a middle-aged woman. She looked at me uneasily and with a questioning expression. But the young lady, who had been playing the piano, though she was at first confused, immediately recovered when I said, as best I could in Polish, that her beautiful playing had led me like one bewitched through all these rooms, against my will and contrary to any sense of decorum; and that if my coming through the kitchen seemed strange to her, I would ask her to remember that I was in no position to choose my path.

She answered in a pure Polish accent that she was pleased that chance had granted her my visit. They asked me to sit down, and I asked her to continue playing, which she immediately did. When she had finished, she

---

Phèdre, Act 5, scene 6. In rage and pain the monster bounded, fell/a-roaring at the horses' feet, rolled over/and opened wide to them its inflamed jaws,/which spewed upon them fire and blood and smoke. *Three Plays of Racine*, trans. by George Dillon (Chicago: Univ. of Chicago Press, 1961).

started speaking to her mother in Russian. I was surprised at her correct pronunciation, and told her so.

"I am Russian," she answered.

"Oh, good heavens! Then why am I twisting my tongue all around trying to speak with you in Polish?"

"I don't know," she answered, laughing—the young Mme. Vyrodova, that was the name of my new acquaintance. This adventure had very pleasant consequences: the mother and daughter were so taken with me, and valued my society to such a degree, that they could not spend a single day without me. And if one day I didn't come, they would reprimand me and definitely didn't want me to skip a whole day without seeing them. I willingly agreed to this, because I had nowhere found such intelligence, pleasant manners, kindness, friendship, fine education and brilliant talent as in the young Vyrodova.

The good old woman, Vyrodova's mother, loves me like a son, calls me Sashenka and kisses me on the cheek. I told Vontrobka, who is quartered with me, about this acquaintance. Although he is sick now, cannot put on his uniform, and consequently cannot visit her, his desire to see this phenomenon of Dombrovitsa is so great that he has decided to devise some trick, just to find a means of entering their home. He thought, re-thought, and finally came up with this: that I should send him with some books for Vyrodova, that for this mission he should put on a soldier's jacket, and that protected under this aegis from the ladies' attention, he could examine at leisure what he calls my *conquest*. I gave him the books, and almost dying from laughter to see him transformed into a soldier, sick, thin, pale, with haggard eyes and stooped neck. He set off, and I stayed to await the denouement. A quarter of an hour later, Vontrobka returned and told me that his campaign had been extremely unsuccessful. The chambermaid took the books, and when he tried to glance in through the door, which had opened slightly at the noise of his arrival, the girl, who thought he was drunk, wouldn't let him in and shoved him out the door. I told him that Vyrodova will be flattered when she learns the reason for his transformation into a drunken soldier.

The young widow, my acquaintance, is frequently visited by Countess Plater. This seventy- or eighty-year-old lady is a great enthusiast for hunting rabbits, wolves, boars, and quite a master at marksmanship. She often rides on horseback through Dombrovitsa, and always past our guardhouse. Her white horse is just a bit younger than its rider. Her riding-master follows behind her with his whip. When the countess decides to go at a gallop, she says just one word: *gallop!* On that command, the riding-master touches the horse with his whip and she begins a smooth, light gallop. We have all had occasion and time to notice that the white horse gallops only in front of our guardhouse and the porch of our chief's quarters, where there are always many hussar officers gathered. I don't understand why the countess is so displeased with us. She calls us Capuchins! Why? Because we seldom visit her house? Then it is more her fault than ours. Have you ever heard of a ball ending at eight o'clock? At the count's, that is the prescribed time for supper; and often the chiming of the fatal eighth hour, which silences the thundering music, is heard just as unexpectedly and reluctantly as the chiming of the hour of death, especially for some of our young hussars.

I don't know what to do! My money disappears like smoke, and where, I don't understand. I do not play cards, I don't drink wine, I don't buy anything; but as soon as I change the banknotes for silver, all these *zlotys*, *groszes*, and *dwudziestówkas* drive me mad, and scatter like grains of sand. I'm ashamed to ask the Sovereign for money again, and so soon, but I have no other resource. My father won't give me any, and in any case I wouldn't trouble my dear parent for the world. Oh, he so poor, and already old! Will I see that happy time when I am in a position to help him? Will God bless me with that joy? Will I comfort my father's old age? Will I repay him for his care in my childhood? Oh height of happiness for obedient children, will I achieve you!

The Sovereign deigned to grant me a thousand rubles. I received them from Arakcheyev, who writes me that, "upon replacing Count Liven in the Sovereign's household, I have undertaken, among other matters, the duty entrusted him to bring to the attention of the Emperor all of your requests and desires." He concluded his letter with assurances of his readiness to do anything within his power for me.

Today I am on duty with the herd, and will be in that capacity all week. In the middle of the meadow assigned as pasture for our horses, they built me a straw hut. I spent almost the whole first day walking through the surrounding fields, and admiring the play and races of our four-legged friends.

Yesterday I was frightened for the first time in my life; and now I have some idea of what fear is. Our herd is grazing seven versts from the squadron's quarters. I have often walked that distance on foot without the slightest fatigue. Yesterday, I rode as usual on horseback to Stankovich with my report on the welfare of our horses, and stayed for dinner. I entrusted my horse to the hussar who accompanied me, and ordered him to ride back to the herd, intending to return myself on foot. After dinner, when I thought to leave, Stankovich, who did not know that I had sent my horse off, prevailed on me to stay until tea. I agreed, reasoning that it would not be so hot in the evening. After tea, Stankovich said, "Where are you hurrying off to, Alexandrov? Have supper with us. The moon is shining, the night is fine. You can go after supper." The words, "the night is fine," persuaded me to stay for supper. I happily anticipated my night-time journey through the silent fields in the captivating moonlight.

After supper I finally parted with Stankovich, and buckling on my sharp sword, set off. But to avoid a long detour, I decided to go straight from Stankovich's quarters through the vegetable gardens and fields to the road that leads to the place where our herd was. I would have gained a lot if my plan had succeeded, but I was mistaken in my calculations. In the deceptive moonlight, everything seemed smooth and level, but when I had to walk through these places, I thought there would be no end to the ditches, pits, and plowed-up fields. At first I easily jumped over the ditches and gullies, and quickly ran across the plowed fields, but when I saw that there was a second field beyond the first, and then a third, and then another field, and another, and there was no end in sight, I lost courage and set off quietly. Finally the ditches and vegetable gardens ended, but the fields still stretched out in a black carpet for a great distance which I had to cross, whether I wanted to or not. Too late, I remembered with regret the folk saying, "If the path is straight, only the ravens fly it!"

Finally I came out on the road. The moon was almost in the middle of the sky, and its light poured silver over all the boundless expanse of the fields. A deep silence reigned all around. Once I came out on the smooth and even road, with no more clods underfoot, nor soft earth, I was about to set off at a quick, light pace, but suddenly terror and amazement struck me motionless. I stopped. A totally inhuman cry rang out over all the expanse of fields and continued without stopping, and with such terrible twists, turns, peals and a sort of moan, that fright seized my heart and mind, and I turned back to run away. However, the shame of such an act, so uncharacteristic of me, and the greater shame of letting it be known to my comrades, forced me think again and continue my path. I took out my sabre and set off toward the unknown cry, which bellowed, howled and roared at the same pitch. Straining my eyes to see what sort of creature had appeared in the field, I could not make anything out, and I needed all the strength of my reason and faith not to think this cry the cry of an evil spirit. I walked about a half-verst further, and finally saw something black approaching me and crying furiously. I walked faster. I had not gone a hundred paces when I saw that it was a peasant of enormous height. Assured that it was not an animal, nor a monster, nor an evil spirit, but just a man, I put my sabre in its scabbard, approached the peasant and asked him why he was crying so. He couldn't answer me—he was dumb, and lived in our village on charity. By means of various signs he managed to give me to understand that he had come from a village nearby, and that because he was afraid of wolves, he tried to imitate a dog's bark to scare them away. As he explained all this, he used such terrible gestures that anyone would be frightened by them alone. He goggled his eyes, ground his teeth, and snarled in a wild voice.

I made him a sign that he should continue on his road, and he set off with the same absurd howl that I had thought so frightening, but that now became desirable and necessary. I faced real danger—not supernatural, not romantic, but the most mundane, crude and terrible!—the danger of being eaten by wolves. In Little Russia, and even here, these animals prowl in great number through the fields and around the villages. Now I walked rapidly, looking carefully and uneasily at every object; and as the beneficial howl of the dumb peasant faded in the distance, my anxiety increased. My heart beat quickly in anticipation of a danger which neither strength, nor courage, nor skill in handling arms would be of any use to me. What could I do against eight, nine or more ferocious, hungry beasts? My discouraging reflections were interrupted in the most pleasant manner: I clearly heard the cries of the watch by the herd, and even their songs, sung under their breath.

I arrived at my hut. I didn't ask for lights, and lay down without undressing on my bed of hay. Awaiting the coming dawn, and having no desire to sleep, I began to consider, review, sort out and turn over the adventures of the night. I could not but admit that I was scared when I heard the dumb peasant's cry. My fear vanished when I saw that it was a man crying, but it was soon replaced by my dread of meeting with wolves. Why in battle, in the face of a thousand deaths, close and terrible, was there not the shadow of fear? What does that mean? Pain, suffering, death—isn't it all the same whether it's from an enemy bullet or sabre, or from the teeth and claws of savage beast? I just cannot figure out the real reason for either my fear, or my fearlessness. Perhaps it is because death on the field of battle is tied to glory, while in a field with wolves, only with pain.

Journey to Petersburg

The regiment is going to Slonim, but I have a twenty eight-day leave to go to Petersburg. Count Arakcheyev's place is now occupied by Barclay de Tolly. Will he be as obliging to me as Arakcheyev? Scarcely! They say that he is a very stern man. However, it would be strange if they managed to find a sterner man than the count; but Arakcheyev had two sterling qualities—a sincere devotion to the Sovereign and blind obedience to His will.

I saw our beautiful capital again! the charming residence of our adored Tsar, our dearly beloved Father—gentle and merciful! No, the human tongue is too poor in expression for so many virtues united! Every day I hear with what love people speak of our Alexander! I see tears of emotion in the eyes of those who tell of His acts, and all of them are filled with mercy, and all of them have only the happiness of the people as their goal! I have to make an effort to stop writing about Him. I would never finish if I obeyed the heart-felt emotion for Him expressed by all the inhabitants of vast Petersburg!

Barclay de Tolly ordered me to report to him, and when I arrived at his office, he gave me 500 rubles with a very kind expression, saying that the Sovereign Emperor supposes the sum sufficient for my uniform. What was I to do? I took the money, bowed, and went off to order myself a uniform and various other things. With that kind of money, you could have a hussar's uniform made only by some sort of miracle, but since the age of miracles is past, I decided to transfer to the uhlans. I wrote of my desire, and the reason for it, to the Minister of War, asking him, as was permitted me, to bring my request to the attention of the Sovereign, and furthermore, to give me a certain sum of money for my transfer from one regiment to another, and a complete uhlan uniform. Once I had written and sent this note to the Minister of War, I made haste to leave Petersburg, supposing that the minister would curse me soundly and present nothing to the Sovereign, but if I wasn't there, and there was no one there to curse, with time he would reconsider and find that I had been given too little money. It's expensive to serve in the hussars. But what do I care about him? As it pleases the Sovereign!

When I returned to Slonim, I didn't find my regiment. It had not yet arrived. The Jews clustered round me with offers of their services, but when they found out that I had gold only for a uniform, they left. And I am alone, with no servant, living in the house of an old, retired sergeant of the Guards, who tells me anecdotes of his youth and his service under Catherine from morning to night.

Finally the regiment has come. The squadrons went off to their quarters, which are almost all in charming, romantic spots. How sweet Poland is in so many ways! The merry, hospitable Poles! The beautiful and tender Polish ladies! The healthful climate! The picturesque spots, and the humble, obliging folk.

Our whole regiment is now together. The first battallion, which had been quartered in Odessa, has come here to Slonim.

Transfer to Another Regiment

April 1, 1811

I am on my way back to Dombrovitsa. I am already an *uhlan, Lithuanian Regiment.* I was transferred.

With great sorrow I parted from my worthy comrades! With regret I took off my shining uniform, and sadly put on the dark blue jacket with crimson lapels!

"It's too bad, Alexandrov," the elder Pyatnitsky said to me. "It's too bad that you have switched to such disadvantage. The hussar uniform was made for you. I always admired you in it. But this jacket—what made you transfer?"

Colonel Klebek summoned me. "What is the meaning of this, Alexandrov?" he asked. "Why have you requested a transfer? I find this most unpleasant!" I didn't know what to answer. I was ashamed to say that the hussar's uniform was too expensive for me, and all because of my inability to handle money. I said a sad farewell to my brave cohorts, to my golden uniform and black steed, got into a post chaise and raced off at a full gallop down the road to Pinsk. My orderly, Zanudenko, was transferred to the uhlans with me. He sat on the coachman's seat, twirling his grey mustache and sighing: "The poor man! He's grown old in the hussars."

Here I am in Dombrovitsa. In the absence of its chief Tutolmin, the Lithuanian Regiment is under the command of Vadbolsky, the very one I knew in Tarnopol. I think that I soon shall be consoled over the loss of my hussar's uniform. The sight of the uhlans, their pikes, helmets, pennants evoke in my soul memories of my service in the Konnopolsk Regiment, of military maneuvers, my unforgettable Alcides, and all those events and dangers! It all, all is resurrected, and rises in a brilliant picture in my imagination! That first year of my entrance into a military career will never be erased from my memory. That year of happiness, of complete freedom, of full independence, is the more dear to me because I myself, alone and without any help, was able to acquire it Four years have passed since then. I am now twenty-one. Ch*** says that I have grown up, that when he saw me in Tarnopol he thought me a boy of about thirteen. That's not surprising! I had a very youthful appearance and something childish in my face. Everyone says the same, even Panna Nowicka before she awoke from the attractiveness of my companionship and exclaimed twice: "My God! Such a young child and he's already in the army!".

I have been assigned to the squadron of Lieutenant Podyampolsky, my previous colleague in the Mariupolsk Regiment. Thanks to my guardian angel, even here my squadron comrades are educated people: Shvarts, Chernyavsky, and the brothers Tornezi, regimental officers outstanding for intelligence, breeding, and education. Podyampolsky has not yet given me my platoon. I am staying with him. Every day the squadron commanders come to visit him, and we pass the time very pleasantly.

The regimental chief has returned. I am often at his place. He loves to live well and knows how to do so. He often gives balls for the ladies of the neighboring manors. Countess Plater does not call uhlans Capuchins, and the count does not order the table set at eight o'clock. On the contrary, at their house we dance until four in the morning, and the old countess takes a very lively and active part in our amusements.

The young widow Virodova married Shabunevich, the regimental adjutant. She related to me that after my departure for Petersburg Vontrobka became acquainted with her, was captivated, and knew how to please her, that they were always inseparable, read together, sketched, sang, played, brewed coffee and drank it—in a word their life was heavenly and their love sincere, that mutual respect and wonder complemented one another.... But I couldn't listen for long.

"How could it happen, I ask you, how after all this did you become Shabunevich's wife?"

"This is how it happened," she answered. "Your regiment was ordered to go to Slonim. Vontrobka left me with true sorrow, and swore to remain faithful, but said nothing of his hand. He wrote to me very tenderly from Slonim, but again not a word of our eternal union, from which I concluded that his attachment was but one of the scores of attachments he had had previously. He loves to test the heart he has taken, and when he is assured that he is loved, his own love cools. Not wishing to submit to this lot, I stopped answering his letters and forced myself to stop thinking about him. Love rewarded me for this offense, brought on by my own tenderness. Shabunevich, a young and handsome uhlan fell in love with me with all the strength of his ardent soul, and proved the truth of his words: he offered me his hand, his heart, and all that he had, or would have. I married him, and now, a happy woman, give thanks every day to God, that He didn't make Vontrobka my husband. It would be an infernal life, my dear Alexandrov, to live with a man like that, who tests everything, trusts nothing, and from excessive experience fears everything. My priceless Yuzya is not like that. He trusts me implicitly, and I love him more each day."

The beautiful Erotiada concluded her story, sat at the piano, and asked me in jest, "What pieces would you have me play, Mr. Alexandrov?" I named them, handed her the music, and sat by her instrument to listen and dream.

Tutolmin is a handsome man. Although he is already forty-four, he looks no more than twenty-eight. To the last, the girls and young ladies of the surrounding estates cannot remain indifferent to him; every one of them, they all have plans for him. But he!... I had never seen anyone who could more coldly, or with less concern than he, observe all the signs of interest, attention, and hidden love. I attribute that to his rather too high opinion of himself. Oh, in a heart filled with pride, there is no room for love!

Yesterday, Shvarts and I went riding. We rode a long way with no object through the sandy knolls and shrubbery, and finally lost our way and our direction, that is, we lost the road and any notion of how to find it. We circled for more than an hour around the spot we supposed the road should be, and then caught sight of a village in the distance. Shvarts had started to lose patience and get angry. He galloped off in that direction, and I after him. We came up to the kitchen-gardens. In one, a woman was spreading flax. Shvarts rode up to that garden and shouted, "Listen, auntie! What's this village called?"

"What did you say, sir?" asked the peasant-woman, bowing from the waist.

"What's the name of the village? Damn your bowing!" shouted Shvarts, his eyes flashing.

The woman was frightened, and started to say, droning on, and hesitating at every word, that there was more than one name for this village, that when it was built it was called something strange, she didn't remember, but that now...

"To hell with you, your village, and the people who built it!" said Shvarts, spurring his horse. We raced off, Shvarts swearing and cursing, and I barely restraining my laughter. We galloped about a half-verst straight ahead, and saw another woman, also spreading out flax in a glade surrounded by bushes, through which ran a little-used road.

"Allow me to question this woman," I said to Shvarts. "You just scare them with your shouting."

"Please, go ahead. You'll see what rubbish she'll hand you."

I rode up to the woman. "Listen, my dear. Where does that road go?"

"I don't know."

"Can't you get to Kornilovka on it?"

"No."

"Well, can you go to the devil on it?" asked Shvarts, losing patience, with malicious irony and a tone of voice that scared even me.

"Yes, yes," said the quailing peasant-woman, bowing low to us both.

"Don't listen to him, my dear. Just tell us, do you know how to get to Kornilovka? Can we go straight through the fields? I think it shouldn't be too far from here."

"Where did you come from?" asked the woman, looking timidly at Shvarts. I told her. "Oh, then you've lost your way. You have to go back the way you came, and come here all over again!..." I almost died of laughter, as they say, at her answer.

"Excellent questioning," said Shvarts. "Shan't we follow her advice?" We rode off, and after being lost for another two hours or so, discovered our enchanted Kornilovka, and arrived there.

At last Tutolmin's steel heart has softened! The hour of his subjugation has struck!... Countess Manuzzi, a beauty of twenty-eight, came to visit her father, Count Plater, and with the flame of her black eyes set afire our entire Lithuanian Regiment. Everyone has become unusually animated! Everyone dances, extemporizes, twirls his mustache, sprinkles himself with cologne, washes in milk, jingles his spurs, and draws in his waist *à la circassienne!* The countess is truly enchanting in her white satin house-dress, with a silken lace scarf on her head, half covering her beautiful dark eyes. She sits in a big armchair, and looks with a sweet indifference and carelessness upon our uhlan Adonises, walking, standing, shining and silhouetted before her! She is tired from the journey. She so charmingly leans her head on her mother's shoulder and whispers, *"Ah! maman, comme je suis fatiguée!"* But the fire in her eyes and her satisfied smile speak to the contrary. The uhlans believe them more than her words, and do not hurry home. Finally, the eighty-year-old Plater's drowsing gave the captive cavalry-men to understand that perhaps the countess really was tired.

The handsome Tutolmin and the beautiful Manuzzi are inseparable. A ball at Tutolmin's is followed by a ball at Plater's. We dance in the morning, we dance in the evening. After the mounting of the guard, which is now done to music every day and in full parade uniform, and always in the presence of our Inspector-General, the Countess Manuzzi, we all go to the colonel's. There, we have breakfast, dance, and finally return to quarters to prepare for the evening's ball! This new Armida fails to turn the heads only of those among us who are too old for such things, who have not seen her, or who are involved in affairs of the heart, and of course me. All the rest sigh over her!

Everything has calmed down!.. The music no longer plays!.. Manuzzi is weeping!.. Not a soul from our regiment visits their house!.. Manuzzi is alone, in her bedroom, weeping bitterly!.. Weeping! And yesterday we all pranced about to some ridiculous dance!.. Yesterday, as we parted, we arranged to gather earlier, dance longer, and again spend the whole evening foisting the old countess on our Gruzintsov!.. But lo, how transient are our earthly pleasures!—*We march at 12 midnight!*.. Magical words! They are the cause of Manuzzi's tears, and of the merry bustle of the young soldiers! Because of them, the singing and dancing of yesterday are sullenly reckoned up and paid off with this and that! Reikhmar says that he is stunned by the order! Solntsev, Chernyavsky, Lizogub, the Nazimovs and Tornezi, though they were true comrades-in-arms in Tutolmin's philandering, have not the slightest regrets, and have all raced off to their squadrons. Tornezi and I rode off to Strelsk.

"Have you finally come to your senses?" Podyampolsky asked us. "I thought you were terminally giddy!"

We answered that the sounds of the last cotillion still rang in our ears.

"Very good! But now we'll start a cotillion whose figures will apparently be quite difficult... Farewell, gentlemen! We have our hands full!" We set off to our squadrons.

Part Two

The War of 1812

11 March

Today we said our final farewells to Plater's hospitable home, to our merry quarters in Dombrovitsa, to all we loved and all we found charming! We are marching to Byelsk, we sharpen our lances, our sabres, and march on.

The old hands among the uhlans say that every time the Russian army moves, all the bad weather moves with it. On this occasion, one was obliged to believe them. From the day we set out, we were accompanied by snow, cold, blizzards, rain and penetrating wind. The skin on my face hurts so that I cannot touch it. Upon the advice of officer Tornezi, I wash my face every night with whey, and this remedy eases the pain somewhat, but I have become so very, very swarthy that I know of nothing darker than I.

Podyampolsky is occupied with accounts at headquarters. I am the senior officer after him, and in command of the squadron. However, I am merely king for a day—in two days my reign will end.

Kastyuknovka

A day's rest for our squadron is fixed in this settlement. A peasant hut serves as quarters for the four of us—Chernyavsky, the two Tornezis, and me. It is blackened, covered with soot, permeated with smoke, with a dilapidated straw roof and an earthen floor. From the outside it resembles a crushed turtle. The front corner of this hovel is ours. Our batmen have arranged themselves by the door and the stove, diligently occupying themselves cleaning bits, curb-bits, stirrups, oiling harnesses, and other such cavalry chores. Must we really stay in a kennel like that all day with such society! We decided to ride over to Sokolovsky's for the day—the landlord of this settlement.

He received us very kindly, and we spent the day at his home merrily and pleasantly. I was very happy to learn that he was the same Sokolovsky of whom Kotzebue wrote in his *A Voyage of Discovery*. Kotzebue calls him Sokolov, apparently by mistake. Sokolovsky told us how he lived in Siberia, despaired, hoped, hunted, and anxiously but philosophically awaited a change for the better. I asked if Kotzebue indeed lived in Siberia as he describes, and if he was wretched.

"He enjoyed himself," answered Sokolovsky, laughing. "He played cards every day, he always won, and to all appearances was very little concerned about what would happen to him."

Settlement **

I do not know if we will be stopping here long. I have been assigned quarters at the home of a Uniate priest. His young wife very sweetly troubles herself to furnish me with all the best her household offers. Every morning she herself brings me coffee, cream, and candied fruit, while for her husband she prepares just a glass of warmed beer and cheese. Her dinners are always tasty, refined; and only so as not to thoroughly enrage her spouse does she prepare some dish to his taste which, I must confess, is quite coarse.

Yesterday our pastor was angry about something. All during dinner he frowned and pushed aside the dishes his wife—pleasantly smiling the whole time—served him. Fortunately, his rage did not have occasion to be expressed in words. No one spoke with him, and we tried not even to meet his gaze. His wife was the best at this maneuver.

Our hostess exasperates me. Not a day has passed that she has not said to me, "You surely must be Polish!"

"Why do you think that?" I ask, and in reply get some utter nonsense.

"You speak so pleasantly. Your manners are so noble!" She has lost her mind!

"Is it really your opinion then that pleasant conversation and noble manners are the exclusive property of Poles? How have all the other nations offended you, pray tell? Why do you deny them those advantages?"

In answer, she laughs, escapes with jokes, and then once more begins to discover in me the various gifts of a Pole. Employing every possible argument to refuse the honor of being Polish, I mentioned in passing to my hostess that if she notices in me something not entirely Russian, it may be because I am partly of Little Russian and partly of Swedish blood; that my grandmothers, on my mother's and my father's side were Little Russian and Swedish, respectively. My hostess then began to praise Swedes, extolling to the skies their bravery, steadfastness and rectitude. My host was visibly losing patience. Unfortunately, at this very moment, they served him his favorite dish—buckwheat porridge, swimming in lard, and sprinkled with fried up pieces of more lard. I don't know why or wherefore, but in Poland they are called *Swedes*. My host grasped the plate, set it before him, and in a frenzy began to beat those innocent pieces with his spoon, repeating, "I don't like Swedes! I don't like Swedes!" Splashes of lard flew on my uniform and epaulettes. I hastily got up from the table, wiping my face with my handerchief.

"Oh, my heavens!" cried my hostess, attempting to snatch the spoon from his hand. "He's gone mad, completely mad!"

About three days after that scene, my hostess brought my morning coffee as she did every day, but this time she did not wait for me to take the cup from her hands. She set everything before me on the little table and, without saying a word, sat down pensively by the window. "Why so sad, my fine lady?" I asked.

"*Nothing, Lieutenant, sir!*" She was silent for a moment, and said, "Won't you help me?"

"I will, I swear by my honor I will!"

"Give me a pledge of this promise."

"Please tell me, what you would like?"

"This ring!" She took my hand, lightly squeezing my little finger, on which I wore a gold ring.... I hadn't expected that. Silent, in confusion, I looked at the young priest's wife who fixed her black eyes on me, and I didn't know what to do!... The ring had been given to me by Miss Pavlishchev, and I had sworn to her that I would never part with it. Meanwhile, my hostess was waiting for an answer and, naturally, was in some confusion upon seeing that I did not take off the ring that very second to give it to her.

"What is the meaning, my love, of your sitting in the lieutenant's room and forgetting that I have not yet had my breakfast?" So spoke my enraged host. He had opened the door of my room, and, seeing that his wife held my hand, stopped on the threshold.

She rushed toward her husband. "Oh, my dearest, my beloved, please forgive me! Everything will be ready this moment!" Having said this, she shot like lightning past her husband, and left him standing like a statue on the threshold, straight across from me. Reassured by this happy turn of events that had at first threatened to deprive me of my ring, that priceless pledge of friendship, I asked my host to come in.

"I have some good news for you, Lieutenant," said my host as he came into the room.

"What could that be, Reverend Father?"

"You're setting off on the march tomorrow."

"Tomorrow! How do you know?"

"I was just at your captain's. I was about to request that you be moved to someone else's house. I hope you won't be angry about that. I am not so rich that I can provide an officer with board and other advantages for more than two or three days, and you have been staying with me for about two weeks. I presented all this to your captain, but he said that that very minute orders had been received to take to the field, and that tomorrow at eight o'clock in the morning your squadron will leave here."

"Congratulations, my kind host! This is, of course, better news for you than it is for me. The weather now is not very good for marching—rain and snow and cold and dust, all at the same time! I thought that we would wait here until spring had finally arrived."

"What can you do? When you're ordered, you must obey." Having said this, my host bowed to me with an ironic smile, and went off to drink his warmed beer.

And so the march! And all for the best—if we're going, let's go! In these quarters we are just getting soft unnecessarily. We are getting used to dainties, comforts, pleasures. White satin hands pat your cheek, pull tenderly at your ear, give you sweets, jams; they make up a soft bed, and it's so easy, so pleasant to grow accustomed to it! After all that, suddenly the march; and suddenly you must go from voluptuousness to austerity, move from the velvet sofa to a swift steed, and so on; contrast in everything. I had not managed to complete my ruminations, when the captain sent for me.

"Well, my friend," he said as soon as I opened the door to his chamber, "say farewell to that black-eyed priest's wife of yours! We're on the march tomorrow!"

"Thank heavens, Captain!"

"Thank heavens? That's news! Weren't you her *piekne dziecko* and *czerwone jabłko* [her beautiful child, her red apple]? Ingrate!" The captain's joke reminded me that I was in truth ungrateful. I could pay for my hostess's love neither with love, nor with a gold ring; but I still had to give her something as a keepsake, and of course not money! I returned to my quarters. My hostess sadly set the table; my host stood by the window, playing some mournful song on the violin and looking ironically at his wife.

There was still a whole hour until dinner. I went to my chamber to see if I could not find something to give my hostess. Digging through my things, I found two dozen Sarpinsky handkerchiefs, shining opalescent. I had bought them in Sarept and sent them to my father; but when I visited him, he gave them back to me, and they lay in my things unused. I took them out and laid them out on the table. Continuing the inspection of my property, I found in a corner of the case my silhouette, taken when I was still in the hussar regiment and in that uniform. I put it with the handkerchiefs and again started reordering everything that was in the case. Finally, tired of looking and finding nothing, and to get it all over with at once, I picked the case up from the bottom, turned it upside down and shook everything in it out on the floor and sat down there myself. At the very moment when I had delightedly seized a paste belt buckle in one hand, and in the other, a large shawl given to me by my sister, my hostess came in.

"Dinner is ready! What on earth are you doing?"

"You wanted to have something as a keepsake. Do me the favor of choosing whatever you like," I said, showing her the handkerchiefs, the silhouette, the buckle and the large shawl.

"I chose the ring."

"I can't give it away. It's a present from a friend."

"A friend's gift is sacred! Keep it!" She went up to the table, took the silhouette and without even glancing at the other things, went toward the door, saying that her husband was waiting for me for dinner. Her choice of present touched me, and I ran after her, clasped her in one arm and earnestly requested her to take at least the paste buckle as well.

"It's true you love me, isn't it, my dear hostess! Why don't you want to take a thing you would wear so close to your heart?" She made no answer and did not even look at me, but pressed my hand to her breast, took the buckle gently from it and went downstairs without saying a word. A minute later I followed. My host was sitting at the table, and my hostess was showing him the buckle.

"And what am I to understand by this?" he said, pushing her hand and the buckle away. Seeing me, he stood and asked me to sit down at the table. "And so, my love? Today we should treat the Lieutenant to dinner of a better sort, for he is leaving us probably forever. What are having today?"

"You'll see." After this short answer, pronounced with some annoyance, she sat down at her place.

"My wife is angry with you," my host began. "You pay her too dearly for these two weeks we have had the honor of providing you with some trifling pleasures."

"I feel I've paid you nothing. That shiny bagatelle cannot be taken as payment. It's simply for..." I wanted to say "the memory," but my hostess glanced at me and I fell silent—at a most inopportune moment, one will note.

My host finished my thought: "a keepsake, isn't that so? But we would remember you without that." All day, right until evening, my host was in a good mood. He joked, laughed, played the violin, kissed his wife's hands, and asked her to sing to his accompaniment "Vous me quittez...," asking me to help him persuade her. "You still do not know how beautifully my wife sings!"

Finally his wife lost patience, looked reproachfully at her husband, her eyes full of tears, and went out. That upset my host. In confusion, he hastily hung the violin on the wall and set off after his wife. I went to the captain's and stayed there until midnight, precisely to avoid meeting either of my hosts that evening, if possible. But I miscalculated. Both of them had waited for me for supper, and were apparently in complete accord. Seeing how my hostess amorously leaned on her husband's chest, I almost thought that my suspicions were baseless, and rejoicing at my discovery, I began to speak with her merrily, trustfully, as a friend. But disappointment was in the offing. Her husband turned to the door to give an order to his man. My hostess quickly took my silhouette from under her scarf, showed it to me, kissed it and hid it again. She did all of this in two seconds, and when her husband turned to us again, she clung to his shoulder.

I rose at dawn, dropped in to see my host and his wife for a minute, wished them good-bye, and set off to the captain's to await the hour set for the march. That joker Tornezi rode by me the whole way, singing, "*Nie kochaj się we mnie, bo to nadaremnie...*"["Do not fall in love with me, for it would be in vain"]

We are marching at an easy pace, the day's marches are not long, and then once again we are ordered to stop *until further orders.* And as luck would have it, we got the most unfavorable quarters. This village is poor, nasty and ravaged, one must suppose, by the inordinate demands of its landowner. All four of us are quartered in one large cottage, and we set up, Chernyavsky with the elder Tornezi on the benches by the windows, and I with the younger on the bunk on the stove. Right across from us on the stove, right under the ceiling, sits an old woman in her nineties. I do not know why she constantly holds her nose with two fingers, saying at the same time, in the thinnest voice, *"Khm!"* and then puts these two fingers up to the wall. The first couple of days, Tornezi and I laughed like madmen at our Sibyl's routine, but now we're used to it; and despite the piercing sniveling, we sometimes forget that there's something breathing over our heads.

Spring this year is sad, wet, cold, windy, muddy. I always considered it a mere stroll to make the rounds of the stables of our platoon, but now I do not prepare for these rounds every morning so willingly. I dress lazily, I tarry, I look out the window twenty times to see if the weather isn't clearing; but since there's nothing for it—I absolutely must go—I go, clinging to the walls, clutching the fence, jumping over rivulets, feeling my way along the stones, and still landing with my whole foot in the mud a few times. Returning from my muddy journey, I find my comrades all still together: Chernyavsky is reading Racine, Cesare smokes his pipe and always puts a little piece of aloe on top of the tobacco, saying that that's what the Turks do. Ivan Tornezi occasionally presents a ballet—*Ariadne* on the island *Naxos*—and he always plays Ariadne. That would make a dead man laugh; and I instantly forget the difficult voyage through the muddy streets.

Podyamolsky went off to headquarters for some reports for about three days; my comrades were sent to get oats and hay for our horses; and I stayed on as commander of the squadron and master of the whole village by right of might. I had taken so little trouble to know anything about this village, that I didn't even know if there was a post office or not. This morning I had occasion to find out. Having completed all of my official duties, I picked up some tale by Voltaire, to reread it for the hundredth time for lack of anything else to do, and lack of anything else to read. And when I had reluctantly opened the book and was about to lie down on my campaign divan—a bench with a rug—the door suddenly opened and in stepped an infantry officer.

"Tell me please, who is in command of the squadron here?"

"I am."

"Be so kind as to order that I be given some horses. I am hurrying to catch up to my regiment. Here is my traveling pass. The Jew who is keeper of the post office won't give me horses. He says that they've all been disbursed, but he's lying. I saw a great number being taken to be watered."

"You'll have your horses this very minute. Please sit down. Send in the orderly officer!" The orderly came. "Go to the post office immediately and order horses harnessed to this officer's carriage—any they have, even if the Jew says, as they usually do, that he only has courier horses." The orderly set off and returned two minutes later with the Jew who was keeper of the post office. The Judas bowed and said that he would not give any horses, because there were only courier horses left.

"Well, we'll see whether you will or not!" I turned to the orderly: "I ordered you to have those horses harnessed without fail. Why did you come back with the Jew?" At the conclusion of this question, the orderly and the Jew vanished in a second. They were carried out the door as if by a whirlwind, and in ten minutes, the officer's carriage rolled up to the porch of my quarters.

The officer stood. "Didn't you serve at some time in the hussars?" he asked.

"I did."

"In the Mariupolsk Regiment, I believe? Aren't you Alexandrov?"

"Yes. How do you know?"

"We were acquainted in Kiev. We served together as orderlies under Miloradovich. Don't you remember me?"

"No."

"I'm Gorlenko."

"Oh, good heavens! Only now do I remember your face. I'm so pleased! Please sit down a moment longer. Tell me of our other comrades. Where are Shlein, Shtein, Kosov?"

"God knows. I haven't met them anywhere, just as I hadn't met you till now. We'll all see each other again somewhere. The time has come for the gypsy life, I mean constant walking, riding, marching, transfers, hither and yon—we'll bump into each other again. I wasn't so close friends with them as with you. Do you remember how we always sat at the foot of the table, to be as far from the general as possible, and eat sweets at liberty? Your bag was always loaded with enough for both of us for the whole day."

"No, you're joking now. I somehow don't remember loading my bag with dessert."

"Well, I remember! Goodbye, Alexandrov! Please God we see each other again just as we are now at parting!" He got into the vehicle, and rushed off down the bumpy road in a cloud of mud spatters. I returned to my smoky hovel, very pleased that I had forced that damned Jew to give him some horses. I still had not forgotten the carping and delays that I suffered at the post-stations when I went on furlough. All the station-masters' tricks came back to me as soon as Gorlenko said that they wouldn't give him any horses on the pretext that they had all been disbursed, and I was pleased at the chance to revenge myself upon at least one of his estate.

On Forage

My comrades returned: Chernyavsky with nothing; Cesare with some unimportant acquisitions. Ivan brought something more. In two days I was to be dispatched.

Finally even I was being sent for forage! Like the others, I was given a detachment and orders with the signature and seal of the commander of the regiment to ride round to the surrounding estates, request oats and hay from the landowners, gather it all, and in exchange give them inventories, which they can send off with their village headmen to the squadron to get receipts to be taken to headquarters. There they will likewise be given receipts, and with those receipts the landowners are to appear before a commission for receipt of payment in cash.

At dawn I left our muddy village and my smoky quarters with its hundred-year-old inhabitant and three brave youths, that is, my comrades, and, following the uhlans of the 20th, set off. The first stage of my operation was the estate of chamberlain L***, three versts from our quarters. My mission seemed rather delicate to me, and for that reason, I was in great confusion when I caught sight of the home of Pan L*** just ten paces away... How shall I begin! What will I say! What if the man is well-respected, old, the head of a family. What if he receives me cordially, considers me a guest, and I—I'm going to ask for oats practically for nothing! I do know that the Poles don't willingly hand over their goods for our receipts, and use every means to avoid them, which is quite natural. However correct the payment on the coupon, it's more pleasant and correct to receive cash on the spot than go riding hither and yon with receipts. Considering, pondering, and blushing at the thought of the drama about to begin, I nevertheless rode up, rode into the courtyard, went into the house; and my forebodings did not deceive me.

I am met by a man of about sixty. His face is sad, his glance uneasy. It was clear, however, that we, the uninvited guests, were not the reason for this. He couldn't even see my uhlans; and, looking like a seventeen-year-old boy, I couldn't frighten him. So, it was some domestic grief that was etched on his genial face. Poles are always very polite; he invited me to sit down before he had asked to what he owed the honor of seeing me in his home. Finally a beginning was made; the question that so terrified me popped out of my host's mouth. I blushed as red as one can get, and answered that my charge from the regiment was to find forage wherever I could, and buy it... of course, not for cash, but in exchange for a receipt.

"I cannot help you in this matter," said the landowner indifferently. "A week ago, everything was burned—the oats, the hay, the wheat, the rye. I've just sent round to the surrounding landowners to buy what I need, if they'll sell it. Your billeting, you gentlemen of the cavalry, is very profitable for those of us who have something to sell you; but it is a great blow to those who, like me, seek to buy." In the course of this conversation, we were served coffee.

L*** continued: "You have a very difficult mission. Excuse my candor, but in exchange for receipts, not a single landowner will sell you the fruits of his earth. I wouldn't sell, even if we all didn't have another way to market them. Judge for yourself, should people give their crops away now if they have the chance to sell them for cash?"

I stood in indecision, and didn't know what to do: leave without another word, or show him my orders?

L*** also stood. "Are you going already? I'm very sorry that I cannot fulfil your request. I would enjoy the pleasure of seeing you in my home longer, if I were not in deep sorrow. I buried my son yesterday!" He could not say anything more. His eyes filled with tears, and he sat down, unable to stand. I hurriedly left, mounted my horse, and galloped off with my uhlans.

Toward evening, I came to the estate of the subprefect's wife, Ts***, and now walked into her rooms a bit more boldly. Unfortunately, I had to deal with old age here as well. I was received by a lady of about eighty. When she learned what I required, she had her steward summoned and asked me to occupy myself until he arrived. Saying this, she opened the door to another room. It was a vast hall in which were gathered all manner of entertainments: shuttlecock, billiards, roulette, cards, cut-outs, a harp, a guitar.... I found there a company of young people, and they were all engaged in different games.

"These are all my grandchildren," said my hostess, introducing me to their circle. They instantly asked me to take part in their games; I immediately agreed, and completely gave myself over to the pleasure of playing each game in turn. While throwing and catching the shuttlecock, I heard the charming sound of the harp, played by one of the young ladies, and the delightful singing of another. How I wished that the steward not come! To the sounds of the harp and the beautiful voice, how could I think without trembling of the commission which lay like a sleeping serpent beneath my uniform? I need only take out my orders and they would all be alarmed. But now, how merry these young people! How they liked me! How amicably they press my hand, embrace me, kiss me. The young ladies ask me to dance themselves, and sport and play! Now, we are all nothing so much as a group of grown-up children, but in something like a half an hour, it will all change: I'll become a desperate uhlan, with the power and authority to gather forage on their estate.... And my captivating hostesses...what will become of their joyful faces, their lively and merry conversation! Oh, why weren't all the oats burned here, or one of the grandchildren die? Then it would be easier for me to leave without it all...but now?

Here I am some fifty versts from my squadron, and I still haven't done a thing; and I probably won't, because any landowner with a drop of sense won't give me anything in exchange for just an inventory. I could demand peremptorily, but in case of refusal, it would still be necessary to take what is needed, and send it off to the squadron, drawn by their horses, having given the landowner for all that an inventory! How can one think of that and not fall into despair! At least at first I cursed my uhlan's calling. During the dances, laughter and sport, I shuddered every time the door to our hall opened.

Fortunately, the steward did not come until just before supper; and to my great happiness, my hostess said that she could give me ten quarters of the rye, and four wagon-loads of hay, provided her men were paid for the transport, and that her village headman and my non-commissioned officer took the inventory to the squadron with the wagons. With great happiness and gratitude, I agreed to her arrangements and kissed her hand. I would have kissed it even had I not been obliged to do so by Polish custom and my own attire, because her indulgence had lifted a terrible weight from my heart, and spared me the necessity of disturbing the serpent which I now carry onward.

Having sent off the wagons with the forage, I returned to the merry company. They were waiting for me for supper, and the difficulties of dispatching the wagons had delayed supper an hour. When we sat down at the table, the hostess seated me next to her. "You are too diligent in your work, young man," she began. "Was it necessary to supervise yourself, and wait until the forage had been loaded and left the village? That is a bit too much. From your appearance and youth, I would not have supposed to find you such a good worker." The incautious old woman did not know that with her interests at stake, I would not have let the uhlans out of my sight for a minute. Could they perhaps have searched out somewhere something better than oats? Will people always judge by appearances?... They wanted me to spend the night, but I was already feeling discontent, and no longer found any pleasure in their society.

When I left the home of the subprefect's wife, I decided to ride all night, in order to visit at dawn the village of retired Captain M***, a Polish official. The Jews told me that he has a great deal of oats and hay in store, and precisely for sale. I hope that fate will be so kind to me as to not let my sleeping serpent wake.

This old nationalist, at whose home I arrived at ten o'clock in the morning, received me with all the cordiality of a cavalry man: "Sit down, sit down, my dear uhlan, what can I serve you? You probably don't drink wine this early, right? Well, then coffee. Hey, Marysia!" At this cry, Marysia appeared, grey-haired, withered, tall, with a gloomy expression. "Have them serve us coffee, my dear." It was flattering to my self-esteem that Marysia (although she was approaching fifty) looked at me tenderly and smiled, while her glance at the veteran expressed at once annoyance and disdain. She answered that it would be ready shortly, left, and in a quarter hour returned with the coffee. She told her master that the steward was asking for him and took a place next to me to pour the coffee. I was not surprised by this familiarity. The housekeepers of old bachelors have all the privileges of mistress, and in Poland they are almost always of the gentry, that is, the *szlachta*.

Finally my host returned, learned the purpose of my visit, shook his head and shrugged his shoulders. "Well, if I don't give it to you in exchange for an inventory, then what?"

"Then I won't have it," I answered.

"You are more patient than I expected, and that does you great honor. Why don't your superiors send you out with money, instead of the power to hand out inventories?"

"I don't know. I think that that is a question of the regiment's economic resources. But it makes no difference to you whether you get an inventory or money; the only difference is time. You'll get paid a little later, because you have to go to headquarters."

The old nationalist burst out laughing. "Oh, how young you are still, dear fellow! Well, but let's go. I'm sure that you have no time to waste. Let's go. I'll give orders that you be given twenty quarters of rye—more than that I cannot give, and I do not want to give up to you what I've already set aside for sale, for money no less." I was so pleased with these twenty quarters, which exceeded my expectations and allowed me to return to the squadron and finally free myself of this odious duty to pillage, that I grabbed the hand of the old nationalist and nearly ran off with the speed of a fallow doe, dragging him with me.

"Careful, careful, young man! I'm sure you're pleased to get so much oats for so little trouble, but my time for running is past. And on top of that, I was wounded in both legs, so let's go at a walk." I was ashamed of my inappropriate delight, and walked silently beside my benevolent host. We walked through a beautiful orchard and came out to his barns and granaries; there stood the steward and my uhlans. Finally, everything was ready. I sent off all my uhlans with the booty, keeping just one with me, intending to spend the day with my kind nationalist and return to the squadron tomorrow. With the greatest pleasure, I took my orders from my uniform jacket, tore them into tiny pieces, and threw them in the lake.

I was so happy! All my good humor returned, and the old captain was so pleased with my company that he asked me most earnestly to stay with him a day or two more. "Your blooming youth, animation, good humor bring to mind, and raise in my soul, my own happy youth. That's what I was like at your age. Please stay, young man," he said, embracing me. "Give an old man these two days. An old man who has come to love you like a son."

I stayed. In reward for my tractability, my host invited two or three families from the surrounding estates. I spent a very pleasant time at the gallant nationalist's. We danced, played all sorts of games, ran from room to room like fifteen-year-olds; and as much as Marysia frowned, the noise, the talk, the laughter, the dances did not slacken in the least. And what is more, our host exceeded our expectations, setting up a huge buffet of pastries, jams, and delicacies of all sorts. And poor Marysia! She couldn't walk past that buffet without making some convulsive grimaces.

Two days passed. I said farewell to my kind host and rode back to the squadron. Thus ended my unpleasant posting, and I hope to God it will not be repeated! When I returned home, I didn't say anything to the captain, except that I had had no need to resort to force. In our quarters just Cesare and I were left. Chernyavsky and the elder Tornezi had gone off searching again.

Today my comrades returned, and it's today we march. For long? For some reason I don't quite understand why we march at this irregular pace.

We covered about a hundred versts and stopped again. They say that Napoleon has crossed our borders with a huge army. I've become more indifferent, for some reason; no more of those high-flown dreams, those outbursts and impulses. I think now that I wouldn't go with every squadron on a charge; I've probably become more sensible. Experience has taken its usual toll, even from my ardent imagination; I mean, it has given it a more appropriate path.

We are staying in a poor little village on the banks of the Nareva. Every night our horses are saddled, we are dressed and armed. At midnight, half the squadron mounts their horses and rides out of the settlement to support the picket and make up mounted patrols. The other half remains in readiness on horseback. During the day, we sleep. This sort of life is very like the description given in Zhukovsky's "Lyudmila":

> Close by the Nareva is my crowded house:
> Just as the celestial moon
> Rises above the valley
> As midnight strikes,
> We saddle our horses,
> And leave our dark cells.

That's just like us, the Lithuanian uhlans: every night at midnight we saddle up and ride out; and the little house I occupy is crowded, too small, and right on the Nareva. Oh, how this location has again enlivened all my feelings! My heart is full of emotions, my head full of ideas, plans, dreams, intentions. My imagination paints pictures that shine with all the lights and colors that exist in the realms of Nature and possibility. What a life, what a full, happy, active life! How can one compare it to the life I led in Dombrovitsa? Now I live every day, every hour, and I feel that I am alive. Oh, a thousand, a thousand times better my current manner of life!... Balls, dances, philandering, music... Oh, God! How trivial, how boring!

Really, I didn't think that I would find a use for the wine they pass out to us, two glasses a day, just like the soldiers. But it is obvious that one must not disdain anything. Yesterday, passing through a certain village, our squadron had to go across a narrow dam. Some difficulty the first section met with forced the whole squadron to come to a halt. Other troops approaching pressed us from the rear, and our horses, jostling and bumping one another so as not to fall into the wide moats by the side of the dam, began to rage, kick and rear. In all this disorder, I was pressed to the center of my platoon, and squeezed so much that although I saw that the horse in front of me intended to strike me with its well-shod hoof, I was powerless to do anything but courageously await and endure the blow. I gasped from the fierce pain! That worthless horse had both the will and the opportunity to break my leg, since I was in such a crush. Fortunately, when the horse was preparing to repeat the blow, the squadron moved forward, and everything fell in line. When we made camp, I examined my leg and I was horrified. It was swollen and bruised to the point of bleeding. From the heel to the knee, it ached unbearably. For the first time in my life I would willingly have ridden in a carriage. It was agonizing to ride on horseback, but when there's no choice, one must bear it. We haven't had a single carriage in some time. Now the wine came in handy. Every day I wash my sore leg with it, and see to my alarm that it becomes more purple by the day, although the pain is subsiding. The sole of my injured foot has become as black as coal. I'm afraid to look at it, and I can't understand why the sole has turned black when the injury was right between it and the knee.—The field doctor Kornilovich says that they'll have to cut off my foot. What nonsense!

What does it mean? We are falling back, and very hastily at that, and we still haven't been in battle even once.

Today we marched through the woods, no road. I thought we were hastening directly against the enemy, but nothing happened. We ran out here to extend our front in tall hemp fields. Some reason to hurry! But there is fighting up ahead... It's bad to be without a real superior officer! Our regimental commander, Tutolmin, reported sick back in Byelsk, and left us to the mercy of fate. Now we are commanded by Shtakelberg, Lieutenant-Colonel in the Novorossiisk Dragoons. Kreits, head of that regiment, is our brigade commander.

We are still stationed in the hemp fields. The day is unbearably hot. Captain Podyampolsky asked me if I wanted to have a bath. And when I answered that I would very much like to, he ordered me to take command of fourteen uhlans, whom he had detailed to get water at a nearby rivulet, which was also not far from the fighting. "Now you have a chance to bathe," said the captain. "Only be careful. The enemy is close by."

"Why don't we fight them?" I asked, getting off my horse to go to the river.

"As if we all have to fight! Just wait, you'll get your share. March! March! Don't hang about! And please see to it, Alexandrov, that your young falcons don't fly off."

I marched behind my party and ordered my non-com to march in front; and in that formation, I ordered them to the rivulet. Leaving the uhlans to fill their canteens with water, wash, drink and refresh themselves as they might, I went off a half-verst upstream, quickly undressed and with inexpressible pleasure threw myself into the fresh, cold stream. Of course, I couldn't remain there blissfully for long; about ten minutes later I got out of the water and dressed even faster than I had undressed, for I could hear shots quite near. I led my party off, refreshed, cheerful, and carrying the salutary liquid to their comrades.

Our whole squadron has been assigned sentinel duty. It's my turn to post, place and make rounds of the sentries. For this I was given a half-squadron. Podyampolsky was set up in the village with the other half. The captain gave me orders on how and in what circumstances to act, what precautions to take, and what to observe while posting the guards, and I set off with my half-squadron up the hill to the monastery, where I had to place the first sentry. I assigned half my men to fixed points, and the other half was ready to relieve them at regular intervals. Riding up to the village, which was situated not far from the hill where the monastery stood, I ordered the uhlans to ride on the grass, press their sabres to their saddles with their knees, and not to ride too close together so as not to jangle their stirrups. Just at the village, I halted my party and rode on alone to see if the enemy were hiding somewhere. Complete silence reigned everywhere. All the houses had been abandoned by their inhabitants; everything was quiet and empty. Only the black depths of the peasants' open barns and stables yawned fearfully at me. Zelant, who had the bad habit of neighing when he was away from the other horses, this time apparently held his breath and stepped so lightly on the hard road that I could not hear his tread.

Satisfied that there was no one in the village, I returned to my uhlans and led them through the village toward the base of the hill. Then, with two uhlans and one non-com, I left the rest of my party and rode up the hill toward the walls of the monastery, to relieve the head sentry.

"We can hear something from the field, your honor," said the uhlans, "and we've spotted things, here and there, like men on horseback, but we can't make them out properly. Could almost be the French." I said that if on the challenge they don't give the password, to fire on them. I took the uhlans who had been relieved and rode off to the party I had left at the bottom of the hill.

Riding through the wood surrounding the monastery, I was very surprised to see one of the men who should have been waiting for me at the foot of the hill coming toward me on foot. "What is the meaning of this?" I asked. "Where is your horse?" He answered that his horse had thrown him. "What? Standing still?"

"No. The French attacked us. The non-com in whose charge you placed us was the first to run. There was nothing we could do, and we scattered. I wanted to ride after you, to let you know, but my horse reared and threw me and ran off."

"Where are the French?"

"I don't know."

"Wonderful!..." I had no right to call a soldier to account when the non-com had run, but I was extremely displeased and alarmed by this circumstance. When we rode out of the wood, I saw a crowd of mounted men moving about indecisively: some rode off, some stayed, some reined in their horses and leaned toward one another. I stopped to make out what this was all about, but hearing Russian, I immediately rode up to them and asked who they were.

"Cossacks," one of them answered. "Good thing you stopped, or we would have attacked."

"Why should you attack without giving the challenge, without asking the pass-word, without knowing for sure whether it's the enemy or one of our troops? And what do you mean: 'Good thing you stopped'?"

"What? But you've been running from us for a long time!"

Now the whole affair was cleared up. A few Cossacks, roving all over the place as usual, rode into the empty village to see if there wasn't something or someone there. Then they set off for the monastery, and when they saw a cavalry detachment at the foot of the hill, took them for the enemy. Just now they had been deliberating on whether to whoop down on them or not. My own brave men, likewise taking *them* for the enemy, considered it not worth waiting around, and, following the example of my rascally non-com, galloped off in different directions. This scattered flight and the speed of their horses saved my men from pursuit by the Cossacks, who had ridden up the hill, looked round the monastery, and having found nothing and no one, came back. But seeing me with three uhlans, they took us for the same, as they thought, Frenchmen, who at first sight of them had fled. And if I hadn't ridden up to them with my question, they would have attacked us with their lances.

"We would have taken you, but good!" said one gallant Cossack of about fifty.

"Not possible," I answered with some annoyance. "Our lances are stronger than yours. You wouldn't have found a place to run." And without listening to any more of their arguments, I rode off on my way.

I was displeased and discouraged beyond all expression. What awaits me in the future? Can one set out on the path of glory with such a cohort? At the first sign of danger they will run away, betray you, shame you. Why did I leave my valiant hussars? They're Serbs, Hungarians! They breathe valor, and glory is inseparable from them! For me, all seemed lost for the future; but what awaits me now? The cowards have no doubt alarmed the reserves. Podyampolsky could send to general headquarters with this infernal dispatch: "Sentries under command of Lieutenant Alexandrov routed by the enemy. By this operation they have now broken through the front line guard." And so the order and security of the army is disturbed, just because Lieutenant Alexandrov, either a coward or a fool, allowed himself to be routed without defending himself, without letting the reserves know, without firing a single shot. Otherwise the enemy could never have so easily broken through the front chain of sentries! And I am told *that even a shadow of a blemish on the name Alexandrov will never be forgiven me!*

Thoughts and feelings, black as night, weighed on my mind and heart. I rode at a walk, accompanied by the three uhlans I had left. Suddenly, the loud tramp of a half-squadron at a gallop struck my ear. Ahead I saw Cesare Tornezi, rushing like a whirlwind, with his half-squadron flying after. Catching sight of me, he cried out in amazement. He stopped his horse: "It's you Alexandrov! For God's sake, tell me what happened!"

"Happened to what, brother? It goes without saying that what happened will always happen to our cowards. They were scared of the Cossacks, and without so much as lifting their weapons, they ran like rabbits."

"Podyampolsky is in despair. The non-com said that you were taken prisoner and the whole guard slaughtered."

"What a strange choice of words! *Slaughtered!* But the scoundrels weren't asleep, so they couldn't have been slaughtered. They could only have been hacked to pieces. What about Podyampolsky?"

"I told you, he's in despair: 'How could he forget what I told him? I explained everything so clearly, in such detail,' said our gallant chief with sorrow and disappointment. But here he comes himself. We set off to free you from the enemy, even if it cost the whole squadron."

I rode up to Podyampolsky. "Don't reproach me, Captain! I would rather be defeated and taken prisoner than see myself covered with undeserved shame." (This was the first time I had been given a mission, appointed to a post of some danger, and requiring courage and vigilance, and this is how I so excellently accomplished my mission.) I told the captain all that had happened in detail. We returned to our village, leaving the poor sentries with no relief until dawn. It wasn't yet time to relieve them.

Podyampolsky, an outstanding officer, brave and experienced, nevertheless did not want to let news of the non-com who fled his guard and filed that ridiculous report to go any further without first using every means of righting the unfortunate affair. And he decided that it was better to die with the whole squadron, to fight to the last drop of his blood, than to allow such a shameful incident to be made public. Thanks to this heroic resoluteness, my name was saved from tarnish, but the events had made a deep impression of mistrustfulness on my soul. I grew afraid of each new post, each mission, if I had to execute it with my detachment. Never, never could I trust them again! Yermolov spoke the truth when he said that *a cowardly soldier does not deserve to live.* Once, such an assertion had seemed severe, but now I see that it is the truth, grasped by the great mind of an exceptional man. The lazy farmer, the spend-thrift merchant, the free-thinking priest, all have vices contrary to their callings and interests; but no one follows their example, and they harm only themselves— poverty and disgrace are their lot. But the cowardly soldier!! I cannot begin to express the magnitude of the harm one insignificant, timid scoundrel can do to a whole army! And in the present case, what misfortunes might have fallen on my head only because a coward who was frightened of his own shadow and ran off, carrying others along with him, would have been the cause of a false report and the pointless alarm of the entire army! No, the timid soldier has no right to live. Yermolov was right!

Such reflections occupied me until dawn. Our sentries were replaced. The cowards were severely punished, the non-com more so. Now that punishment has been executed, a new thought gives me no peace, frightens and shames me; and there is no way that I can drive it out of my mind. I blush to write these lines: Was not I alone responsible? Do not I alone deserve censure and punishment? I am an officer. I was entrusted with the detachment. Why did I leave them alone, and with a non-com like that, who had never even seen battle?

We are riding by quick marches into the depths of Russia with the enemy on our backs. They wholeheartedly believe that we are running from them. Good fortune blinds one!... I am often reminded of Starn's prayer before the sacrificial altar to Odin, when he begs Odin to send down upon Fingal's mind bewilderment, *auguring the fall of the mighty*!... Despite Napoleon's innumerable admirers, I make bold to think that for such a great genius as they consider him, he is too confident, both in his good fortune and in his abilities, too credulous, careless, ill-informed. Blind fortune, coincidence, a ruined gentry and a deluded populace might help him mount the throne, but to remain on it, to occupy it with dignity, will be difficult for him. Beneath the imperial mantle, they will soon see the artillery lieutenant who is at his wit's end from his unprecedented good fortune. How is it possible, based only on geographical information and spies' reports, to have decided to wage war on a vast, rich nation, renowned for its greatness of soul and the selflessness of its gentry—the unshakable supports of the Russian throne; renowned for its troops' organization and great numbers, their strict discipline and courage, their physical strength and sturdy build, which give them the power to endure any hardship; a nation that encompasses so many peoples, so many climes, but for all that has as its bulwark faith and tolerance? He will see this glorious army retreat without a fight, retreat so quickly that it will be difficult to keep up; and he will believe that it retreats in fear of meeting the enemy! He will believe in the timidity of the Russian army within the borders of its Fatherland!... He will believe all this and run after our army, try to overtake it. What terrible blindness!! And terrible must be the end!

The French are doing their utmost to overtake us and fight, and we are doing ours to flee and not fight. This maneuver comforts me greatly. It's amusing to see with what speed we lead our gullible enemy into the depths of our forests!... however, it doesn't always seem funny. Imagining the terrible end of our retreat, I involuntarily sigh and grow pensive. The French are an enemy worthy of us, noble and courageous; but an evil fate, in the guise of Napoleon, leads them to Russia; here they will lay down their lives, here their bones will be strewn and their bodies decay.

For two days I have not closed my eyes and scarcely have I got down from my horse. Shtakelberg has sent me to occupy a position for camp. I was given four uhlans from each squadron, and with me ride the engineers for the Novorossiisk Dragoons and the Akhtyrka Hussars. When we have occupied a position for camp, I am to ride to meet the regiment; and when it is settled in, I am to await further orders, and upon receipt, immediately set off. Our marches are rather long. I almost always ride out at night, arrive at the position around noon, and until the entire rear guard is dispersed to their positions, I wait my turn to occupy the position assigned for our regiment. Then I must immediately ride to meet it, accommodate the squadrons and, after all the chaos and new orders, set off.

A third day has passed. Camp was made near the small town of Kadnev. I can't stand it any longer. Returning to town from camp, I sent an uhlan out to the road to watch for the regiment and let me know when it came in sight, while I went to my quarters, intending to have something to eat and then get some sleep if I could. Awaiting dinner, I lay down on my host's bed, and don't remember anything more.... When I awoke late that evening, I was very suprised that I had been allowed to sleep so long. There was no light in the chamber, and no people. I quickly arose, and opening the door to the hall, called my non-com. He reported.

"Hasn't the regiment come yet?" I asked. He answered, no, that only the Kiev Dragoons had. "Why didn't you wake me?"

"We couldn't, your honor. You slept like the dead. At first we tried to wake you quietly; but later we shook you by the arms, the shoulders, sat you up, brought a candle right up to your eyes, and finally threw cold water in your face. All in vain—you didn't even stir. The mistress, who was here when all of this happened, started crying when she saw that we couldn't manage to wake you, and laid you back down on the bed. 'The poor child! He's almost dead! Why do you take such young men in the service?' She bent down to hear if you were breathing. Since I was next in command, I ordered the uhlan to ride up farther to meet the regiment, but he soon returned with the information that our regiment's line of march had been changed, and that only the Kiev Dragoons were coming here, under the command of Emanuel."

I immediately rode off to the camp. They hadn't yet turned in, and I found both of my comrades, the engineers from the dragoons and the hussars. The first had asked Emanuel to take him and his party under his own command. The hussar and I, once informed of what route our regiments had taken, set off to find them, which we managed to do very shortly.

Occasionally there are minor clashes between our rear guard and the enemy's, so there is some cause to retreat.

I'd just like to run away!... I don't know what to do. I'm deathly afraid of exhaustion. Afterwards, this would be ascribed not to excessive work, but to the weakness of my sex! We march day and night. Our rests consist only of brief stops when we are allowed to dismount for a half hour. The uhlans immediately lie down at their horses' feet, while I just lean my elbows on the saddle and put my head in my arms. But I do not dare to close my eyes, lest I unwittingly fall asleep. Not only do we not sleep, we don't eat: We are hurrying somewhere!—Oh, our poor regiment!

To ward off sleep, which overcomes me, I dismount and walk on foot; but I am so exhausted that I quickly mount again, and lift myself into the saddle with difficulty. Thirst scorches my insides. There is no water anywhere, except for the ditches by the side of the road. I got down from my horse again, and with great discomfort got some disgusting water, warm and green, from the very bottom of the ditch. I put it in a bottle, mounted my horse with this treasure, and carried it about five versts further, holding the bottle before me on the saddle, lacking the resolution to either drink it or throw the muck out. What cannot necessity do? Finally, I drank the infernal liquid...

If I had millions, I would give them all just now for leave to fall asleep. I am utterly exhausted. All my senses thirst for rest.... I took it into my head to look at myself in the bright blade of my sabre: my face was as white as a sheet and my eyes were swollen! The others had not experienced such great changes, and probably for the reason that they can sleep in the saddle. I cannot.

That night, Podyampolsky reproved Cesare and me because the men in our platoons reel in the saddle and let their helmets fall off their heads. The day after that dressing-down, we saw him riding with his eyes closed, quite sound asleep on his walking horse. Taking some comfort in this spectacle, we rode alongside to see how this would end. But Cesare thought it absolutely essential to take revenge for the dressing-down. He spurred his horse and galloped past Podyampolsky. His horse raced off for all it was worth, and we had the pleasure of seeing the fright and haste with which Podyampolsky picked up the reins which had fallen out of his hands.

Cesare and I have fallen into incomprehensible discord! We always start by riding out ahead of the squadron; at first we talk very amicably, but later we begin to argue, and finally, having made some politely caustic remarks to one another, we ride off to opposite sides of the road. On one of these sorties, we rode off toward the ditches on the side of the road, got off our horses and lay down; but fortunately, we had not yet fallen asleep when the squadron came up. Podyampolsky, supposing that we were with our platoons, was surprised and angry to see us peacefully settled in the ditch by the road. "You should be ashamed, gentlemen!" he said. "Instead of looking after your soldiers so they don't fall asleep, or fall, or drop their helmets, or damage their horses, you rode up ahead and went to sleep on the road!" Struck by the same spirit of discord that set us against each other, we replied that it was just two days ago that he himself put it to the test and demonstrated that our current difficulties surpass the strength of man! Podyampolsky made no objection, but ordered us to be without fail at our posts, with our men. "We are obliged to set them an example," he added kindly. "It will be easier for them to bear any difficulty if they see that their officers bear it with them. A soldier will not dare to grumble at any loss if his officer shares it with him." I sensed the truth of Podyampolsky's words, and fully intended always to be governed by them.

Finally we were given a day of rest. With what indescribable pleasure did I spread out my great coat on the hay, lie down, and that very minute fall asleep. I think that I slept about ten hours, because the sun hadn't yet set when I crawled out of my hut—crawled in the literal sense, because the hole that served as a door was no more than a half-arshin high. I beheld a lively and beautiful scene: crowds of officers—uhlans, hussars, cuirassiers—walked all round the camp. The soldiers cooked kasha, cleaned the ammunition. Orderlies and adjutants galloped hither and yon. Our regiment's wonderful band sounded forth to the delight of the great multitude of officers of all regiments who had come to hear it. Shtakelberg, the current commander of our regiment and future amateur and connoisseur of musical art, had devoted himself to the improvement of our regimental band, and had led it to such heights of perfection that now in neither army, neither the First nor the Second Western, was there its equal.

Our regiment was stationed near a chain of rather steep hills. When night came, there were innumerable campfires, and the valley rang with noise, the soldiers' conversations, the neighing of horses, and the clatter of their hoofs. I watched this noisy, animated scene for about half an hour, and finally, I don't know why, went over to the other side of the hills. Going down into the valley, I didn't hear the slightest sound, as if no soldiers, no war, no army had ever existed on earth! I went up the hill again, watched for a time this scene of feverish activity, of constant bustle and motion, and once more descended into the quiet and tranquillity of the valley! This quick change from incredible noise to complete silence makes an impression on my soul which I can neither understand nor describe.

Near Smolensk a State manifesto was proclaimed in which it was stated: *"that our Sovereign will no longer restrain our courage, and frees us to take vengeance upon the enemy for the tedium of our involuntary retreat, which until now was necessary."* Our soldiers jumped for joy, and their eyes shone with courage and pleasure. "Finally!" said the officers. "Now it's our turn to be in pursuit!"

Smolensk

Again I hear the dreadful, majestic rumble of the cannon! Again I see the flash of bayonets! My first year of martial life is resurrected in my memory!... No! A coward has no soul! Otherwise, how could he see and hear all that and not blaze with courage! For two hours we awaited orders beneath the walls of the fortress of Smolensk. Finally, we were ordered to march on the enemy. The city's inhabitants, seeing us march by in order, in formation, with heroic bearing and confidence in our powers, accompanied us with joyous cries. Some, and especially the old men, constantly repeated: "God help you! God help you!" in such an exceptionally solemn manner that it made me shudder, and moved me....

Our regiment is placed on both sides of the road. Podyampolsky's squadron on the left. Farther left, brick barns. The spot we drew was so inconvenient for cavalry maneuvers that at the first enemy onslaught we could not hold it. The whole field is so dug up, overgrown with bushes, and cut through with ruts, that in any fast exercise, the squadron would, at every step, have to leap over a ditch, or a bush, or a pit. Since they took clay for bricks here, there was a great number of pits, and what is more, they were all full of rain water. We were ordered to hold back the enemy. So, to set things up, Podyampolsky set the squadron in combat formation and ordered the flankers to ride out. "Which of you, gentlemen, would like to take command?" asked the captain. The elder Tornezi immediately volunteered. He and about twenty of the best horsemen set out against the enemy. An hour later they all returned, except for Tornezi, whom the French had hacked to pieces. They say that in a temper he was carried into a crowd of them, and that however much they cried: *"Rendez vous! Rendez vous!"* he hacked at them on the right and the left; and finally, in a frenzy, they fell on him and in an instant he was gone.

When Podyampolsky asked the flankers how they could allow their officer to be hacked to pieces, they said in their excuse that Tornezi galloped into a crowd of the enemy, and without accepting their proposal to surrender, hacked them and cursed them without mercy, and that they all fell on him at once. A multitude of sabres flashed above the unlucky Tornezi, and he fell at the feet of his horse lifeless and dead.

We all very attentively watched the right side of the road, where an engagement was already under way, and where some of our squadrons fought extremely well. We might have paid dearly for this gaping about, if our priest Vartminsky, the most intrepid man in our whole regiment, had not ridden up to us and pointed to the left with his whip (the only weapon he ever used, for horses or the enemy). Looking where he pointed, we saw enemy cavalry galloping towards us on our flank. In an instant, Podyampolsky commanded: "Second half-squadron, right march!" And facing the enemy, he ordered me to take command and to fire on the cavalry racing toward us. A delicious moment for me! I no longer remembered the shameful flight of my uhlans from the guard; I saw only the opportunity to win fame.... But suddenly my command: "Forward, march, march!" merged with our chief's loud voice, ringing out behind our line: "Back! Back!" In a second, my half-squadron turned back and galloped off at breakneck speed to the highway. I was left behind the rest. The squadron galloped out of formation, in a dense crowd over bushes, mounds and ruts. Zelant, my fiery, arrogant steed, strained under me, but I did not dare give him free rein. He had the bad habit of running with his head up, and I was faced with a very difficult choice: give free rein to Zelant and immediately fall with him into a pit, or fly headlong over a bush; or if I rein him in, be overtaken by the enemy, flying at our heels. I chose the latter as the less dangerous. I had long known of the mediocrity of the French cavalry, and I could be assured that in the entire detachment that was chasing us, not one horse could equal Zelant in speed. And so, reining in my steed, I rushed at a full gallop after my squadron. But hearing the tramp of horses behind me, and distracted by involuntary curiosity, I could not help but glance back. My curiosity was well rewarded: I saw galloping behind me, just an arshin from my horse's haunch, three or four enemy dragoons, who were trying to get their broadswords in my back. On seeing this, though I didn't increase speed, without quite knowing why, I threw my sabre over my shoulder, point first. I passed over mounds and pits, and Zelant like a whirlwind carried me away from the enemy pack.

Coming out on a level place, we repaid the enemy for our disorderly flight. Obeying the orders of their officers, the squadron instantly came to order, drew up, and in a dreadful cloud rushed at the enemy. The earth groaned under the hoofs of our ardent steeds; the wind whistled in the pennants of our lances. It seemed that death with all its terrors rushed at the head of the brave uhlans. The enemy could not bear this sight, and while attempting to escape was overtaken, beaten, dispersed, and routed, much more completely than we were when we were forced to retreat at full speed over mounds and ruts.

Now our squadron is installed on the right side of the road, and the uneven field occupied by the chasseurs. "It should have been that way in the first place!" said Podyampolsky, twisting his mustache in vexation.... We are to guard the fortress here, and so we wait with nothing to do, but well-prepared—meaning mounted and with lances at the ready. Ahead of us the riflemen of the Butyr regiment are exchanging fire with the enemy. A brave, outstanding regiment! As soon as they started their operations, enemy bullets no longer reached us.

We will be in this position until tomorrow. The Butyr regiment has been relieved by another, and now not only do the bullets reach us, they wound. Podyampolsky found this very annoying. Finally, tired of seeing one after another taken off the front lines, he sent me to Smolensk, to Shtakelberg, to tell of our critical situation, and ask what he would have us do. I did what I was ordered, told Shtakelberg that we had many wounded men, and asked what were his orders. "Stand fast," answered Shtakelberg. "Stand, and don't move a pace from the spot. Strange, that Podyampolsky should send to ask about this!"

With great pleasure I set off with this fine answer to my captain.

"Well, what are the orders?" Podyampolsky shouted from some distance.

"To stand fast, Captain!"

"So we'll stand fast," he said calmly, and turned to the front line with that fearless look so characteristic of him. He wanted to encourage the soldiers, but he found to his satisfaction that they had no need of it. The eyes and faces of the brave uhlans were merry; the recent victory had revived their courage. Their entire aspect said: *Death to the enemy!* Toward evening the second half-squadron set off, and I, having the liberty to leave my post, set off to my captain's to ask about all the incomprehensible events of the day. Podyampolsky stood by a tree, leaning his head on his hand and watching a skirmish with no concern. It was apparent that his thoughts were not in the present.

"Tell me, Captain, why did you send me to Shtakelberg, and not a non-com? You wanted to protect me from the bullets, isn't that right?"

"That's right," Podyampolsky answered pensively. "You're still so young, you look so innocent, and in these terrible scenes, so happy and carefree! I saw you gallop behind the whole squadron during our disorderly flight from the brick barns, and I imagined a lamb chased by a pack of wolves. My heart breaks at the very thought of seeing you killed. I don't know, Alexandrov, why I think that if you were killed it would be a murder. Please God, I will not be a witness! Oh, bullets don't distinguish. They would as soon pierce the breast of an old soldier, as the heart of a blooming youth!...."

I was surprised at my captain's melancholy, and his unusual concern for me, which I hadn't noticed earlier. But then I recalled that he had a brother, whom he loved dearly, who had stayed with the Mariupolsk regiment, alone, left to the mercy of fate and his own wits, and I found it quite natural that my appearance of an immature youth, and the dangers of war, reminded him of his brother, his tender years, and his position, in which he might fall during such a hard war.

Night was coming on. The second half-squadron mounted their horses, but the first hurried off. The firing had stopped. I asked the captain for permission to dismount. He agreed, and we continued our conversation.

"Please explain to me, Captain, why we have so many wounded officers. The rank and file are such a dense mass. They could kill more of them, and more easily. Are they purposely aiming at the officers?"

"Of course," answered Podyampolsky. "That's the most effective means of breaking and weakening the enemy's ranks."

"Why?"

"What do you mean, why? Because one brave and skillful officer can do more harm to the enemy with his knowledge, perspicacity, and ability to take advantage of terrain and of the mistakes of the other side; and especially an officer gifted with that lofty sense of honor that would have him meet death unflinchingly, and act calmly in the greatest danger. Such an officer, I repeat, can alone do the enemy more harm than a thousand soldiers in no one's command...."

Our conversation continued some two hours in this vein. I attentively listened to Podyampolsky's opinions and observations—the best officer in our regiment, brave, experienced, as hard on himself as he was with others. The second half-squadron's turn to dismount cut short our conversation. The captain mounted his horse, and told me that if I wanted, I could sleep for half an hour. I did not make him repeat that. I immediately availed myself of his leave and, wrapping myself in my soldier's cloak, lay down under a tree, with my head at its roots. At dawn, in a light sleep, I heard something rattling in my helmet. Now wide awake, I raised my head and saw, standing not far away from me, Lieutenant-Colonel Lopatin and Podyampolsky. They were speaking about something, looking, and occasionally pointing in the direction of the enemy riflemen. Ashamed that they had found me asleep, I hurriedly got up; and at that very instant, a spent bullet hit my helmet, which explained the first cracks. I gathered the bullets lying near me, and brought them to show the captain.

"Well, so what?" he said, laughing. "Is that any wonder to you?"

"What do you mean? They didn't bang in here, but they flew this far, why didn't they injure me?"

"They didn't have the power. But enough. Mount up, we're going to be relieved!" A squadron of dragoons came to take our position, and we went into the fortress and settled in to rest by its walls.

Smolensk has been given up to the enemy! By night, our rear guard had already mounted the heights above the river. Rayevsky gazed regretfully at the burning city. One of the crowd of officers around him shouted, "What a beautiful sight!..." "Especially for Engelgardt," one of the general's adjutants answered. "Two of his buildings are on fire!"

We are all in retreat. Why did they tell us that our Sovereign would no longer restrain our courage? It seems our bravery was exposed to a very minor test. As I see it, we are retreating into the depths of Russia. It will be bad for us if the enemy stays in Smolensk! Only Napoleon's boundless self-confidence would permit us to lure him further. But all of this is beyond my understanding. Couldn't we have met and smashed the enemy at our nation's borders? Why such dangerous maneuvers? Why lead the foe so far into the heart of our country?... Perhaps it is being done with a great aim; but until it is achieved or fathomed, the army could lose heart. Just now, one hears surmises and conjectures, one more doleful or absurd than the next.

It was my turn to serve as Konovnitsyn's orderly. The general loves to be as close to the enemy as possible, and apparently considers any danger a mere trifle. At any rate, he is as calm in the midst of battle as in his quarters. There was a small engagement started here. The general rode up to the front line, but since his retinue immediately drew the enemy's attention and fire, he ordered us to disperse. I don't know why, but we did not obey at once, and during the interval his horse was wounded under him. The enemy concentrated its riflemen on our party, which forced Konovnitsyn to ride off a bit farther from the flankers' line. When we all turned back after him, my annoying Zelant, who has a big stride, moved a bit ahead of the general's horse. When Konovnitsyn saw this, he asked me, quite severely: "Where are you off to, officer? Don't you know that you are supposed to ride behind me, and not ahead?" In shame and annoyance, I reined my horse. The general probably thought that it was fear that made me quicken my pace!

Konovnitsyn had to send to Count Sivers, on the left flank, to find out if, in case of a retreat, the roads were safe and suitable, whether he had sufficient troops, and if he required reinforcements. I volunteered for the mission. "Oh, no!" said Konovnitsyn, looking me over. "You're too young; I can't entrust this to you. Send someone a bit older."

I blushed. "Won't your excellency try me? Perhaps I will be able to understand and carry out your orders."

"Ah... Very well! Excuse me," said Konovnitsyn hastily but kindly. He gave me his orders, adding that I should leave as soon as possible. I was not yet out of his sight when he, troubled by doubts, sent a second officer after me with the same orders. And this was evidence of God's protection, because the enemy already held the positions I was riding through to Sivers. On my return, I met the other officer, from whom I learned that there were enemy riflemen where we had ridden before. When I reached Konovnitsyn, I told him in complete detail of the Sivers detachment's position, of the roads, fords, resources—in a word, of everything I had been ordered to find out. When he had heard my report, Konovnitsyn showered me with praise, asked pardon that he had hesitated to give me the orders because of my youth, and apparently wishing to smooth things over, sent only me off everywhere for a whole day, saying with every order: "You are more meticulous than the rest." Racing all day over the fields from one regiment to another, I was exhausted, tired, dying of hunger, and not at all happy to have gained the reputation of being a meticulous orderly. Poor Zelant began to look like a borzoi.

The sun had already set when we reached camp. I had just dismounted when I had to mount again. Podyampolsky said that it was my turn to get hay for the whole regiment.

"I have ten men from my squadron for you. The rest will be here shortly. May God be with you!" Then he added under his breath, "And see if you can't manage to get something to eat—a goose, a chicken. Just bread for so many days, I'm sick to death of it!" Fifty uhlans were under my command, and I set off with them down the first road that came to hand to track down some haymaking, because at that time of year they already start to mow. The night was very hot, and very dark as well. The moon was not out. When we had ridden about six versts from camp, we caught sight of a village about a half-verst away, and in three minutes we were already there, because we were so happy at our swift find that we rode there at a trot. A wide meadow adjoined the village; a rivulet was visible, and beyond it some small copses. I ordered the uhlans to take their horses into the meadow, and I remained alone in the deserted village. I tied up my horse and set off to look around the empty dwellings. It was something strange to see all the doors open; everywhere, dark, silence and desolation reigned. Nothing was locked—the stables, barns, granaries, storerooms and houses were all wide open! But in the yards cows and sheep were walking, lying, standing, and flocks of geese were sitting. The poor geese! The sight of them reminded me of Podyampolsky's request, reminded me that one of them must surely die! Oh, I'm so ashamed to write that! How shameful to admit to such inhumanity! With my noble sabre, I cut off the head of a harmless bird!! It was the first blood I had shed in my whole life. Even though it was only a bird's blood, believe me, you who will someday read my *Memoirs,* that the memory hangs on my conscience!

An hour later, my uhlans returned, leading their horses, loaded with hay. "Haven't you loaded them too heavily?" I asked, seeing the huge sheaves of hay that hung at their sides.

"No, your honor! Hay is light!"

I believed them, not once suspecting that a weight unknown to me lay concealed there, and that for that reason they had purposely tied up such horrible mountains of hay. I mounted my horse, ordered someone to take the dead goose, and rode off ahead of my party, which marched on foot, leading their horses by the rein. We had already covered more than half of our way, and were within two versts of camp when an uhlan suddenly galloped up: "Hurry, your honor, the regiment is about to move out." I ordered the men to march as fast as they could. They began to run, and naturally, the horses set off at a trot. I was very surprised to see sheep falling here and there from my detachment's horses. I had not had time to ask why they took so many of them, when a second uhlan galloped up with an order from the regiment to abandon the hay and make haste to the regiment. I ordered the men to leave everything there—the hay, the sheep and my goose—mount their horses and return to the regiment at a trot. We overtook them already on the march.

"What does this mean, Captain, that the regiment set off so quickly?"

"That's a strange question, what does it mean? We were ordered to, so we marched. We're not out for a stroll, this is war!" I fell silent. The captain was in poor spirits, and probably because he was hungry. I was hungry too, and what is more I hadn't slept all night.

We have a new commander-in-chief: Kutuzov! I heard this standing in a circle of orderlies, adjutants and many other officers, crowding by the camp fire. A general in the hussars, Dorokhov, said, stroking his grey mustache, "Please God, Mikhail Larionovich will come as soon as possible and halt us. We ran off as if it were downhill all the way."

Kutuzov has arrived!... The soldiers, the officers, the generals are all delighted. Calm and assurance have replaced apprehension. Our whole camp breathes and seethes with courage!

A cold, penetrating wind numbs my body. It's not that my greatcoat isn't wadded, it doesn't have a lining. My uhlan jacket is lined with taffeta, and that is all my protection from a wind as cold as during winter.

Borodino

That evening our entire army settled into bivouacs near the town of Borodino. Kutuzov wants to wage the battle we have all wished for and waited for so long. Our regiment as usual occupies the front line. That night, no matter how I curled up and muffled myself in my greatcoat, I could neither get warm, nor fall asleep. Our cabin had been built *à jour,* and the wind whistled through it like through a broken window. My comrades, whose greatcoats are warm, sleep soundly. I would gladly lie by a fire, but there isn't one, and none was made.

August 24

The wind has not died down! At dawn the signal cannon roared threateningly. Its rumble flew, rushed, and flowed over the whole expanse occupied by our army. Happy to see the day, I immediately left my uneasy berth! The cannon's rumble had not quite died away when everyone was on his feet! In a quarter of an hour everything got into motion, everything was made ready for battle! The French are marching towards us in dense columns. The whole field has turned black, covered with their countless multitude.

The twenty-sixth

A hellish day! I am nearly deaf from the wild, constant roar of both artilleries. The rifle bullets which whistled, screamed, and fell on us like hail attracted no attention. Even those they wounded didn't notice; what time had we for them?... Our squadron went on the attack several times, at which I was most displeased. I have no gloves, and my hands are so stiff with cold that I can barely bend my fingers. When we stand in place, I put my sabre in its scabbard and hide my hand in the sleeves of my greatcoat; but when we are ordered to attack, I have to draw my sabre and hold it in my bare hand in the wind and cold. I was always very sensitive to cold, and to physical pain generally; now, enduring day and night the brutal northern wind, against which I am defenseless, I feel that my courage is not what it was at the beginning of the campaign. Although I have no timidity of spirit, and my color has not once changed, and I am calm, I in any case would be glad if we stopped fighting.

Oh, if I could get warm, and feel that I have hands and feet! I can't feel them now.

My wish has come true. It is not important how, but it has come true. I am not fighting, I am warm, and I can feel that I have hands and feet. My left leg especially lets me know quite perceptibly that I have it. It is swollen, bruised and aches unbearably. I got a contusion from a cannon ball. The sergeant-major kept me from falling from my horse, held me up and led me off behind the front. Despite all the battles I had been in, I had no concept of a contusion. I thought that if you got one, you weren't wounded; and so, since I didn't see any blood on my knee, I returned to my position. Podyampolsky, turning round, and seeing that I was standing at the front, asked with surprise, "Why did you come back?"

"I'm not wounded," I answered.

The captain, supposing that I had been hit by a spent bullet, was reassured; and we continued to stand and maintain fire until nightfall. Then the enemy started to light our lines with candle bombs, which flew picturesquely along our front. Finally, this amusement ended too, and all grew quiet. Our regiment moved back a bit and dismounted, but Podyampolsky's squadron remained on its horses. I did not have the strength to stand longer the torments I endured from my aching leg, the cold, my frozen blood, and the cruel pain in all my limbs (I think because I had not gotten off my horse all day). I told Podyampolsky that I could no longer stay in the saddle, and that if he would allow me, I would ride back to the rear, where the field doctor, Kornilovich, would see what was wrong with my leg. The captain gave me permission. At last the time had come when I myself willingly rode to the rear! The rear, which I had so disdained formerly! I rode off without being severely wounded!... What can bravery do against the cold!!

Leaving my squadron, I set off in the company of one uhlan on the road to the rear, barely able to keep from moaning. But I could ride no farther than Borodino, and stopped in that village. It was filled from one end to the other with wounded. Searching, unsuccessfully, for a cottage that would let me in, and refused everywhere, I decided to enter and occupy a place without asking for consent. When I opened the door of one peasant cottage, vast and as dark as the grave, I was met with twenty voices, painfully crying to me from the depths of that murk: "Who's there! Why have you come? Close the door! What do you want? Who has come?..." I answered that I was an officer with the uhlans, wounded, that I cannot find quarters, and that I beg them to allow me to stay there overnight.

"Impossible, impossible!" yelled several voices at once. "There's a wounded captain here, and we're already cramped!"

"Well, then the wounded captain should know himself that it's hard to find quarters in this location; and however cramped you may be, you should invite me to stay with you, and not drive me away."

In answer to this sermon, someone answered curtly, "Well, if you stay, there'll be no place for you to lie down."

"That's my problem," I said and, happy to be out of the cold, climbed up on the stove and lay down, not just fully armed, but without even taking off my helmet. My limbs began to thaw, and the pain abated. Only my injured leg was as heavy as a beam; and I could not move it without pain. Exhausted with cold, hunger, fatigue and pain, I fell into a deep sleep in a minute. At dawn, I apparently wanted to turn over, but since I was sleeping on the edge of the stove, my sabre dropped over the edge and crashed down. Everyone woke up and cried, "Who's there? Who's there?" Their voices betrayed great fright.

One of them put an end to the alarm by reminding his comrades about me, saying quite obligingly, "It's that uhlan's fault—the one the devil brought us last evening." After that, they all fell asleep again, but I could no longer sleep. My leg hurt badly, and instead of yesterday's chills, I had a high fever. I got up, and seeing through the cracks in the shutters that it was already dawn, I opened the door to go out and leave the hospitable roof beneath which I had spent the night. My uhlan was standing at the very threshold with both horses. When I tried to mount, and put my left leg in the stirrup, tears involuntarily flowed from my eyes. After riding just about a half-verst, I wanted to dismount, lie down in the field, and trust myself to the will of fate. My leg had swollen up and was causing me unbearable pain! Fortunately, my uhlan caught sight of a cart in the distance. There was just an empty barrel in it, that had been used to take wine to the army. He immediately galloped off and brought the cart to me. We threw out the empty barrel, and I took its place, lying on the same hay that it had lain on. The uhlan led my Zelant by the rein, and in this fashion, I arrived at the rear, where I found my good friend, Buryi, the regiment bursar—and now I'm sitting in his warm cabin, in his sheep-skin coat, holding a glass of hot tea in my hands. My leg is wrapped in bandages, soaked in alcohol. I hope that that will help, for want of any better means. Kornilovich is not here, he's with the regiment.

I am completely recovered! Good soup, tea, and warmth restored strength and flexibility to my limbs. It is all forgotten, like a dream, although my leg still hurts. But why think of that! What's more, it does seem to me that my contusion is a very mild one.

After spending two days in Buryi's cabin, I hastened to return to the regiment. I was to take off a small detachment of twenty-four uhlans to reinforce the squadron.

We are retreating to Moscow, and are now within just ten versts of it. I asked Shtakelberg to permit me to ride to Moscow to have a warm jacket sewn for me. With his permission, I gave my horse to an uhlan and set off on a pair of jades, barely alive, that had been hired in the village. I had wanted to stay near the Kremlin, at Mitrofanov's, a dear friend and cohort of my father, but I learned that he had gone off somewhere. As I asked for news of him, I was obliged to drop in on the many tenants of the huge building in which his rooms were located. One of these forays was made to the chambers of a young merchant's wife. As soon as she saw me open her door, she immediately started to say: "Come in, come in, Mr. officer! Please, do me the favor of having a seat. You're limping. Wounded of course? Won't you have some tea? Katyenka, bring some instantly." While saying all this, she seated me on the divan, and Katyenka, a cute fourteen-year-old girl in the full bloom of mercantile beauty, already stood before me with a cup of tea. "Well, sir, is the foe very far? They say that he is marching on Moscow."

I answered that they wouldn't let him into Moscow.

"Ah, please God! Where would we go then? They say he forces everyone to accept his faith."

What was I to answer to questions like that? The little girl echoed in her thin voice: "It's said that they brand all their prisoners on the chest." Saying this, she pointed to her own heart.

"That could very well be," I answered. "I heard something to that effect." They would have importuned me with more questions, but I stood up and said that I must hurry to my post.

"Well, God be with you, Sir," said both sisters, leading me through the vestibule to the stairs.

I had my jacket sewn, put it on, and wanted to leave the city immediately; but that was not so easy to do. The enemy was close, many of the cabmen had left Moscow, and those that were still there asked fifty rubles to take me to headquarters; but since I hadn't one, not to mention fifty rubles, I set out on foot. I had walked about three versts on the highway when I was forced to lie down on the ground just past the city gates. My leg had started to hurt again and swell up, and I couldn't stand on it. Fortunately, some baggage-wagon was passing by, loaded with saddles, saddle-clothes, mess-tins, packs, and all sorts of military rubbish. An officer rode with it. I asked him to take me on the wagon. At first he would not agree, saying that he could not throw off any of the things; but putting to him that a simple soldier, not to mention an officer, was more valuable to the Sovereign than twenty baggage-wagons, I convinced him to make place for me. At headquarters, I got out, thanked the officer and limped off to find Shvarts, to ask him for some sort of horse—mine was still with the regiment. I found Shvarts in the quarters of Count Sivers. After the Battle of Borodino, we had not seen one another. He was very surprised to see me, and asked why I was not with the regiment. I told him of my contusion, of the pain, of Moscow, of the jacket, adding to all this that I wanted to return to the regiment as quickly as possible, and that to do that, I needed a horse. Shvarts gave me a Cossack horse with a long thin neck, ugly, and saddled with a nasty saddle with a huge cushion. On this horse, which even in its time had had no fire, no speed, I arrived at the regiment. Impatient to mount my own fine Zelant, I discovered to my great irritation that he had been dispatched with the post horses to a village about five versts away.

Having passed through Moscow, we stopped two or three versts farther on. The army continued its march.

For some time the ancient capital has been burning in many places!

The French are completely brainless. Why should they burn our beautiful town? Or their magnificent quarters, which they have rented at such expense? Strange people! We have all watched sorrowfully as the fire has become larger and a bright glow has covered almost half the sky. The taking of Moscow has caused us some confusion. The soldiers are somehow frightened, and sometimes they blurt out: "It would have been better for us all to lie down dead here than to give up Moscow!" Of course they say this to one another quietly, and in that case an officer is not obliged to hear it.

The left flank of our regiment touches some miserable little village, in which there is no longer a single person. I asked the captain if we were to stay there long.

"Who knows?" he answered, "We have not been ordered to start fires, so that means we must be ready at any minute. And what's that to you?"

"This. I would like to go to the house at the edge of the village to sleep a little. My leg hurts a great deal."

"Go ahead. Have the corporal stand by the hut with your horse. When the regiment moves, he can wake you."

I ran straight to the house, went into the hut, and, seeing that the floor and benches were broken, could find no place better than the stove to lie on. I crawled up onto it and lay on the edge. The stove was warm, so it was clear that someone had stoked it recently. It was rather hot in the hut owing to the closed shutters. Warmth and darkness! What two blessed comforts! I fell asleep at once. I think I slept more than half an hour, because I soon awakened to the repeated exclamation, "Your honor! Your honor! The regiment has left! The enemy is in the village!!" Having awakened, I hastily arose, and while trying to support myself with my left hand, felt something damp under it. I turned to look, and as it was dark I had to lean very close to the thing on which I had rested my hand. It was a corpse, apparently a militia man. I do not know whether I would have lain on the stove if I had seen this neighbor beforehand, but it didn't occur to me to be frightened now. Such strange encounters occur in life, especially in the present war! Leaving the silent inhabitant of the hut to sleep the sleep of the never-to-awaken, I went out onto the street. The French were already in the village, and our people were firing at everyone. I hastened to mount my horse and overtook the regiment at a trot.

Shtakelberg sent me after hay for the regiment's horses, and I, willy-nilly, had to ride a horse which was stubborn, lazy and ugly as a donkey. Sending my command on ahead, I followed, thinking about my unpleasant predicament. Shame and misfortune awaited me in the first battle with such a steed: it wouldn't advance toward the enemy and it wouldn't retreat from the enemy.

"There are our remounts!" said one of the uhlans to his comrade, indicating a nearby settlement.

It was a verst off the road along which I was leading our detachment. The thought that I might procure my own horse lightened my thoughts, calmed me, and chased away my gloom. I instructed the corporal to lead the detachment at a walk to the nearby forest, while I, not galloping, jolted on as fast as possible to reach the village where I hoped to find our remounts.

Fate soured against me. I did not find my horse there. These weren't our regiment's remounts. The uhlans' remounts were still farther, three versts from the village.

The miserable hungry ass on which I sit, consumed by a chagrin which you can hardly imagine, will not move faster than a walk, and even that is excessively slow. I have never experienced a more tormenting situation. If I were given the choice of being in two more battles of Borodino or having this horse under me only two days, I would this minute choose the first option without wavering a second.

I looked for and found my Zelant, but how dearly this cost me! Having decided at whatever costs to free myself from my unpleasant situation, with spur and sabre I forced the poor horse to carry me at a trot to a second village, and there, to my delight, the first thing which presented itself was Zelant. Having mounted him, I flew like an arrow to the forest where I had ordered my detachment to go. I had hoped to find them by their tracks, but the multitude of roads going right, left and crosswise, and the countless numbers of hoof prints on all of them confused me. Having ridden about three versts randomly along a road which seemed wider than the others, I arrived at a manor house of pretty architecture. The flowerbed in front of the portico leading into the orchard was all trampled by horses. The alleys were strewn with expensive laces and silks: signs of pillage were visible everywhere. Not meeting a single person and not knowing how to find my command, I decided to return to the regiment. Shtakelberg, seeing me alone, asked, "Where is your command?" I related frankly that, desiring to get a horse in the nearby village, I had commanded the detachment to go at a walk toward the forest and to wait for me there, but that when I returned I did not find them at the designated place and did not know where they were.

"How dared you do that!" cried Shtakelberg, "How dared you leave your command? You should not have been away from it for a second. Now it is lost. The forest is occupied by the enemy. Get going, sir! Find me your people, or I shall report you to the commander-in-chief and you will be shot!"

Deafened by this salvo, I went again to the damned forest, but enemy snipers were already there.

"Where are you going, Alexandrov?" asked an officer of the squadron which was located in the front line of our snipers.

I answered that Shtakelberg had driven me to look for my foragers.

"And did you lose them?"

I told him everything.

"Well, brother, what a trifle. Your foragers, probably, went roundabout by a safe route and now must be in the village occupied by the remounts of our rear guard. Go there."

I followed his advice and indeed found my people with their bales of hay in this village. At the question, "Why didn't you wait for me," they said that hearing firing and galloping in the forest, they thought it was the enemy, and, not at all wanting to be taken captive, they had gone on eight versts further. They had found hay there, loaded it on the horses, and had come to wait for me here. I led them back to the regiment, reported to Shtakelberg, and went straight to the commander-in-chief.

Feeling terribly insulted by Shtakelberg's threat to have me shot, I did not wish to remain under his command any longer. Without dismounting, I wrote to Podyampolsky in pencil: "Inform Colonel Shtakelberg that not wishing to be shot, I am going to the commander-in-chief, with whom I shall seek to remain as an orderly."

Arriving at the headquarters, I saw "To the Commander-in-Chief" written in chalk on some gates. I dismounted and, having entered a vestibule, met some adjutant.

"Is the commander-in-chief here?" I asked.

"He is here," he answered in a polite and kind tone. But when I said that I was looking for Kutuzov's room, at that moment the appearance and voice of the adjutant changed. "I do not know; he is not here; ask there," he said disjointedly, not looking at me, and immediately left. I went further and saw on the gates, "To the Commander-in-Chief." This time I was where I wanted to be. In the front hall I found several adjutants. I went up to the one whose face seemed nicer than the others. This was Dishkanets.

"Report my presence to the commander-in-chief. I have business with him."

"What sort? You may make it known through me."

"I cannot. I must speak to him myself and without witnesses. Do not refuse me this indulgence," I added, bowing politely to Dishkanets.

He immediately entered Kutuzov's room and, in a minute, having opened the door, said, "Please," and with this went again to the vestibule. I entered, and not only with the necessary respect but even with a feeling of reverence bowed to the gray hero, the venerable old man, the great commander.

"What do you want, my friend?" Kutuzov asked, looking fixedly at me.

"I should like to have the good fortune of being your orderly throughout the continuation of the campaign, and I have come to ask you for this indulgence."

"What is the reason for such an unusual request, and moreover the way in which you make it?"

I related what had forced me to be so decisive and, overcome by the memory of the undeserved insult, I spoke with feeling, ardor and daring expressions. Among other things I said that, born and raised in military camps, I had loved the military service since my day of birth, that I had dedicated my life to it forever, that I was ready to devote all my blood to defending the interests of the Sovereign, whom I esteemed as I did God, and that having the mentality and reputation of a brave officer, I did not deserve to be threatened with death. I stopped as much from overflow of emotion as from a certain confusion. I noted that at the words "brave officer" a faint smile appeared on the face of the commander-in-chief. This caused me to blush. I guessed his thought and, in order to justify myself, decided to tell him everything.

"In the Prussian campaign, Your Serene Excellency, all my commanders continuously and unanimously praised my bravery, and even Buksgevden himself called me exceptional, so after all that I believe I have the right to call myself brave without fearing to be considered a braggart."

"In the Prussian campaign? Surely you didn't serve then. How old are you? I thought you were not older than sixteen."

I said that I was twenty-three and had served in the Konnopolsk regiment during the Prussian campaign.

"What's your name?" the commander-in-chief asked suddenly.

"Alexandrov!"

Kutuzov arose and embraced me, saying, "How happy I am finally to have the pleasure of knowing you personally! I have heard about you for a long time. Remain with me, if you wish. It will be very pleasant for me to provide you some rest from the burden of military duties. As for the threat to shoot you," Kutuzov added laughingly, "you took that too much to heart. Those were empty words, spoken in anger. Now go to Konovnitsyn, the duty general, and tell him that you are to be my permanent orderly."

I was about to go, but he called me again: "You are limping? Why is that?"

I told him that in the battle of Borodino I had received a shell wound.

"A shell wound! And you haven't been treated! Tell the doctor immediately to look at your foot."

I answered that the wound was very slight and that my foot hardly hurt. I was lying when I said this: my foot ached and was all purple.

Now we are living in Krasnaya Pakhra, in the Saltykov home. They gave us some sort of board hut in which we (that is, the orderlies) shudder and shake from cold. Here I found Shlein, who was with me in Kiev, serving as orderly to Miloradovich.

I am exhausted by fever. I shake like an autumn leaf. Twenty times a day I am sent various places. To my misfortune, Konovnitsyn remembered that I, having been his orderly, was the best of all of those who served him. "Oh, hello, old friend," he said, catching sight of me on the porch of the house occupied by the commander-in-chief. From that day on I have had no peace. Whenever it is necessary to send someone quickly, Konovnitsyn calls out, "Uhlan orderly to me! And the poor uhlan orderly runs like a pale vampire from one regiment to another, and sometimes even from one flank of the army to the other.

Finally, Kutuzov ordered me to appear.

"Well," he said, taking me by the hand as soon as I had entered, "is it easier for you with me than in the regiment? Have you rested? How is your foot?"

I was obliged to tell the truth, that my foot was hurting unendurably and because of this I had a fever every day, and that I was able to sit on my horse only mechanically, through habit, and that I didn't even have the strength of a five-year-old child.

"Go home," said the commander-in-chief, looking at me with fatherly compassion. "You have indeed become thin and are terribly pale. Go, rest, get well and come back."

My heart contracted at this proposal.

"How can I go home, when not a single person is leaving the army?" I said sadly.

"What's done is done. You are ill. Do you think it would be better to stay in some hospital? Go! There is no action going on now, and maybe we'll stay here for some time. In that case you will be able to find us in the same place."

I saw the necessity of following Kutuzov's advice, for I could no longer stand the demands of military life even for a week.

"Will you permit me to bring my brother back with me, Your Serene Excellency? He is already fourteen. Let him begin his military career under your leadership."

"Very well, bring him," said Kutuzov, "I will take him under my wing and be a father to him."

Two days after this conversation Kutuzov again ordered me to appear: "Here is your travel pass and money for the trip," he said, giving me first one and then the other. "Go with God! If you need to, write directly to me, and I shall do everything that is mine to do. Goodbye, my friend!" The great general embraced me with fatherly tenderness.

Fever and the cart shake me without mercy. I have a courier's pass, and that is the reason all the drivers, not paying attention to my order to go slowly, gallop at breakneck speed. My red lapel and trouser stripes frighten them so that, although they hear me say when I get into the conveyance, "Go at a trot," they don't believe their ears, and making their spirited steeds spring forward, they don't stop them until they reach the next station. But there is no misfortune without some good: I am no longer freezing, for the tormenting shaking continuously causes me to be feverish.

At the posting station in Kaluga some person, apparently a clerk, having waited until no one else was in the room, came up to me quietly as a cat and even more quietly asked, "Permit me to learn the contents of your dispatches."

"My dispatches! It would be funny if they told couriers what was written in the papers they are carrying! I don't know the contents of my dispatches."

"Sometimes these things are known to the courier gentlemen. I am discreet, no one will know about this from me," the tempter continued to whisper with an affable expression.

"Nor from me either. I am discreet, like you," I said, rising in order to move away from him.

"One word, old fellow! Moscow...."

I did not hear the rest. I took my seat in the carriage and drove off. Such scenes were repeated in many places and by many people. Clearly it was nothing new for them to interrogate couriers.

Kazan

I stopped over at the noblemen's club to dine. The horses were waiting, and my dinner was coming to an end when a government official with a quiet gait, squinty eyes and a cunning face approached me.

"Where are you going?"

"To S***."

"Are you straight from the army?"

"Yes."

"And where is it located?"

"I don't know."

"How can that be?"

"Perhaps it has moved to another place."

"But where did you leave it?"

"On a field between Smolensk and Moscow."

"They say that Moscow has been taken, is that true?"

"That is not true!"

"What? You don't want to say so. Everyone says that it has been taken, and that's for sure!"

"If it's for sure, what more do you want?"

"Then you agree that this rumor is correct."

"I do not agree! Goodbye, I have no time either to chat or to hear rubbish about Moscow. I was on the point of leaving."

"Wouldn't you like to pass some time at the Governor's? He has invited you to his house," the cunning person said in a quite different tone.

"You should have told me this in the beginning and not amused yourself with inquiries, and now I don't believe you. Moreover I am a courier and don't have to visit anyone."

The clerk hastily went away and in two minutes appeared again. "His Excellency urgently invites you to his place. He has sent his carriage for you." I immediately went to the governor's. The honorable Mansurov began his conversation with thanks for my good sense in handling the indiscreet questions. "I was very pleased, he said, "to hear from my clerk with what caution you answered him. I am greatly indebted to you for this. A certain scoundrel who had fled the army recently has caused a lot of trouble here. He has spoken so much rubbish and disturbed the people's minds so that I was obliged to put him under guard. Now I can ask you to be candid with me: Has Moscow been taken?"

I delayed my answer. It would be silly to deceive the governor, but some clerk or other was still standing there, and I didn't want to answer such an important question in his presence. The governor guessed my thought: "This is my true friend, he is just like myself! I beg you not to hide the truth from me. The Sovereign himself considers me worthy of his confidence. Moreover, I need to know about the fate of Moscow in order to take measures in matters concerning the city. Rebellious Tatars are gathering in crowds and awaiting a chance to do violence. I must prevent this. Thus, has Moscow actually been taken?"

"I may assure Your Excellency that it was not taken but given up freely, and this is the enemy's last triumph on Russian land; now his destruction is inevitable!"

"On what do you base your assumptions?" the governor asked. His face expressed grief and fear at the words "Moscow has been given up."

"These are not assumptions, Your Excellency, but complete accuracy. The calmness and happy appearance of all our generals and the commander-in-chief himself guarantees the destruction of the enemy. It would be unnatural if, having allowed the enemy into the heart of Russia and having given him our ancient capital, they could preserve tranquillity of spirit without being convinced of the enemy's rapid and inevitable destruction. Consider all this, Your Excellency, and you will agree with me yourself."

The governor talked with me for a long time, asking about battles and the present situation of the army. Finally, in parting, he spoke flatteringly, and in conclusion said that Russia would not have gone to the extremes of giving up Moscow if there were more officers such as I. Such praise and from such a person as Mansurov would have turned the head of anyone, and all the more of me, for a flood of rumor, of conclusion, speculation and gossip awaits as soon as my sex is disclosed! Oh, how I will then need the testimony of people like Mansurov, Yermolov and Kono- vnitsyn!

The Tatar's Tale

Beyond Kazan begin forests which are broad, dense, virgin and impenetrable. In winter the highway going through them is as narrow as those in villages. Village roads are even better than the highway, since on them one can get closer to where one is going and always more cheaply. The latter circumstance was not unimportant to me, and so after the second station I turned off the highway to a small road which hour by hour led deeper into a pine forest. Night arrived. Nothing stirred in the virgin forest, and the only thing to be heard were the exclamations of my driver and the dreary songs of an old Tatar, who was traveling with me from Kazan. He had asked my permission to sit on the driver's seat, and in exchange was acting as my servant on the trip.

"*Gaida, gaida, Khamitulla!*" he sang in the drawn out and dreary tones of his people. This was the refrain to some endless song. Weary of hearing the same thing for a whole hour, I asked, "What is this Khamitulla, Yakub, with which you are buzzing my ears?"

Yakub turned around angrily on the driver's seat. "What is Khamitulla? Khamitulla was the most handsome of all our kind!"

"Of your family, Yakub, or of the entire Tatar tribe?"

Yakub did not answer. I thought that he had become angry as usual, but the gray Tatar looked gloomily into the depths of the forest and sighed. I left him alone to think, apparently about Khamitulla, and, having covered my head with my cloak, was about to go to sleep. Suddenly Yakub turned completely around facing me:

"Master! We are traveling now through the very forest where Khamitulla roamed and hid out so long! Where his name alone and his imagined robberies caused terror to travelers! Where they sought him, pursued him, and finally caught him! Poor Khamitulla! I could not believe my eyes when I saw him in chains. He, a good and honest man, an exemplary son, a brother, a friend! In chains for a crime! For robbery! What do you think, master, what was this crime and what kind of robbery? Do you want to know?"

"Of course, Yakub, tell me."

"I love to talk about him. He amazes me and I pity his miserable fate with all the heartfelt pangs of a father. Yes, I loved Khamitulla like a son!

"He was seventeen, when I, having paid the groom's fee for my second wife, went to live with my father-in-law in the village to help him with his labors. The house of Khamitulla's father was next to ours. I was then forty-two, had no children, and with my whole soul I attached myself to that brave youth, who also loved me like a father. He was not only the handsomest of our young people, but also the best shot and most outstanding rider. Sometimes, having quieted an angry unbroken horse and leading it up to me, he would say, 'Look, Yakub, I like to ride only this sort! What good is a broken one? I wish there were no broken horses on earth at all!' I would laugh.

"'Do you wish, Khamitulla, that we should all break our necks riding crazed horses? It's all right for you, you are young, strong, a wonderful horseman, but I, or your old father? What would we do?'

"'True, I hadn't thought about that.' And the scamp would lead his beloved animal out to pasture.

"But the time arrived when neither a good horse nor a tight bow could please Khamitulla any more. His fiery steeds, shaking their manes, flew about the hills and valleys, but Khamitulla didn't even think about saddling any of them. He liked staying at home and from time to time passing by the window of Zugra, the daughter of one of the village's wealthiest Tatars. Zugra was a dark, statuesque, tall Tatar girl, of course with black eyes and brows, although the latter charm is no rarity among Tatar women—they are almost all dark-eyed. But the blackness of Zugra's eyes and brows was a kind of captivating black! Something in them caused Khamitulla's heart to ache terribly."

"Yakub, how is it that Khamitulla was able to see his beloved? Tatar girls are kept hidden from menfolk."

"Not from those they wish to please. In that case they know very well how to make themselves seen. It was enough that Khamitulla was able to distinguish the charming darkness of his Zugra's eyes and brows from the similarly dark eyes and brows of twenty pairs of different eyes!

"'Her eyes burn and her brows glisten! I swear to you, Yakub, I swear by the Koran!' the lover would repeat to me.

"'Have you lost your mind, Khamitulla? Haven't you comrades of your own age? Why do you come to me to talk such nonsense and even to swear by the Koran?'

"'Talk to my comrades! Tell my comrades about Zugra? Oh, they know all about her well enough and I shall certainly not pour oil onto the fire.'

"'Well, what do you want? Have you asked your father to give a groom's fee for her?' I asked. 'What did he say?'

"'Not with money, we aren't in any position to do so. Zugra's father wants a groom's fee which no one in our village can give, and I least of all.'

"'In that case, there is nothing to be done, Khamitulla. Be intelligent, try to forget her, conquer your feelings. Busy yourself with some trade, for example. Go to Kazan.'

" 'Yes, I must go,' my young friend said dejectedly. 'I shall go. My father is sending me to sell robes and I shall be there until spring.'

"'And how soon are you leaving?'

"'In a week.'

"I was pleased with this, assuming that in Kazan, a beautiful and populous city, among cares, amusements and various things, the young Tatar would not have time to be occupied with his passion. How little I knew Khamitulla!

"He went, wrote to his father often, gave a detailed account of his sales, sent the money entrusted to him, did not hasten his return and never mentioned a word about Zugra. I was pleased, thinking that the separation had done its work, that the youth had become reconciled, but how little I knew Khamitulla!

"Meanwhile, as he traded, worried, despaired, hoped and waited for the first flowers of spring in order to return to his parental roof, groom's fees for the beautiful Zugra were offered to Aburashid, her father, from all sides. As they multiplied, so did the greed of the old Tatar. Finally a rich merchant arrived from a distant hamlet and offered a groom's fee which Aburashid was unable to resist. They betrothed Zugra and gave her away. On the evening of that day on which Zugra with bitter tears sprinkled the magnificent sash on her breast, a gift from her young husband, on the evening of that very day Khamitulla arrived.

"No one saw on the young Tatar's face any sign of sadness, or fury or despair, which one might have expected, judging by the first reaction with which he heard about Zugra's marriage. I encountered him first, accidentally, at the entrance to the village, and assuming that it would be easier to hear such fatal news from me, I told it to him with all the consolation and sympathy of a father. From the first words Khamitulla became pale as a sheet and all his limbs shook. Convulsively he reached for the hatchet lying on his cart, but instantly came to his senses and, to my inexpressible surprise, quite coolly listened to the whole history of the matchmaking, the tears, the resistance, and finally the marriage of his poor Zugra. I was pleased with this indifference and blessed the inconstancy of the human heart. But oh, master, how little I knew Khamitulla!

"That night Zugra disappeared from her husband's bed and Khamitulla from his father's plank-bed. Both were nowhere to be found. Zugra's husband almost went out of his mind. He went to town and made a complaint. A judge arrived, an investigation began, searches were made. Finally, it was discovered that Khamitulla was living with his Zugra in a virgin wilderness of more than forty versts expanse, that is, in this very one through which we are now traveling. Well, was there any possibility of finding him here, or even more of catching him? With all my soul I was overjoyed at this situation, for it, at least for the present, calmed my fears for Khamitulla. But what will happen later? Where will he find shelter for the winter? What will he eat, what will he wear? How can one live in the forest at such a time of year, when it is so terrible in our parts! Meanwhile Zugra's father and husband went forth each day into the forest, accompanied by an escort of all their relatives. The local police also sought Khamitulla, who, according to a rumor, now here, now there, took bread from passersby, and sometimes money, but without ever harming anyone at all. Almost the whole summer passed in these searches and rumors. Autumn arrived. Rumor now had it that Khamitulla was a robber, although he never even pushed anyone with his hand, and if he took something from them, it was always such a small amount as only to suffice to buy some bread. But now the local police and deputies were looking for Khamitulla-the-robber with all the zeal of committed officials!

"One rainy night, when the moon had ceased to shine and it was so dark that it was impossible to see anything two paces ahead, I sat longer than usual. I was saddened, the most woeful thoughts passed through my mind one after another—all were of Khamitulla. The conclusion of my favorite's sad tale was close, winter would disclose everything and put an end to everything. It was terrible! Finally, I lay down on the bed, my eyes already closed, it seemed that I had fallen asleep, but a quiet knock at the window and the whisper of a familiar voice made me rise quickly from the bed with terror and involuntary joy. 'Khamitulla!' I cried out tearfully, and could say no more. My words froze. I could only squeeze the trembling hand of my poor friend. I could not invite him into the hut, nor could I offer him shelter, warmth or food. My heart wanted to burst! 'Khamitulla, flee! the village is full of deputies. The police chief himself is looking for you. Flee as fast as possible!'

"'Come out to me, Yakub,' Khamitulla said in a scarcely audible voice. 'Come out to me. We will cross behind the village and then into the forest. I have much to tell you.'

"I went out, and, taking each other by the hand, we went from the village to the field. The forest loomed a verst away and we took refuge there. I wanted to stop.

"'No, father, let us go further. I need you. You shall do me a favor, perhaps the last one!'

"Not having the strength to speak, I followed silently where Khamitulla led me. The pouring rain whipped me mercilessly on the head and face—in my haste I had fled without my hat. We went at our fastest pace more than half an hour.

"'Look,' said Khamitulla, stopping suddenly and stopping me. 'Look, Yakub, there is my poor Zugra!'

"He bent over some sort of mound resembling the top of a stump or a pile of straw. I went up behind him and saw Khamitulla pulling a woman from under the pile of pine branches. It was his Zugra! With soul-rending moans Khamitulla pressed her to his heart. 'Zugra! My Zugra! My one earthly joy! We must part!'

"He fell onto the grass in despair and embraced the knees of the sobbing Zugra. She sat down beside him, put her head on his chest, embraced him, pressed her lips to the pale face of the weakened youth, and, kissing him passionately, poured forth the bitterest of tears. I sobbed. Oh, master! What feelings are sometimes hidden under our rude appearance and in the depth of the wild impenetrable forest of our cold land!

"When the first paroxysms of the most terrible of all love's suffering—the suffering of parting—had somewhat quieted, Zugra began to speak.

"'For the time being we must be submissive to fate, my kind friend. We shall be apart while you seek a place where we can again be together. I shall go to my father, but I shall not go to my husband, I shall not go for anything! He is not my husband. My consent was never sought. Let my father return the groom's fee. I am yours, eternally yours! I have never had another husband.'

"'Oh, Zugra, Zugra, we are parting forever!' the young Tatar said dejectedly, but, gradually becoming enraged at the thought of eternal parting, he began to beat his chest fearfully, crying out in a despairing voice: 'Zugra, I shall never see you again! Kill me, Yakub, kill me! What is life to me without Zugra!'

"Meanwhile dawn began to break. I tried to bring Khamitulla to his senses, and, indicating the growing light in the east, said that if he didn't want to be captured by the deputies then he had better decide on something.

"'I still do not know why you led me into this forest. You said something about some favor. What can I do for you? Here are the heart and hand of a father. Use them, demand from me all that might soften the severity of your fate.'

Khamitulla got up, embraced Zugra again, and held her a long time in his embrace, spasmodically pressing her to his chest. Finally, handing her to me, and paling as even a corpse cannot pale, he said in a sinking voice: 'Take her, Yakub! Hide her for the time being from her father's and husband's anger, from the mockery of evil people. Take my Zugra. Zugra, Zugra! Yakub, why don't you want to kill me!'

"Fearing new paroxysms of despair, I seized the young Tatar girl by the hand and ran to the village as fast as my strength permitted. She was choking from tears. Arriving home, I gave Zugra into the hands of my wives and went into the meeting hut to find out what was being undertaken to capture Khamitulla. They told me that watchmen had been placed on all paths in the forest, that the major himself was making all the arrangements, that the lateness of the year helped their maneuvers, because the leaves had fallen, leaving the forest bare, permitting one to see farther into the thickets. Unhappy Khamitulla will be captured, inescapably captured! Returning home, I found Zugra asleep. Poor thing, she was pale and thin. She shook constantly and, sobbing, muttered disconnectedly, 'Khamitulla, oh, Khamitulla!'

"I could talk for a long time, master, about everything that I learned from Zugra. How they lived in the forest, how they were inexpressibly happy, and how, finally, at the sight of the falling leaves a deadly anguish and presentiments of misfortune oppressed them. The forest, becoming more bare with each day, began to seem not a refuge to them, but a transparent prison, and that is why Khamitulla had decided to give Zugra over to me and to flee further until a more favorable time. But he was not successful in doing that. The local police, under the leadership of their superior (an army major), took such resolute measures that after several days of uninterrupted investigations and searches my poor friend, the valiant, brave Khamitulla, notwithstanding a heroic defense, was seized, fettered, hauled to town and put in prison. He was tried and.... No, I can speak no longer! The memory of this has opened again an old wound in my heart. He was not guilty of human blood. However, they treated him like a cutthroat. The chief crime with which they charged him was that in the fight with the deputies he had wounded the superior himself and left him for dead, prostrate on the road. That was all the blood which Khamitulla had shed in the course of his calamitous wandering about the forest."

The Tatar covered his face with his hands and sighed, or, to put it better, groaned, bending his head almost to his knees. Having given this fit of grief some time to become stilled, I asked, "What became of Zugra?"

"Zugra's father took her back. She threatened to kill herself if they gave her back to her husband. Her beauty, her unhappy love, her silent grief, her inconsolable tears made her an object of the deepest sympathy from everyone, but she was dead to everything except memories of Khamitulla. Day and night she cried for him, sitting behind her screen, and it was she who composed the song which you have heard from me. In it she presents the happy time of their love in their virgin forest, their fears of the coming parting, the terror at the resounding voices of the deputies, who seek traces of her beloved in the forest, and at last the final parting. Our whole village sings this song."

"What is the meaning of the refrain '*Gaida, gaida, Khamitulla?*'"

"'*Gaida*' means to hurry or to go or let us go, depending upon how the word is used."

Yakub fell silent.

Forest, virgin forest, in your impenetrable thicket, the haven of wild beasts, there burned a love which cannot be expressed in words! Khamitulla is long gone, but the sound of his voice still resounds in those places where he was so happy. Where he loved and was loved so boundlessly! How many times has the echo of this forest repeated his name, pronounced now with the whisper of love, now with the awful voice of the pursuer, now, finally with the mournful song of the young Tatar girl, poor orphaned Zugra!

At last I am home! My father greeted me with tears. I told him that I had come home to get warm. Papa cried and laughed, looking over my cloak, which no longer had any color, was shot through, singed, and had holes burned through it. I gave it to Natalya, who says that she will use it to sew a capote for herself.

Having told my father about the commander-in-chief's favorable disposition towards me, I convinced him to let my brother go with me. He agreed to this parting, which was terrible for him, but with the condition we wait until spring. However much I insisted that this was impossible for me, Papa would not hear otherwise.

"You may go," he said, "as soon as you regain your health, but I will not let Vasily go in winter—not at his age! And in such a troubled time! No, no! Go yourself when you want. His time has not come, he is not yet fourteen!"

What am I to do? I will leave it to time to accustom Father to the thought of parting with his dearly beloved son. Not waiting for that, I am writing to Kutuzov that "impatiently desiring to return to service under his glorious banners, I cannot hope to have the fortune of standing under them with my brother, because our old father does not want to let this immature lad onto the field of bloody battles in such a severe time of year and is persuading me, if at all possible, to await a warmer season, and that now I do not know what to do at all."

I received an answer from Kutuzov. He writes that I have the full right to fulfill my father's will, that having been dispatched by the Chief of the army, I am obliged to him alone to account for an extension of my leave, that he permits me to await spring at home, and that by doing this I will not be diminished in people's opinion, because I have shared hardship and danger with my comrades to the end, and that the commander-in-chief is an eyewitness to my valor.

This letter was written in the hand of Khitrov, Kutuzov's son-in-law. Father knew his hand very well, because Khitrov lived for some time in V*** and my father had occasion to correspond with him. I showed the letter to Papa, and my old father was so touched by the kindness and attention shown my by the famous commander that he was unable to refrain from crying. I wanted to preserve this letter as a memento of the favorable disposition toward me of the most famous of Russian heroes, but Papa, taking this paper for himself, caused me to blush twenty times a day by showing it to everyone and letting everyone read it. I was obliged to remove the letter secretly and burn it. When my father learned of my action, he was very offended and severely rebuked me, accusing me of unforgiveable indifference to the flattering attention of the first person in the government. I heard father's recriminations with respectful silence, but in any case I was satisfied that the ceaseless reading of Kutuzov's letter had ceased.

Five captive French officers live here, three of them very well educated. Their confidence in the wisdom of Napoleon does honor to their own wisdom. They indicate Smolensk on the map and say to me, "Monsieur Alexander, the French are here." I don't have the spirit to dissuade them from their happy error; what will I gain by telling them that the French are in a trap!

Finally, after a number of postponements, Papa decided to let my brother leave, and high time! The snow had already melted, I burned with impatience to return to military action. Having received permission to prepare for departure, I set to with such activity that everything was finished in two days. My father gave us a light two-seat carriage and his own servant as far as Kazan, and from there we will travel alone. Father was very opposed to letting my brother go without a servant, but I told him that this might have very unpleasant consequences, since nothing would prevent the servant from telling everything he knew. So it was decided that we would go alone.

1813

On Monday, the first of May, at dawn, we left our father's home! My conscience bothers me because I did not cede to my father's request not to go that day. He had a superstition that Monday is unlucky, and I should have humored him, especially under the circumstances. My father released his beloved son, and parted with him as with his life! Oh, it was wrong of me, very wrong! My heart will not cease to reproach me. I imagine that Papa will pine and worry much more now than if we had left a day later as he wished. Man is incorrigible! How many times have I repented, after acting stubbornly, only because I thought I was in the right to act so! We are never so unfair as when we think that we are fair. And how could I, how dare I have opposed my father's will—I, who think that children should consider their father a god? What devil sent upon me such mental derangement?...

Three stations from Kazan, our carriage was smashed to pieces. We were thrown down a slope into a wide ditch. Our carriage cracked up, but fortunately, we were both unhurt. Now we are riding in a cart. How strange my fate! How many years now have I been riding about in precisely that means of conveyance which I cannot abide!

Moscow

Mitrofanov gave us some sad news: *Kutuzov is dead!* Now I am in a most difficult position: My brother is registered in the Mining Service and is on its list, but I drove off with him without taking any document from the authorities. How can I deliver him to the armed forces now? Under Kutuzov, this thoughtlessness would have had no consequences, but now I'll have all sorts of difficulties. Mitrofanov advises me to send Vasily home, but at his first words on the subject, my brother stated resolutely that he wouldn't think of returning home, and that he would serve in the military and in no other service.

The Smolensk Road

Riding through the woods, for a long time I could not understand the reason for the bad smell the wind carried to us from time to time from the forest depths. Finally, I asked a coachman about this, and received an answer that could not have been more horrible, pronounced with all the indifference of a Russian peasant: "A Frenchman is rotting somewhere nearby."

In Smolensk, we marched along the ruined walls of the fortress. I recognized the place near the brick barns where we were so unprofitably positioned and from which we retreated in such disorder. I pointed it out to my brother, saying, "Over there, Vasily, my life was in danger." The flight of the French had left horrible traces: their bodies rot in the depths of the wood and infect the air. Such misfortune! Never before had anyone's arrogance and conceit been so severely punished as theirs! Horrors are told of their sorry withdrawal.

When we returned to the station, the stationmaster wasn't home. His wife asked us to come into the office and enter our travel orders ourselves. The horses will be here immediately, she said, sitting down to her work and tenderly kissing a sweet looking girl who stood next to her. "Is that your daughter?" I asked.

"No, she's a French girl, an orphan!" While our horses were being harnessed, our hostess told us the touching story of the beautiful girl. The French marched upon us sure of victory and a long stay, and in that surety, many of them took their families with them. Upon their fatal withdrawal, or rather, their flight homeward, these families attempted to hide in the forests both from the cold and from the Cossacks. One such family settled in the vicinity of Smolensk, in the woods. They built themselves a cabin, made a fire, and set about preparing some meager food, when suddenly the whooping of Cossacks rang through the woods.... Such a misfortune! This line might apply to them:

Jusqu'au fond de nos coeurs notre sang s'est glacé.

They all raced off, just following their noses, and tried to make it to the densest part of the woods. The eldest daughter, a girl of eight (the very one who stood before us, leaning on the knees of her benefactress, and crying from the tale), ran to an impenetrable thicket, deep in snow, with nothing on but her little shift. The poor child, quite stiff with cold, finally crawled out on the highway at dawn. She did not have the strength to walk, but crawled on her hands and knees. Just then a Cossack officer was riding by on horseback. He might not have seen her, but the girl had enough presence of mind to muster all her strength and cry to him: *"Mon ami! Par bonté prenez moi sur votre cheval!"* The surprised Cossack stopped his horse, and looking carefully at the thing stirring by the road, was moved to tears to see that it was a half-naked child, for all of her clothes were torn to pieces, and her hands and feet were quite frozen. Finally, she fell motionless. The officer took her in his arms, sat her on his horse, and rode off toward Smolensk. Riding past the station, he saw the stationmaster's wife standing by the gate. "Do me the favor, Madam, of taking this girl in your charge." The stationmaster's wife answered that she had no place for her, that she had many children of her own. "Well, then I'll smash her head on this corner, right before your eyes, to spare her future suffering!" Struck as if by lightning by this threat, and thinking she would in fact see it carried out, the stationmaster's wife quickly took the unconscious girl from the officer's arms and took her to her chamber. The officer galloped on. For more than two months the child was near death. The unfortunate creature was completely frozen. The skin peeled in sheets from her hands and feet; her hair fell out; and finally, after a high fever, she returned to life. Now the girl is living with the stationmistress as a beloved daughter, she has learned to speak Polish, and thanks to her tender age, she does not regret the lost advantages to which she had a right by reason of her exalted birth—she was from one of the best families in Lyons. Many fine ladies to whom the stationmaster's wife told this tale, just as she had to us, invited the pathetic orphan to live with them; but she always answered, embracing the stationmistress: "Mommy brought me back to life. I'll always stay with her!" The stationmaster's wife began to weep on finishing her tale with these words, and pressed the sobbing child to her breast. This scene touched us to the depths of our souls.

They took my courier's travel orders and gave me others, only as far as Slonim, where all the officers who have for some reason become separated from their regiments remain under the command of Kologrivov, and the same fate awaited me! On the road, we met Nikiforov, an officer in the hussars, extremely civil and obliging, but a bit strange. My rascal of a brother finds some pleasure in angering him at every station.

Slonim

I am here again, but how everything has changed! I couldn't even find my former quarters at the old guardsman's. Kologrivov received me with the most terrible imperious look. "Why did you spend so long at home?" he asked.

I answered, "Because of illness."

"Do you have proof from a doctor?"

"No, I don't."

"Why not?"

"I saw no need to get any." This strange answer angered Kologrivov in the extreme.

"You, sir, are a rogue..."

I walked out without letting him finish the obligatory speech. So...now what do I do? With a minor brother on my hands, whom I can't place in the regiment because he's already enlisted in the Mining Service. Where will I go with him? Such were my thoughts, while I covered my face with my hands, my elbows on the Jew's big table. A light tap on the shoulder brought me back to reality. "Why so pensive, Alexandrov? Here's an order for you from Kologrivov. You are to ride to Laishin to Captain Bibikov, and get from him some horses, which you are to graze in green meadows, on silky swards!"

I had absolutely no desire to joke. What will I do with my brother? Where will I place him? Take him with me to the regiment, and present him with the picture of an uhlan's life, such an immature youth?.. Oh, why didn't I leave him at home? My shows of intelligence broke my father's heart by separating him from his dearly beloved son, and far from bringing me any gain, has brought only trouble and vexation!.. Sorrow and anxiety so changed my appearance, that Nikiforov, my travelling companion, was touched: "Leave your brother with me, Alexandrov; I will do everything for him that you would, and he will receive the same friendship and care from me that he would from you." The proposal of the noble Nikiforov lifted a burden from my heart; I thanked him with all my soul and entrusted my brother to him, begging the latter to lose no time, but write to our father and ask for discharge from the Mining Service. I entrusted him with all the money, said farewell, and set off for Laishin.

Captain Bibikov, Ruzi, Burogo and I are assigned to fatten up the tired, wounded and emaciated horses of all the uhlan regiments. To my lot fell one hundred and fifty horses and forty uhlans to tend them. The village in which I am quartered is some fifteen versts from Laishin, surrounded by woods and lakes. Days on end I spend riding or walking in the dark forests, and bathing in the lakes, clean and clear as crystal.

I occupy a vast barn—it is my hall. Its floor is covered with sand, the walls decorated with garlands of flowers, bouquets and wreaths. In the middle of all this I've set up a luxurious bed, in all senses of the word *luxurious*: on four low stumps, three wide boards are laid out; on them soft, fragrant hay is spread, almost all the same color, to a height of three-quarters of an arshin, and covered with some sort of velvet rug, with bright shining flowers; a large black morocco pillow with crimson decoration completes my wonderful bed, which serves me as divan and armchair as well. On it, I sleep, lie, sit, read, write, dream, dine, sup, and doze.

It is now July. In the course of the long summer day, I have not been bored for a minute—I rise at dawn at three o'clock, that is, I wake, and then the uhlan brings me coffee, of which I drink a glass with black bread and cream. After my breakfast, I go to view my herd, distibuted among the stables. Under my supervision, they are taken to be watered. By their hale and hearty leaps, I see that my uhlans follow their superior's example— they are not stealing the oats, or selling it, but giving it all to these beautiful and obedient animals. I watch their shapes, formerly too thin, take on their beauty, fill out, their coats fill in and become glossy, their eyes shine; their ears, which were practically hanging, start to move quickly and point ahead. I stroke and pat the most beautiful of them, order saddled the one that bounds most merrily, and go off for a ride wherever my curiosity or a charming view might take me. At twelve o'clock, I return to my hall of plaited brushwood. There, my bowl is already waiting—some very tasty Ukrainian cabbage soup, or some borshch and a small piece of black bread. After dinner, which always leaves me a little hungry, I go riding again, either through the fields or along the river. I return home at around two to write a few lines, take a nap, dream, build castles in the air, tear them down again, or look through my *Memoirs,* but without changing anything—

and what would be the point, why should I? Just my family will read them, and they're good enough for them. Toward evening, I go riding again, swimming, and finally return to attend the evening watering. After all that, my day concludes with a scene that is invariably repeated every evening. This is harvest season, and so as night comes on, all the young men and girls return from the fields with endless singing (and I've never heard singing more obnoxious), and in a thick crowd they walk towards the village. At the entrance, my uhlans are waiting for them, also standing in a crowd. The two mix and meld; the singing dies down; I hear talk, laughter, squeals and curses (the latter always from the men). With all this din, they run into the village, and finally go off to their houses.

I go to bed too, on my luxurious, soft, sweet-smelling couch, and fall asleep the same moment. But tomorrow, it will be the same way, the same scenes. Calm, happiness, sweet dreams, health, high color—all of this is mine in my present mode of life, and I haven't been bored for a minute. Nature, which planted in my soul love of freedom and for her own beauties, has given me an inexhaustible source of happiness. As soon as I open my eyes in the morning, feelings of contentment and happiness immediately awake in my whole being. It's absolutely impossible for me to imagine something sad—everything in my imagination glitters and burns with a bright light. Oh Sovereign! our adored Father! not a day passes that I do not in my mind embrace Your knees! To You I owe a happiness that has no equal on earth—the happiness of being completely free! To Your mercy, Your Angelic goodness, but most of all to Your wisdom and great soul, which had the power to grant the possibility of great valor in the weaker sex! Your pure soul proposed in mine nothing unworthy of me! did not fear evil use of the calling given me! Truly, the Sovereign has penetrated my soul. My thoughts are completely pure—nothing occupies my mind except the beauties of Nature and the duties of service. Now and then I am enticed by dreams of returning home, of high rank, of a brilliant reward, of heavenly happiness—of tending my kind father in his old age, assuring him ease and plenty in all things! That's the one time I cry.... Oh father! my indulgent, kind-hearted father! Let merciful God grant me the unspeakable happiness of being the comfort and support of your old age....

I've noticed that there is some sort of vague, indistinct rumor of my existence making the rounds in the army. Everyone talks about it, but no one knows anything; everyone considers it possible, but no one believes it. More than once, I've been told my own story with all sorts of distortions. One described me as a beauty, a second, as deformed, a third, as an old woman, a fourth gave me a giant's stature and bestial features, and so forth.... Judging from these descriptions, I could be sure that no one's suspicions would ever attach to me, were it not for one circumstance that threatened finally to attract the notice of my comrades: I should wear a mustache, but I have none, and of course I won't. The Nazimovs, Solntsev and Lizogub already joke at me, saying: "Well, brother, when can we expect to see your mustache? You're not a Laplander are you?" Of course, it's a joke. They don't imagine that I'm more than eighteen. But sometimes the noticeable civility of their remarks and modesty of their words suggest to me that if they are not completely convinced that I will never have a mustache, then at least they strongly suspect that it is possible. But my cohorts are very kindly disposed towards me, and think very highly of me. I lose nothing in their eyes—they were my witnesses and comrades in my martial career.

I am ordered to turn over all the horses and men to the senior non-com in my detachment and set off to a squadron of our own regiment in command of Staff-Captain Rzhensnitsky. There are two of them. The elder is rather eccentric, a real *Schleicher,* knows everything, has seen everything, been everywhere, can do anything, but doesn't much care for work and does little of it. He is in his element at headquarters. But his brother is a fearless, experienced, true officer, devoted with all his soul to the noise of camp, his keen sabre, and his good horse. I was very happy that I was going to be in his squadron. I cannot bear worthless squadron leaders—they're a disaster in wartime, and in peace time, a joke and a bother.

When I rode up with Rzhensnitsky, I found the squadron mounted and ready to take the field. I had not expected that at all, and was very upset by the swift change from complete peace to the greatest activity and business.

"Hello, my dear Alexandrov!" said Rzhensnitsky. "I've been expecting you for some time. Do you have a horse?"

"Neither horse nor saddle, Captain! What should I do?"

"You will have to stay here for a day and find a saddle to buy. Take one of the government-issued horses. But try to catch up to the squadron at the next stop-over." Then he rode off with the squadron, and I set off to our Lieutenant Strakhov's. I found many officers of our regiment, and one of them sold me a wretched French *archak* saddle for one hundred and fifty rubles. Even though I knew the price was ungodly, what was I to do? If he had wanted five hundred rubles for his saddle, I would have had to pay it.

The next day, I rose at dawn and immediately rode off after my squadron. At about five o'clock in the afternoon, I arrived at the village set for their stop-over. The first thing I saw was the sergeant-major, in just his shirt, tied to a porch. At first I didn't make this out, and intended to give him my horse; but finally seeing that he was tied up, I tied up my horse as well.

"How did you get tied up?" I asked the poor captive.

"By my hands, as you see very well," he answered rudely.

In Brest-Litovsk, before crossing the border, we had to undergo an inspecting officer's review. For two whole hours a pouring rain poured down on us from head to foot. Finally, wet to the bone, we crossed Russia's boundary. The sun came out from behind the clouds and shone brightly. Its rays, and a warm summer breeze soon dried our uniforms.

Our detachment is composed of several squadrons from various uhlan regiments. Our commander is Captain Stepanov. A few squadrons of horse-chasseurs joined us, under the command of Seidler, also a captain, and apparently Stepanov's superior.

Prussia

We are going to the fortress of Modlin, and we will be there under command of Kleinmikhel.—Yesterday it rained all day and a cold wind was blowing. We have to cross a river, not a very wide one, but since the ferry cannot take more than ten horses, our crossing will be very protracted. All our uhlans look terrible: their faces have turned blue from the cold! This cold wind with the constant showers is worse than a winter frost. I decided to go warm up in a little house on the hill, right above the river. I scrambled up the steep, slippery path and went into the hall, where a fire set on the hearth poured forth its salutary warmth, when I was greeted with a stern: "Why have you come?" This was asked by Captain Stepanov, who had set up here to wait until his whole detachment had crossed. I answered that since the Lithuanian squadron had not yet started the crossing, and its turn would not be for some time, I came up to warm up a bit.

"You should be at your post," said the captain dryly. "Be off, immediately!"—I left, and in my mind cursed the captain with all my heart for driving me out of a warm dry hall into the cold, damp and dark night! Coming up to the bank, I saw that the squadron was getting ready for the crossing. I was the duty officer, and should have been there constantly, both at the squadron's crossing, and on the march. Having loaded as many men and horses as would fit, I found a little cabin on deck where peat was burning in a small cast-iron stove, and a German woman was making coffee for those who wanted some. Her soft bed stood right next to the stove. I knew that our squadron's crossing would take about an hour and a half, and so I ordered the non-com on duty, whom I knew to be meticulous, to see to it, and when it was done, to let me know. Having arranged things so successfully, I settled down on the German woman's bed and asked her to serve me some coffee. After two cups, I warmed up. It was not just very warm in the cabin, but almost too hot. However, I had no desire to go out on deck—the rain and wind continued. Waiting until they would tell me that the whole squadron had made the crossing, I fell asleep in the high, soft pillows, and do not recall how I fell into such a deep sleep. When I awoke, there was not a sound, not wind nor rain nor men. All was quiet, the ferry did not move, and there was no one in the cabin. Seeing this, I quickly rose, opened the door, and saw that the ferry was standing at the shore, that the whole vicinity was deserted—there wasn't a single person to be seen, and that it was almost day. "What is the meaning of this?" I thought. "Could they have forgotten about me?" Walking up the hill, I saw an uhlan with my horse.

"Where's the squadron?"

"Long gone."

"Why wasn't I awakened?"

"I don't know."

"Who led the squadron?"

"The captain himself...."

I mounted my horse. "Which squadron crossed last?"

"The Orenburg Uhlans."

"How long ago?"

"Over two hours."

"Why didn't you tell me when our squadron left?"

"No one knew where you were."

"What about the non-com on duty?"

"He ordered me to just take your horse and wait here on the shore."

"How far are our quarters?"

"About fifteen versts...."

I rode at an easy trot, very displeased with myself, my uhlan, the non-com on duty, the wind, the rain, and the commander who had driven me out of the cabin so mercilessly. The morning was fine. The wind and rain stopped, the sun came out, and finally I saw our squadron's quarters near a thick wood. When I arrived at my comrades', I found them calm and happy (that is, full). They had had a good breakfast and were preparing to march. And so I stayed, hungry, without having dismounted, but joined with my regiment and off to new quarters.

Modlin

We reached Modlin on the 10th of August. Tomorrow, our squadron is on sentry duty. Rzhensnitsky has placed us all over a distance of two versts. I am in the middle, and the chief commanding officer of this picket. Ilinsky and Ruzi, on the flanks, are to send me reports each morning on everything that happens with them, and I report to the captain. Now I am living in a little cave or dug-out. By night, half my men are in readiness, with horses saddled, and the other half rests.

Yesterday, Rzhensnitsky sent me a bottle of excellent cream, in reward for a small skirmish with the enemy and for the four prisoners I took.

There is apparently a great store of balls and powder in Modlin. All it takes is for some of us to show ourselves in the field, and they immediately fire cannon on us. Sometimes they do this honor to a single man, which strikes me as extremely funny. How can you waste a ball on one man?...

We have left Modlin and are going to join our regiments. We are billeted near Hamburg.

Bohemia. October

The view of the mountains of Bohemia is so picturesque! I always ride up the highest of them and watch our squadrons stretched along the narrow road in a colorful, winding ribbon....

The weather has turned cold and damp again. We are surrounded by dense fog, and in this impenetrable cloud complete our journey through the peaks of the Bohemian mountains. What beautiful views must be hidden by this rippling grey shroud! To add to my displeasure, I have a terrible toothache.

A Night in Bohemia

"Your honor, you are duty officer for the squadron tomorrow."

"When do we march?" The sergeant-major who announced my duty answered that in the orders it said that we were to be at the assembly point at four in the morning.

"Very well, you may go...." I'm deathly tired today! As soon as we arrived at our quarters, I turned my horse, Uragan, over to Kindzersky, and went off down the first path that I spotted, going wherever it would lead, and walked all day, now climbing the hills, now going down into the valleys. I wanted to be everywhere there was a good site, and there were a lot of them. My walk didn't end before sunset. Hurrying back to the squadron, I still could not help but stand and gaze for a quarter of an hour at how the evening fog, like whitish smoke, begins to fill the narrow crevices of the mountains. Finally, I am home, that is, with the squadron (Excuse me, dear Papa! I always forget that you don't like me to use the word "home," when I speak of the squadron), and the first person I meet gives me the duty roster. I summoned my orderly. "Zanuda, wake me tomorrow at dawn."

"Don't worry, your honor, the general march will wake you!"

"Oh, I forgot. Well, then it's not necessary."

What could be more annoying than a general march at dawn?.. The sun wasn't even up when the trumpeters stood in line before my windows and began to play that piece that has the magical power not only to banish sleep, but to force even the laziest of our armed forces to rise and dress that very second. Although I am considered one of the more energetic officers, I had never wanted to stay in bed another half hour more than now. But then Ruzi threw open the door and flew into the room in full uniform.

"What, you're still in bed? What about your duty? Get up, get up! What a fool you are! Didn't you hear the general march?"

"As if I could avoid it, when ten trumpets are playing right in my ear!"

"Ten, indeed, Such exaggeration! There are just two trumpeters riding through the village. But anyway, get up, the captain doesn't play games."

"Fine way to scare me."

"Get up! I'm going to lead the squadron out...." Ruzi went out, and I got dressed in five minutes. It seemed to me for some reason that a full-dress uniform required a plume, and I ordered Zanuda to fetch it; but when he came back, I hadn't the vaguest idea what the old mustachioed gent was holding in his hands. It was some sort of long, yellowish-brown brush.

"What is that, Zanuda?"

"Your plume, your honor!"

"It's a plume... Where did you find it?"

"In your suitcase!"

"And out of its case, no doubt?"

"Yes, your honor!"

"Give it to me, you worthless creature!" I snatched my plume from the hands of the dumbstruck Zanuda, put it in my helmet and went to join my comrades.

Zanuda grumbled after me, "Nothing's good enough for a freak. Who does he expect to stare at him with his plume!"

Seeing me with my frowning brows and my ridiculous looking plume, the officers all broke out laughing: "Don't you look fine today, Alexandrov! That plume really suits you! You were really made for each other!...And why did you deck yourself out so today, pray tell?"

"I'm the duty officer."

"Really? You must be in fine form then. Plume and all?"

"Yes!"

"You look so ridiculous...enough, brother, throw it away, or it will break your head with the next wind." I did not listen.

We set off. On the march, Ruzi gave me command, and since he was in the fourth platoon, we rode together behind the squadron. "Do you know where we are stopping tonight, Alexandrov?

"I do, on Baron N ***'s estate."

"Well, of course, but you can't imagine what pleasures await us there!"

"What sort of pleasures?"

"We are to be quartered in the castle itself. The baron is as rich as Croesus, hospitable. The march isn't long today—we'll manage to get there long before evening. The baron undoubtedly has daughters and a pianoforte. Oh, I foresee something delightful!

"You're crazy, Ruzi. Who assured you that the baron will be inclined to amuse us?"

"The Germans say that he is very kind, and likes to live a merry life."

"Well, and the daughters? What if he hasn't any?"

"He'll find some."

The wind grew stronger by the hour. "Let's move to the other side, Ruzi. It seems you were right when you said that my plume would crack open my head. This annoying wind throws it from side to side." We moved over.

Today, all of Ruzi's hopes were to collapse. The clear sky was covered first with light clouds, then storm clouds, and finally was laid over with a quite black, impenetrable mantle. Rain descended upon us in torrents, with thunder and wind, and mercilessly poured down on the defenseless uhlans. By the time we had put on our raincoats, everything we had on was wet. The guides took us God knows where, and our short march stretched out so that we arrived at our quarters in the middle of the night.

Wet, shivering, spattered with red clay, we finally halted before Baron N***'s splendid castle. Oh, with what joy did I jump down from my horse. I didn't believe that I was already on the ground. All day on horseback! All day in the rain! My limbs were quite stiff! One would long remember a march like that.

"Why did you dismount, Alexandrov?" the Captain asked. "Have you forgotten that you are duty officer? Mount up again and conduct the men to their quarters."

"I can do that on foot, Captain," I answered, and taking my Uragan by the reins, I was about to set off before the squadron.

The captain was conscience-stricken. "Come back, Alexandrov! The non-com can billet the men...."

We went up a stairway, clean, light and as smooth as glass. We entered magnificent rooms, elegantly furnished, and settled down to rest on the armchairs and divans. An evil fate befell everything we so much as touched: where we walked, stood or sat, everywhere, there were traces of the red clay we had been spattered with from head to foot, or rather, from foot to head.

Our cordial host invited us to sit down at table. The captain and my comrades immediately took their seats, conversed noisily, clinking glasses, tumblers, dishes, spurs, sabres, and supposing themselves safe from the rain and wind for the remainder of the night, gave themselves up wholeheartedly to the pleasures of an elegant table and merry conversation.

Taking advantage of their fervent efforts over supper, I went off to the bedroom, or rather the room that had been assigned us. The doors from it to the dining room were open. Several beds stood side by side near the wall. How sad for the baron to have to give up such fine linen for our beds! I did manage to spare the baron's luxury my boots, stuck over with mud. But I lay down just as I was in all the rest on the feather-bed, and wrapped myself in it. How nice all of that was, clean, white, soft, fine, rich! All satin, batiste, lace, and in the middle of it, a wet uhlan, spattered with red clay!..... My situation seemed so amusing that I laughed until I fell asleep.

I was awakened by a loud and heated argument between our captain and Major Nichvalodov of the Orenburg Hussar Regiment. "They don't know how to write in your office," said the captain.

"Excuse me," Nichvalodov sweetly replied, "but in yours, they can't read." They argued, shouted, and finally read the orders again. It turned out that Nichvalodov was right: we are not at our appointed quarters. That's terrible news!

In an instant I jumped out of my warm refuge. The captain was already looking around for me. "Where's the duty officer? Alexandrov! Go sound the alarm, as loud as possible!" But when he saw that I didn't budge, he asked in surprise, "What are you standing around for?" Nichvalodov answered for me, that I was in my stocking feet.

"A fine duty-officer for you! Well, sir, then go in your stocking feet!" Fortunately, the orderly came in with my boots. I quickly put them on and set off at a run so as not to hear the mocking cries of my captain: "An excellent duty-officer! You should have gotten completely undressed!..."

The wind blew, howling and gusting; the rain poured down, and the night was as dark as it could get. Our trumpeters were standing outside. "Go to the village, and sound the alarm very loud," I told them. They rode off. There was no other means of gathering our men, quartered in the village, which extended some three versts along the mountain gorges. The squadron was assembled in about an hour and a half. We mounted our horses; the guides rode with flares up front, behind, and on the sides of the squadron. We rode off, shivering and cursing the march, the storm, the captain, and the distance to our quarters. We had to cover two more miles.

When we had ridden a half-verst, the captain suddenly stopped the squadron. The mind of our indefatigable chief had come up with the ridiculous idea of leaving me alone to wait for men who, he supposed, had not heard the alarm, or could not get to the assembly place in time. "Gather them all, Alexandrov, and lead them after us to quarters!" A fine state of affairs! but there was nothing to be done; it was impossible to object. I stayed behind. The squadron set off, and when the tramp of the horses' hoofs in the mud had completely died away, the wind's wild roar mastered the environs. Listening to the terrible concert, I imagined I was surrounded by evil spirits, howling in the ravines. The captain was really crazy! Why didn't he leave me one of the guides with a torch? What am I going to do now? How can I find the road back to the village? I can't see it, there's no light anywhere, not a single spark. Am I to stand here as if on watch, and stand until dawn? These useless questions to myself were interrupted by my horse's impatient capers. I wanted to calm him, and stroked him with my hand; but this method, which had always worked before, did not help now. He capered, reared, rolled his head, snorted, beat his hoofs on the ground, and moved crosswise now one direction, now another. There was no way to quiet the frenzied Uragan. The noise of the woods around us, and the howl of the wind deafened me; but despite that, I heard another noise, and another howl. Wishing yet fearing to assure myself of my conjecture, I unwillingly and with trembling heart listen more closely. To my inexpressible terror, I find that I was not mistaken—it is a brook falling into a deep abyss, and on that side of the ravine, there's something howling, but not the wind. My imagination painted a pack of hungry wolves, tearing my Uragan to pieces, and I was so taken with this terrible supposition, that I forgot a danger much more immediate and quite real: the ravine into which the brook fell was just two steps from me, and Uragan still would not stand still. Finally I remembered, and was just about to throw myself off my horse, but the thought that he would break loose and run off to the squadron restrained me. Oh, my dear father! What would become of you if you could see your daughter now, on a frenzied horse, on the edge of a ravine, at night, in the midst of forests and gorges, and in a terrible storm!... Death looked me straight in the eyes! But the Providence of God, our Heavenly Father, watches over all of His children. A gust of wind tore off my plume, and quickly carried it off over a ditch, right into some bushes, where I thought I heard the howl of wolves, my terrible comrades on this night watch. A moment later, the howling ceased, and Uragan stopped capering. Now I could get down off him, but my earlier fear that he would break loose again restrained me, and I stood motionless, like an equestrian statue, above the depths of the ravine into which the brook fell.

The rain had stopped some time ago, and the wind had started to die down. The night began to clear, and I could clearly make out the objects around me. Behind me, quite close to my Uragan's hind legs was the abyss! I never jumped off a horse so fast in all my life, and immediately led him away from this dangerous area. Peering intently and uneasily into the black depths of the shrubbery on the other side of the ravine, I could not yet make anything out; but Uragan is quiet, and there doesn't seem to be anything there. I would really have liked to have spotted my plume, but there was nothing white showing anywhere, and if it's not in the ditch, the wind must have carried it off God knows where. Looking carefully around at my surroundings, I made out a great number of roads, lanes and paths leading into the hills, the ravines, and the woods. Where is the one that I should take? No tracks were visible on any of them. While I tried to make out just the slightest sign of them, the fog, herald of morning, began to spread around me like a white cloud, grew thicker, and covered everything with an impenetrable mist. Once again, I dared not take a step, so as not to break my neck or completely lose the road! Weary and sad, I lay down on the grass by an old log. At first I just leaned on it, but my head bowed imperceptibly, my eyes closed, and sleep overcame me.

When I awoke, I was in paradise! The sun had just come up; millions of varicolored lights played in the grass and leaves; the abyss, the brook, the wood, the gorges, everything that seemed so terrible by night, were now so charming, fresh, light, green, dappled with colors! In the gorges, such shadows and grasses! To the last circumstance, I owed the fact that Uragan had not run off. He was walking through the dewy grass and eating it with evident delight. I walked up to him, easily caught him, and mounted him.

More than once I have found that an animal's instinct in certain circumstances is more useful to man than his own reason. I would have discovered the road the squadron took only by chance, but Uragan, whom I left free to choose our path, in a quarter hour came out on one where the deep tracks of a multitude of shod horses were clearly visible. This was our path yesterday! A verst away, in the gorges, I could see Baron N***'s village. But yesterday, the captain left me within a few sazhens of it. All of Uragan's damned row drew me off that far! I turned him back to the village to see if there weren't some of our men there; but he absolutely refused to go, reared up, and very picturesquely turned on his hind legs in the direction the squadron had gone. Obviously, Uragan is smarter than I: how could one suppose that uhlans would stay at lodgings until sunrise, even if they had been left behind by the squadron?

I gave my horse free rein to gallop how and where he would, and rushed fairly fast now from hill to hill, now along the edge of deep ravines. A narrow road turned off sharply to the right near one steep precipice, grown over with shrubbery. Galloping past this place, I saw something white in the bushes. I jumped down from my horse, and taking it by the lead, ran off in that direction, not doubting for an instant that it was my plume, and I was not mistaken. It was. It lay in the branches of a bush, a brilliant white. The rain had washed it as clean as could be; the wind had dried it; and the object of yesterday's ridicule was white, fluffy, and as beautiful as only such a hair plume can be. I put it in my tarnished helmet, and began the difficult maneuver of getting on my infernal Uragan again. I don't know why, but I can't part with this horse. Why do I love it? It's mean, so impatient and arrogant that my head is never squarely on my shoulders when I ride that devil. For a quarter of an hour I circled round with my horse in the bushes. When I tried to get one foot in the stirrup, I jumped around on the other wherever he decided to turn. Finally, I was overcome with anger, and I yanked at the reins as hard as I could, and screamed at him in such an awful voice. The horse calmed down, and I hastened to mount him.

Good God! what strange occupations my fate has set me! That I should scream in such a wild voice that even a mad horse quieted down!... What would my old girl-friends say, if they had heard me shriek so absurdly? I was angry with myself because of my necessary feat: for the injury done the delicacy of the female organ by my heroic cry!

The beauty of the site and Uragan's quick gallop cheered me again. I stopped being annoyed, and found the means by which I had managed to quiet my unruly horse almost funny, and at the same time necessary. But Uragan, it seems, wanted to pay me back for his momentary fear, or perhaps, he sensed that our quarters were near, but he began to snort, twisting his head, and galloped headlong. I was a bit afraid, knowing that when he gets excited, he doesn't understand a thing and gallops in any direction. My hasty and unsuccessful attempts to restrain him were useless. I began to lose my presence of mind. It is surprising how horses can so quickly understand that, and immediately take advantage of it! Uragan flew off like an arrow.

God saved me, truly He did! The furious animal flew off with me where there was no path! At first I was very frightened; but the impossibility of restraining the horse, or of jumping off, quickly brought me to my senses. I tried to keep my balance and hold myself firmly in the stirrups.

In misfortune, just as in illness, there is a turning point: when I saw far ahead of me a black strip crossing my path, I froze with fear and wanted to throw myself from my horse. A minute's hesitation left me no time to carry out my fatal intention. The horse galloped toward the river, swirling between steep banks, and raced straight toward it. I don't remember how I flew with him, or how I stayed in the saddle, but that put an end to Uragan's fury. The stream was no more than three sazhens wide. The now tamed horse swam across it at an angle, burst out on the steep bank with incredible effort, and set off at a walk, obeying the slightest movement of the reins. When he had come out again on a straight road, although he was clearly shaking with impatience to race on to his comrades, he continued at a walk, and when I allowed him to go at a gallop, he galloped obediently at an even pace all the way to our quarters.

"And where have you been travelling, pray?" the captain asked sarcastically. "I seem to remember that I ordered you to wait for the men who were left behind, and that you were to arrive at the squadron together.

What kept you? The men have been here a long time already."

"I stood on the same spot for a long time, Captain. You didn't give me a guide with a flare; and the night, as you know, was as dark as a cellar; so I dared not move anywhere for fear of falling in the ditch."

"Don't tell me you stood there like a bronze statue in the the very place I left you?"

"For a few minutes I did; but of course, I finally tried to find the road back to the baron's village, if my horse hadn't gone mad when something frightened him. Then I was occupied just with him, and..."

"And couldn't handle him," the captain interrupted.

With that inappropriate and unseemly reproach, my irritation was aroused. I took my helmet in my hands to leave, and answered dryly and without looking at the captain, "You are mistaken! I didn't want to handle him. It was neither the time nor the place."

However much I wanted to tell my comrades of the events of that stormy night, I refrained. What would it have served? To them, everything seems either too commonplace, or completely unbelievable. For example, they would not have believed the wolves. They would say that it was dogs, which might indeed be true. And my brave leap into the river is a thing so commonplace that they would have found it funny that I told about it as if it were some marvel. After all, they don't understand that everything that is commonplace for them is very unusual for me.

Prague

We stopped here until nightfall. The city authorities found some difficulty allowing our corps to march through the city. Finally they did, and we marched through hastily, without stopping a minute; they saw to that. However, Ilinsky, Ruzi and I stayed behind in a tavern to have a quick supper, and later set off at a gallop to overtake our squadron, thundering along the stone pavement. The Germans stood aside in fear, and after us there were constant cries of "Schwerenot." The winter here is unusually cold. The Germans ascribe this to the Russian invasion and, huddling by the hearth, say that if they had known in advance of the arrival of the uninvited guests, they would have prepared more peat.

Harburg

Yesterday we made an unsuccessful attempt to upset the tranquility of Harburg. At midnight, with the Horse-Chasseur Regiment, we advanced to the walls of this fortress, and settled in to wait for dawn, when we would bombard it with cannon. My platoon and I were detailed to cover two siege artillery. We were all under the command of one of the heads of the

Hanseatic League forces. Dawn broke. We began to fire shells at the fortress, and did so for about two hours without interruption. Two or three houses had caught fire, but we were not vouchsafed an answer. The Harburg garrison had apparently vanished from the face of the earth. They did not fire a single shot. And I simply cannot understand the purpose of our rising. I thought that there would be an assault; but all of our alarm ended with our firing some dozen shells at Harburg and going back to our quarters. The expedition hurt only me. Waiting for dawn, I lay down next to an artillery piece on some wet sand. And it is spring now, so I think that from the dampness rising from the earth, I caught a head cold and was so badly sick for a whole week that people didn't recognize me, as if I had been suffering constantly for three years.

Hamburg

There is nothing more ridiculous than our rounds of the sentry posts. The passwords, replies, and calls are so distorted by our soldiers, especially the infantry recruits, that if you tried you could not think up cries as absurd as they do, all by themselves—because none of it is Russian. And why should Russian sentries use German cities as pass-words? And what is more, the recruit asks the password in the following manner: "Who goes there? Answer! Or you're dead!" (But that is an empty threat: he is afraid to aim for fear that his rifle might fire.) After this, without waiting for an answer, he yells at the top of his lungs: "Give the password! The password is the city of ***," and then he'll say something absurd. He asks and answers himself, and the officer approaching can only try to keep from laughing. However, there's a bright side to everything. If the slow-witted soldier, whom you simply cannot convince that he is supposed to ask the password, not give it, were to pronounce it properly, the enemy sentries, who were quite close, might hear and employ it to our disadvantage. But since they can only hear things they can neither understand, nor pronounce, they all stay peacefully at their posts.

Last night our colonel almost broke his neck; and while the event was not funny in the least, it became such an amusing situation that the colonel laughed himself when he related it. He wanted to check the readiness of his sentries, and set off to review them alone. He rode about for some time and did not see the guards in the positions where they should have been. The colonel was terribly annoyed at the sloppiness of the sentry officers. He thought that the guards had not been posted at all, but he was relieved of his delusion in a very funny manner, which almost killed him. The guards were all at their posts; but because the night was so black, when they heard a man riding by, instead of hailing him, they held their breath. One of them, to our colonel's misfortune, had fallen asleep by a stump. He awoke from the snorting of his horse, jumped up, and yelled wildly from fear: "Give the password! The word is Gavrilo!" That is, Archangel Gabriel. The horse rushed to one side and fell in a ditch with its rider. By God's mercy, the colonel escaped with a slight bruise.

1814

News of the taking of Paris forced Davout to surrender. The French left Hamburg, and military actions ceased. We are now the peaceable guests of the King of Denmark. Taking advantage of this circumstance, I want to ride round beautiful Holstein, alone, in a cabriolet, with my trusty horse harnessed to it.

Ilinsky volunteered to be my travelling companion. We took a week's leave and first to Pinneberg. Wishing to walk a bit along the beautiful shady allee that leads from Uetersen to Pinneberg, we both got out of our cabriolet. I wound the reins around a brass ring on the front of the cabriolet, and counting on the meekness of my old horse, I let him walk down the road alone. We didn't think that the horse, feeling how light the carriage was, would quicken its pace; but finally I saw that he had gone off far ahead. I ran off to stop him, but this only made the horse start running too, faster and faster, at a gallop, and finally as hard as he could. Ilinsky, mustering all his strength, almost overtook him and grabbed him by the shaft. But the horse knocked him to the ground, ran a wheel over his chest, and galloped off at full tilt toward Pinneberg. Ilinsky jumped up, and rubbing his chest with his hand, ran off anyway after the horse, now disappearing from sight. I think this was because in the front of the cabriolet was our suitcase, with the silver fittings for our uniforms and five hundred rubles in gold. Neither of us wanted to lose all that. However, there was no way he could run all the way to Pinneberg. Nevertheless, Ilinsky and the horse disappeared from view. I too set off at my fastest pace, and found my comrade and the horse right at the gates of Pinneberg. They were surrounded by a crowd of Germans, but the suitcase was already gone.

"What are we to do now?" Ilinsky asked me.

"Their authorities are right here," I said. "You speak German well. Go tell them exactly what sorts of things we had in our suitcase; they can probably find them."

Ilinsky set off. I got into the cabriolet and rode off to find lodging, where I left my horse in the care of the German workman, and then set off to the town mayor's offices. Ilinsky was already there. The German for some reason did not want to search out our lost things. He said that it was simply impossible: "Your horse ran through the woods alone. How are we to know what happened to your goods?" Ilinsky, irritated at such indifference to our misfortune, said that if this had happened in Petersburg, our lost things would be found in one day, even if several thousand people were mixed up in it; and that there was no police on earth that could compare to the Russian police in efficiency, perspicacity, and shrewd use of methods for searching out and discovering even the most subtle of petty crimes. These words drove the even-tempered German mad. He hastily left the room, his face flushed, his eyes glaring, boiling with vexation. Seeing no need to await his return, we went off to our quarters.

We had no means to ride further. We had lost all our money, our things, and even our uniforms. We were both just in our frock coats. That day we had no tea, no supper; and in the morning, a sad lot awaited us—to have no coffee, no breakfast, and ride thirty versts back on empty stomachs. I had two marks left, but we had to use them for the horse. Ilinsky found this unfair, and strongly objected to what he called my partiality to a stubborn animal. "That worthless beast is lucky the money is in your pocket. If it were in mine, pardon me, Alexandrov, your stupid donkey would have to fast all the way back to Uetersen."

"Well, now we are going to fast, my dear friend," I answered. "And what are you complaining about? Pretend that you are on bivouac, in the field, that it's war time, that it's 1812, that our rations and provisions were thrown in the water, that the Cossacks stole the wine, meat and bread from our orderlies, or that those knaves ate it themselves and blamed it on the Cossacks. In short, pretend you're in some such situation and you'll feel better."

"Thanks very much! Console yourself with all of that by yourself," said the hungry Ilinsky angrily, and disappeared into the cupboard. I don't know what else to call these ingenious Germans' beds. They're just like cupboards. You open a double door to find a square bin, filled with feather-beds and pillows, with no blankets. If you want to sleep there, you must crawl into the middle of all that, and you're all set. Seeing that Ilinsky had gone into the cupboard, not to come out until morning, I went off to our hostess to persuade her to light me a candle for nothing. She granted my request, stroking my cheek, and calling me a fine young man, I don't know why. I wrote about two pages, and finally lay down myself on the floor, after I had dragged out all the feather-beds and pillows that were in the other cupboard.

At three o'clock in the morning, I stroked and kissed my good horse, who paid no attention, and continued eating his oats, which I had purchased with my last two marks. Ilinsky was asleep. The workman greased the wheels of our cabriolet, and the hostess asked me from the window, *"Herr Offizier, wollen Sie Kaffee?"* All of these actions were interrupted by the hasty arrival of the irate mayor.

"Where is your comrade?" he asked curtly. He had our suitcase in his hands. Overjoyed to see our treasure once again, when we had nearly lost it, I ran off to awaken my cohort.

"Get up, Ilinsky!" I cried, going up to the doors of his cupboard to open them.

"Leave me alone, for God's sake. Quit joking around," Ilinsky grumbled indistinctly. "Let me get some sleep."

"I'm not joking, Vasily! The mayor of Pinneburg is here with our suitcase."

"Well, then take it."

"That won't be so easy to do. He obviously wants to give it to you personally and, as far as I can tell, with a splendid retort to your expression of doubt yesterday in the competence of their police."

"Well, then at least ask him, brother, into our hostess's chamber, while I get up." In five minutes, Ilinsky came in where we were waiting.

The mayor, silent until then, jumped up from his place and went up to Ilinsky: "Here are your things, to the very last one, and all the money, the very same coin you had. Do not think that our police are inferior to your Petersburg police in any way. Here are your things, and here is the thief," he said, pointing triumphantly through the window to an eighteen-year-old youth who was standing outside. "He saw your horse near Pinneberg yesterday, grabbed the suitcase from the cabriolet, and threw it in a ditch behind some bushes, and led the horse off to the city. Now are you satisfied? We'll hang the thief this instant if you like."

With this terrible proposition, made with true German pomposity, Ilinsky paled. I began to tremble, and my desire to laugh at the amusing ire of the Pinneberger turned into a painful feeling of horror and pity. "Oh, what are you talking about," we both cried at once. "How could we want that? No, no! For God's sake, let him go..."

"I see that I was mistaken regarding your police. Please excuse my ignorance," Ilinsky added in a most courteous tone. The German, reassured, let the unfortunate boy go. He had been standing at our window, his whole body shaking and white as a sheet. Hearing that he had been pardoned, he clasped his hands in such an expression of joy, and so humbly knelt at our window, that I was touched to the depths of my soul, and even the mayor of Pinneberg sighed heavily. Finally, he wished us a happy journey through Holstein and went out.

Now we boldly ordered coffee, cream, sweets, and some cold game for the road.

"Oh, you have such a positive outlook, Alexandrov!" Ilinsky said to me when we got in our cabriolet. "You didn't grieve at all over the loss of our property."

"Why use that grand word *property*, Ilinsky? Are a uniform, a cartridge pouch, and forty crowns property?"

"But you don't have anything else."

"No, so what? But I found your sorrow very funny."

"Why?"

"Because you can't seem to get used to being without money. As soon as a crown or two falls into your hands, you bet it on a card and lose it."

"Sometimes I win."

"Never! At least I've never seen you winning. You're as inexpert at gambling as I am unlucky."

"That's not true! You're no judge of my skill. You haven't the vaguest notion of sport," said Ilinsky with irritation, and he was silent the rest of the way.

Over dinner we were reconciled. We spent the night at Itzehoe, and the next day set off to Glückstadt. The mournful view of the Elbe, which here flows level with swampy banks, the flocks of ravens with their ominous cry, filled us with boredom and sorrow. We hastened to leave the place, and turned off the highway and rode on country roads. At one inn, a new one it seemed to us, we were pleasantly surprised by our kind reception, and good fare. The exterior of this house promised no more than potatoes for dinner and straw for a bed, and when we went in, we ordered dinner as one usually does in such taverns, without paying any attention to the host. But the fine tablecloth, the porcelain dishes, the silver spoons and saltcellars, and the crystal glasses attracted our attention, and with it our surprise. That was not all: as he brought our food to table, our host asked us to sit down, and sat down with us. Ilinsky, who could not abide any sort of familiarity, asked me, "What is the meaning of this? Why has this peasant sat down with us?"

"For God's sake, be quiet," I answered. "Perhaps this will be something from *A Thousand and One Nights*. Who knows what our host may turn out to be?" In the course of this conversation, the host's brother arrived, and likewise sat at the table. I didn't dare say a thing. Ilinsky's irritated look, and the merriment of both the peasants amused me in the extreme. So as not to offend our genial hosts with inappropriate laughter, I tried not to look at Ilinsky. After dinner, we were served coffee in a silver coffee pot, on a splendid tray, cream in a silver pot of outstanding workmanship, with a little spoon, fashioned like a soup ladle, also of silver, heavily gilded on the inside. All of this was brought to the table. Both our hosts invited us to pour ourselves as much coffee as we pleased, and sat down to drink it with us.

"What is the meaning of this?" Ilinsky repeated. "A simple tavern, bare walls, wooden chairs, the people simply dressed—and a wonderful dinner, excellent coffee, porcelain, silver, gilt, the appearance of considerable wealth, taste, yet with country simplicity! What do you think, Alexandrov? What do you make of it?"

"I don't know, but I do think that we can't pay them any money here."

"Why not? I thought just the opposite, that we'd have to pay ten times as much here as in some other place."

We left to stroll in the beautiful surroundings, such as one can only find on such even, flat country as in Holstein. When we returned, I asked Ilinsky to let me take care of everything myself, ordering and paying up, saying that I was overcome with fear, and I expected some sort of marvelous happening. We were served tea with the same kindness, geniality, rich service and taste. Finally, we had to go. Our horse had been superbly groomed, the cabriolet swept out, and our host's brother held our horse by the reins at the porch. I saw Ilinsky jingling two marks in his hand.

"What are you planning to do? You aren't really planning to pay for such pains, such kindness, and fare equal to all the earthly delights, with two marks. Be so good as not to pay anything. Believe me, they won't take it."

"We'll see about that," answered Ilinsky. And with these words, he gave our host the two marks, asking if that was sufficient.

"We have nothing for sale. This is not a tavern," answered our host quietly.

Ilinsky was a bit confused. He put away his marks, and said in softer tones, "But you spent so much on us!"

"On you? Not at all! I am very pleased that you stopped by, but we simply shared what we always have in our family."

"We took you for peasants," said Ilinsky, overcome with curiosity and anticipation of some unusual revelation; but he was immediately brought back to earth.

"And you were not mistaken, we are peasants!..." Finally, after several questions and answers, we learned that these kind people had received an inheritance from a distant relative of theirs, a wealthy Hamburg merchant; that they had built themselves this house less than half a year ago; that others had often made the same mistake we had; and that it was not the first time their house had been mistaken for a tavern.

"And do you entertain everyone cordially, without relieving them of their delusion?"

"No, you're the first!"

"But why?"

"You are Russian officers. Our King ordered us to treat the Russians well."

"But, dear people, Russian officers would like it better if you would not let them think that they were in a tavern quite so long. We ordered everything just as if we were going to pay for it."

"You might have guessed that you would not have to pay, since we dined with you..." At these words, Ilinsky blushed, and neither of us said anything more, but bowed to our kind host and left.

It is late autumn. The dark nights, the mud, the drizzle, and the cold wind force us to gather at the hearths of one or another of our comrades from the regiment. Some of them are outstanding musicians. To the charming sound of their flutes and their guitars, our evenings fly past, quickly and merrily.

The Return March to Russia

There was not one of us who would have happily left Holstein. We all say farewell with deep regret to this beautiful country and its genial inhabitants. We are ordered back to Russia. Holstein, hospitable land, beautiful country! I shall never forget your orchards and flower-gardens, your light, cool halls, the honesty and geniality of your inhabitants! Oh, the time I spent in that flowering garden was one of the happiest of my life!..

I reported to Lopatin to tell him that the regiment was ready to move out. The colonel stood deep in thought before the mirror combing his hair, apparently without noticing what he was doing. "Tell the regiment to march. I will stay here for half an hour," he said, sighing heavily.

"Why did you sigh, colonel? Aren't you glad to be going back to the motherland?" I asked.

Instead of answering the colonel sighed again. As I left his office, I caught sight of a minor baroness, one of our colonel's hostesses—a beautiful girl of twenty-four—all in tears. Now I understand why the colonel doesn't want to leave.... Yes! In a situation like that, as for the motherland—good luck to it!

And so, unwillingly and sorrowfully we left Holstein, and of course probably for good. They liked us there, although not all of us—that's true; but where would they like everyone?.. They liked us in many respects: as allies, as trustworthy defenders, as Russians, as fine guests, and finally, as gallant heroes. The latter is confirmed by the fact that three or four Amazons are following behind our squadron! They are all quite certain of marrying the men that they follow. But disappointment is closer than they think. One of them is being taken by Pel***, a forty-year-old, married madcap. He would have us all believe that his Phillida is following him because of the power of her irresistable passion for him! We listen, barely refraining from laughter. An irresistable passion for Pel***, for a balding scarecrow, ridiculous and stupid!.. Could it be some sort of enchantment? Anything in the world is better-looking than his frog eyes!

What sort of strange planning is this, to pick the very worst season for a march! It is late fall, muddy, dark, rainy. We have no diversion except the funny scenes between our loving couples. Last evening, Tornezi told us that he had been at Pel***'s. The object of his love was sitting there, all dressed in black and deep in thought. Pel*** looked at her with sympathy, which in him is extremely funny and inappropriate. "That's what love can do to you," he said with a sigh. "She's pining away, grieving, she cannot live without me! The fatal passion of love!.."

Tornezi almost choked, trying to keep from laughing. "But you are with her, why should she grieve?"

"Everyone doubts my love for her. She does not expect to keep me at her side forever."

"That stands to reason—you're married. I don't understand why you have brought her."

"What was I to do? She wanted to drown herself!"

"I really don't know where she was going to drown herself," Tornezi said to me. "I don't think there were any rivers in Uetersen."

Pel*** continued this nonsense for some time. But listen to the finale to the episode, and how Pel*** came to learn of it and witness it. I went out to order my horse brought to me. When I returned, I met the pensive beauty in the vestibule. She threw herself into my arms, pressed her face to mine, and burst into tears. *"Cher officier! sauvez-moi de ce misérable! Je le deteste! Je ne l'ai jamais aimée; il m'a trompé!"* She had no time to speak further. Pel*** opened the door to his room. When he saw us together, he was not bothered in the least—so confident was he in the power of his beauty and merit! The damned fool!

Poznan

Here fate appointed that all amorous ties be dissolved. I learned of this by chance. I had to go to the regimental office to see Ya***, who now held the post of adjutant, since our poor Tyzin could no longer follow the regiment, much less hold the post himself—he stayed behind in some little German town with his young, grieving wife. Ya***'s quarters consisted of four rooms. Two were for the office, and in the other two he lived with his little page, whom we all called "the beautiful baron." When I learned that the adjutant was not in, I went to his rooms to see the baron. But when I opened the door, I stopped in perplexity, unsure whether to walk in or turn back. A young lady paced the hall in great sorrow. She was crying and wringing her hands. I glanced around the room, and when I did not see the beautiful baron, I looked more carefully at the weeping beauty, and recognized Ya***'s page.

"O Dieu! à quoi bon cette metamorphose, et de quoi vous pleurez si amèrement?.."

She answered me, in German, that she was very unhappy; that Ya*** was sending her back to Hamburg; and that now, she didn't know how she could show herself in her own country. Expressing my sincere sympathy for her, I left. The next day, on the march, I did not see a single one of our Amazons behind the squadron, and asked Tornezi what fate befell them. "The usual one, the inevitable," he answered. "They were tired of them, and sent them away."

Usually, singers ride at the head of the squadron and sing almost the whole day's march. I can't imagine that it was great fun for them. It would get boring to sing all day, even if you did it by choice, and on orders all the more so. Today, I witnessed an amusing way of getting them to want to sing.—Verusha, a non-com, and the lead-singer, is the most inept of lead-singers. He starts every song singing through his nose in a voice that is more disgusting than any I have ever heard. Tornezi and I always gallop off when we hear it. This time he was in low spirits for some reason—perhaps he was sick—and he sang badly as usual, but contrary to his custom, quietly. Rzhensnitsky noted: "Well, well, what is the meaning of this sickly voice? Sing like you are supposed to!" Verusha continued to sing the same way. "All right, then I'll give you some added courage!" And with that, he started to beat in time to the music with his whip on Verusha's back as he sang....

I saw this tragi-comedy from a distance, galloped up to Rzhensnitsky, and grabbed him by the hand. "Please, enough, Captain! What are you thinking of? Will songs come to mind with a whip on his back?..." I have some power on Rzhensnitsky's mind. He listened to me, stopped encouraging Verusha with his whip, and let him drone on as he pleased.

Vitebsk

We are now once again on our native soil! This has absolutely no effect on me—I cannot forget Holstein! We were there as guests; and for some reason I like being a guest better than a local.

Quarters for our regiment were assigned in the town of Yanovichi, the muddiest town on earth. Here I found my brother. He had been made an officer, and at his request, transferred to our own Lithuanian Regiment. I really don't understand why neither of us ever has any money. Father sends it to him, and the Sovereign to me, and we are constantly penniless! My brother tells me that if we were obliged to march out of Yanovichi, the Jews would grab onto his horse's tail. He could not have explained more clearly how much he owed them.

"What are we to do, Vasily! My only advantage is that I am not in debt myself; but I still don't have any money."

"You will have. The Sovereign will send you some."

"And you have our father. And he will give you his last kopeck."

"Well, that's the truth. Should I really write to Father?"

"Haven't you already?"

"No!"

"Write him, write with the next post."

Waiting until spring comes, we are both living at headquarters, because there is absolutely nothing to do in the squadrons. My brother and I obtained some incomprehensible sort of tea—both because of its low price, and its quality. I paid two rubles silver for it, and no matter how much water we pour into the teapot, the tea is always just as strong. Not bothering to discover the reason for this unusual phenomenon, we drink it with great pleasure.

Yanovichi

The time has come for exercises, for foot and cavalry drills; spring has come. At the insistence of the squadron commander, I am obliged to go to the squadron.

Amusing news! K*** is in love! He came to Yanovichi to take me with him to the squadron. On the way he related how he met a certain lady landowner, R****, and that the young Miss R****, her daughter, could not be driven from his mind. The result is that he sleeps constantly from love and grief. He confirmed the truth of his words in action—he immediately fell asleep. I found all of this extremely amusing, but since I was by myself, it seemed somehow inappropriate to laugh, and I calmly viewed the charms of Nature, blooming once again. However, it was apparent that K*** really was in love; as soon as we arrived at the squadron, he awoke as if by instinct. He immediately sent for the sergeant-major, hurriedly gave him his orders, and ordered other horses harnessed.

"Why don't you come with me, Alexandrov? I'll introduce you."

"To whom, Major?"

"To my neighbors."

"To your R****, I suppose?"

"Of course!"

"Let's go. I will be very happy to see the major's future lady."

"It's all but arranged, my dear sir! For some reason, I think of her day and night."

"Well, then let's go faster."

On the road, I thought that there would be no end to K***'s talk of the beauty, virtues, talents, and all conceivable physical and spiritual charms of the divine Miss R****; but I was pleasantly disappointed in my fears. K*** got in the britska, did not even say, "Be off, and quick about it!" and rode as if he were going, not to see a sweet, beautiful, kind young lady, but to some drill or review. He started discussing the service, horses, sentries, uhlans, pennants—in short, everything, both good and bad, but not the thing, it seems to me, that should have occupied his thoughts and heart.

What a strange man! We had talked about half an hour, as if on order, all about our daily life on the line, when he finally sighed, and said, "It's still far!" He wrapped his head in his greatcoat, leaned in the corner of the britska, and fell asleep. I was very glad. A fine man and a meticulous officer, K*** did not have the education, nor the knowledge, nor even the sort of mind, that make fellowship and conversation pleasant. I was happy to be free to think of what I wanted and look at what I wanted.

Everything is funny about this strange suitor! How can he wake up exactly when he must? Just as we drove up, he opened his eyes as if he had not been asleep for one minute. We got out of our carriage. Going up the steps, I told K***, that he must present me to the ladies.

"Don't worry, I can manage that!" His funny answer made me fear some strange sort of recommendation. But everything turned out much better than I thought. K*** said simply, pointing to me, "An officer in my squadron, Alexandrov."

The one who had captured the officer's heart was a young lady of eighteen, pale, light-haired, tall, svelte, with long blond hair, big dark-grey eyes, a large mouth, white teeth, and the bearing of a brave grenadier. I liked this all very much! If I were K***, I would have chosen her as my life mate too, and loved her as much as he does—ride to her in no hurry, sleep all the way, and wake up at the doorway! I met her right away, and made friends with her. That was over in half an hour. But what amazed me, astounded and charmed me, was her mother, a most beautiful woman! a real Venus, if only Venus could look as if she were forty! In that fascinating face were gathered all the most beautiful of the charms: sparkling black eyes, thin black brows, coral lips, a skin color that defies any description! I looked at her, and could not stop looking. Finally, unable to speak other than I think, I told her directly that I cannot take my eyes off her face, and that I cannot imagine what sort of ravishing creature she must have been in her youth!

"Yes, young man, you are not mistaken—I was a Venus. There was no other name for me, nor comparison to be made! Yes, I was a beauty in the full sense of the word!"

Despite the fact that she was saying this about herself, I thought her very modest. She said "was a beauty," but she is now, this minute, an exceptional beauty! Is it possible that she does not see that?

K*** has proposed to R***. The wedding will be in a week. I am very glad. The young lady is rather well-educated, cheerful, and free and spontaneous in her conduct. I hope that it will be quite merry for me in their home, once she becomes the lady of our regiment. Oh, how I hate those inaccessible she-bears who wish to maintain some sort of high tone, but don't notice that they look more like puffed up merchants' wives than fine ladies. Stupid women!

Yesterday we were invited to a ball. I went with K***. Our bridegroom fell asleep, true to his former habit; and since we had to drive about ten versts, I had sufficient time to talk to the young major's wife. We recounted anecdotes to each other, funny stories, and laughed, with no fear of waking her happy husband. Finally, our conversation took a different tone—we spoke of the heart, of love, of inexpressible feelings, of fidelity, happiness, unhappiness, the mind, and God knows what all we spoke about. I remarked in my travelling companion a turn of thought that made me surprised that she had married K***. I asked her about it.

"I am poor," she answered, "and as you see, no beauty. My heart was free. Mama found K*** a suitable match for me, and I saw no great difficulty in fulfilling her wishes."

"All right, but do you love him?"

"I do," she said, after a moment's silence. "I love him, but of course, with no passion, no fire. I love him as a good husband and a good man. He has an excellent disposition. All of his failings are redeemed by his good heart."

Our military ball was just like all other balls—very amusing in fact, and very boring if described.

Now I must describe something I did of which I have been ashamed now for several days, from morning to night. Let this sort of confession serve as my punishment.

Wishing to walk in the beautiful groves near Polotsk, I requested a week's leave, and with R*** as my companion, I set off to his father's estate. We were given horses that were half-dead, but quite willing to serve in this function. We rode in a simple cart, on a muddy road, and were either dragged or jolted along, since that was the kind of horses we had. We had no adventures on the way, if you don't count the following. Our yawning coachman, driving past a crowd of peasants, grazed one of them with his shaft, knocked him down and ran over him. The outraged peasants came after us with cudgels a half-verst long, calling us, *us* specifically and not our coachman, dogs and terrors.

Finally we came to the river, on the other side of which was R***'s estate. While they were preparing the ferry, my comrade went into a cabin to smoke his pipe, while I stayed on the shore to watch the sunset. Then an old man of about ninety came up to me, I thought to beg. At the sight of his white hair, bent body, shaking hands, fading eyes, his terrible skinniness and ancient rags, I was completely overcome with sympathy, the deepest sympathy! But how this heavenly feeling could combine with a devilish one, I swear I do not understand! I took out my purse to give the poor man some considerable help. I had eight crowns and a banknote for ten rubles. They did not want to take that unhappy banknote at a single post-station, considering it suspect, and I had the shamelessness to give it to the poor old man!

"I don't know, my friend, if they will give you the money they should for it," I said to the happy beggar. "But if they don't, take it to the Reverend Rector, and tell him that I gave you this banknote. Then you'll get ten rubles for it, and the paper will be returned to me. Farewell, my friend!"

I ran down to the ferry. We crossed, and in an hour were beneath the hospitable roof of Pan R***. I spent four days there. I walked through the dark copses, read, had coffee, bathed, and scarcely saw R***'s family, or him either.

"Our guest is a little strange," R*** was informed by his sister. "He goes out to the woods in the morning, and returns for dinner; and then you don't see him again until evening. Does he act that way in the regiment? Is he in his right mind?"

"I don't know. The rector thinks a lot of him."

"Well, the rector's praise doesn't mean much. He has been crazy about him since he found out that he gave ten rubles to old Joseph."

"Why?"

"Here's why: because he'll give to anyone who asks in the name of Christ."

"What! I can't believe that old Joseph begged for alms and his owner permitted it. At his age?"

"Yes, at his age. His owner not only permits it, he orders everyone in his village who can't work, for whatever reason, driven out to this business. It doesn't matter why—old age, weakness, illness, minority, imbecility. Oh, a sizeable detachment spreads out through the neighborhood from his village every morning."

"What a horrible man! But I didn't know that my comrade was so soft-hearted toward the poor."

"Your comrade is an eccentric, and eccentrics all have some sort of peculiarity."

"Do you really consider compassion a peculiarity?"

"Of course, if it's excessive. What's the point of giving ten rubles to one man. Is he so rich?"

"I don't think so. But then, I don't know him well yet."

I overheard this conversation between brother and sister by accident. I returned an hour earlier than usual from my walk, and finding no great pleasure in talking with the elder R*** and his high-minded daughter, I took a book out to the summer house at the bottom of the garden. The young R***s walked to the same spot and sat not five paces from me on a wooden bench. The obliging Miss R*** spoke about me a bit more, constantly referring to me as an eccentric and the rector's favorite. Finally her brother lost patience.

"Oh, stop it, would you please. I'm tired of you and your talk of him! I wanted to talk with you about how to convince father to give me some money. Now our stepmother is no longer alive, there's no one to interfere.

"No, there is."

"For example? Will you dissuade him?"

"How can you say that? I love you, and though I know that any money that falls into your hands immediately goes for gambling, I would be ready to give you my portion, if only I had it under my own control. No, dear Adolph! I won't stop father from giving you money. But his own decision is this—a firm, unalterable determination not to give you a single kopeck."

I heard nothing more, but when I went to the door of the summer house, I saw brother and sister running toward the house. Apparently the last words of Miss R*** drove her brother into a fury. He raced off to his father, and she after him. I hastened in the same direction. It is surprising what powers of self-control the old R*** had. I found them all in the hall. The young lady was pale and trembling. Her brother was sitting on the window ledge, convulsively gripping the back of an armchair, and trying in vain to adopt a calm expression. His eyes burned, his lips quivered. But the old man greeted me very kindly, and quietly asked, in jest, "Do you intend to become a hermit in my woods? I would like to know ahead of time, so I can prepare a nice cave for you, with moss, dry leaves, and everything necessary for a recluse."

I don't know how things ended between father and son, but they parted amicably. The slightly unbalanced Adolph drove his sister to extreme distraction, and me simply to distraction, with his assertions that she and I are very much alike, and that his sister is like a living portrait of him. So, we all three look alike! How flattering! The young R*** looks just like the devil.

Finally, we perched up on our cart and set off. At the first station, when we had to pay the fare, I took out my purse to get the money, and was very surprised to find that two of the eight crowns were missing. I tried to remember if I hadn't left the purse on the table or the bed when I went out for a walk. But no, apparently, it was always with me. Finally, I remembered, and was very happy. The crowns had probably fallen into the banknote, that was stuffed into the purse with them, folded over three times. I took it out and gave it to the beggar without unfolding it; and so, he received through Divine Providence the help I offered him, but was nearly spoiled by some satanic calculations! But only a monster is capable of giving the poor help whose efficacity he doubts! No, in giving him the banknote, I only thought that they would take it at much less than its value, and that they wouldn't take it at the stations because they saw that I had gold, and that the Poles only take coins.

Vitebsk

I am living at Commissioner S***'s. My leave is not up and I spend the time here more merrily than with the squadron. His Royal Highness the Prince of Württemberg loves to have the army officers gather at his lodgings in the evenings. I go there too. We dance, play various games; and the Prince himself occasionally takes part in our amusements.

A Duel

Today at ten in the morning R*** came to me and said that he had quarreled with Prince K***, and that the Prince had called him a scoundrel. "Congratulations! What did you do?"

"Nothing! I said that he was a villain, but apparently he didn't hear that."

"That's wonderful! And you came here to boast that you had been called a scoundrel. This is the first time in my life I have heard that someone who called an honorable person by such a name escaped without a slap in the face." While saying this we were both standing by an open window, and I had no sooner finished than, to make matters worse, Prince K*** walked past. R*** called to him. I guess Prince K*** took R***'s voice for mine, because he bowed politely, immediately approached me, and to my great astonishment, and that of my landlord and two other officers, was met at the door by R*** with the question "Did you call me a scoundrel?" and a quick slap in the face!! S*** asked us all to leave his house. "You want to squabble? Well, not here!" We all went out of town. It goes without saying that a duel was unavoidable, but what a duel! ... I had never even imagined such a comic one as I now saw. It began with an agreement not to wound each other in the head and to fight until the first person was wounded. R*** was bothered about where to find a second and a sharp sabre. I immediately offered to be his second and handed over my sabre, knowing for sure that nothing really would happen except some laughs. Finally the two madcaps started to fight. For the life of me I couldn't keep a straight face. From the start to the finish of this caricature of a duel I couldn't keep from laughing. In order to keep the agreement about no wounds to the head, and obviously deathly afraid of their own sabres, both antagonists were bending almost to the ground, each sticking out his hand with the sabre as far forward as possible and waving it right and left without purpose. Moreover, in order not to have to see the flash of steel, they were looking away. And as far as I could tell they couldn't see anything anyhow, because both were bent over double. As a result of these measures and the need to respect the first condition of the duel, there did actually occur a violation of that condition. R***, not seeing where and how he was waving his sabre, hit the Prince with it along the ear and cut it somewhat. The opponents were very happy to cease their hostile actions. However the Prince decided to make a fuss about why his ear had been cut despite the agreement. But I calmed him down, explaining that there was no way to correct this error other than to be wounded again. The eccentrics went to a tavern, and I went back to S***.

"Well, what happened?" I explained. "You're a crazy man, Alexandrov! Why did you want to incite R***? It would never have occurred to him to challenge someone to a duel and even less to give someone a slap in the face." (It really hadn't occurred to me that I had incited him to an illegal act, and only now I see that S*** was correct.) Old S*** started to laugh, remembering the scene at the door.

We had to part with the halls of the Prince of Württemburg. We had to leave Vitebsk and return to dirty Yanovichi. The squadron commanders are stridently ordering officers to their stations. There is nothing we can do; we travel tomorrow.

Yanovichi

The mud here exceeds all the mud on earth. You can't make your way any further than across the square to visit a fellow soldier except on horseback. True, one could go on foot, but then one would have to press against the houses of the Jews, staying atop the earthen mounds as close as possible to the walls, windows and doors, from which the passerby is assailed with steam and odors of all sorts, as, for example, of vodka, beer, goose grease, goat's milk, mutton, and so forth. You can be sure of a cold in the head after the conclusion of this nasty detour.

Vitebsk

On the present tour here old S***, frightened by the violent scene, did not permit me to lodge with him but took quarters for me in the home of a young and pretty wife of a merchant. As soon as I had made myself at home there, Kherov, a close friend of my brother's, came to see me. "Hello, Alexandrov! Have you been here long?"

"Just arrived!"

"And your brother?"

"He's with the squadron."

"Where are you dining, at the Prince's?"

"I don't know. I'll present myself to the Prince, and, if he invites me, then I'll dine with him."

"Look at these wonderful spurs I bought for myself."

"Are they silver?"

"Yes!" We both were standing at the table, and I leaned on it in order to look more closely at the spurs. At that moment Kherov lightly stepped on my foot. I looked around, and right next to me was standing the landlady. "Gentlemen, are you not ashamed to say such words in a house where only women reside?"

That's original! I assured the landlady that our words could be spoken in the presence of angels, let alone in the presence of women. "No, no! You will not convince me, I heard!"

"Impossible, you misunderstood, dear little landlady."

"I request that you do not call me dear and that you conduct yourself more properly in my house." Having said this, she grandly went off to her own part of the house, leaving us to think what we liked about her departure. Kherov took his shako in order to leave, but, having accidently looked into my purse and seeing some gold in it, he stopped. "Your brother is in debt to me, Alexandrov, won't you pay up for him?"

"Of course! How much does he owe?"

"Two chervontsi."

"Here you are."

"What a fine young fellow you are, Alexandrov! For that I am going to give you my silver spurs." Kherov left, and I, leaving orders to attach my new spurs to my boots, set off to present myself to the Prince.

I returned to my quarters an hour after midnight. My bed was arranged in a small room on the floor. Everything was already quiet in the house, and a light was shining only in the landlady's chamber. Assuming that I was completely alone and in complete charge of my room, I undressed without any precautions. I wanted to lock the door, but, as there was no hook, I simply closed it, lay down, and apparently was already sleeping; in any case, I did not hear the door into my room opening. I awakened with the shuffling of someone's feet walking about my room. My first reaction was to cover my head with the blanket. I was afraid that the person wandering about might step on my face with his foot. I don't know why, but I didn't want to ask who it was walking about, and this was for the best. Immediately I heard a voice asking quietly, "Where are you?"

It was the landlady. Impatiently she repeated, "Where are you?" And she continued shuffling her feet on the floor, saying, "Now just where are you? Look and you will see that instead of earrings in my ears there is something bad! In each something bad is hanging. That is for the devil. What's in each of them is for the devil alone!" At this she gave forth some kind of wild laugh, but quietly. I was terrified. No doubt about it, my landlady was mad. She had escaped the supervision of her serving girls, and had come to me, particularly to me. She would soon find me in this room, which was at most a sazhen and half in length and width. What would she do with me! God knows what turn her thoughts might take. Perhaps she might think me one of those demons which she thinks hang in her ears instead of earrings. I had heard that mad people are very strong, and so in case of an attack I didn't expect to exit honorably from the contest. Thinking all of this, I kept my breathing as quiet as possible and was afraid to move. But it was becoming unbearably suffocating to lie with my head covered. I wanted to open the blanket a bit, but in doing this I touched the candlestick. It fell with a noise. The mad woman's joyful cry froze my blood! But happily this cry awakened her servants, and at the same time as she, crying out, threw herself upon me, they ran into the room and seized her, although she had already fallen upon me with outstretched arms.

Nature gave me a strange and disturbing quality. I love, I grow accustomed to, I become bound with all my heart to the quarters where I live, to the horse which I ride, to the dog which I keep out of compassion, even to the duck or the chicken which I buy for my table. Immediately I am sorry to use them for the purpose for which I bought them, and they live with me until they somehow wander off. Knowing my funny weakness, I thought that I would pity even the dirty people of Yanovichi if I had to part with them. However, thank God, no! We are going on campaign, and I am excessively happy that I am leaving this eternal, saturated bog. This is one place on the earthly sphere to which I should never want to return.

Polotsk

This morning while leaving church I caught sight of R***. He was walking quickly and was, it seemed, bothered by something. His stories about his conquests always amuse me, for he is ever the hero of some happening from which he emerges crowned with myrtle or laurel. Hoping to hear something of that sort, I ran after him, caught up to him, came along side and stopped beside him. "What's bothering you, friend? Do you need another second? I am at your service." My appearance apparently made a bad impression on R***. This surprised me. "What's with you? Where are you going so fast?"

"Nowhere! I am simply walking. Greetings from my father. Excuse me brother. I have done you wrong. I lost your money."

"What money?"

"The two chervontsi."

"I don't understand."

"Didn't you get a letter from the rector?"

"No."

"Well, then you really couldn't know anything about this. The poor old man to whom you gave ten rubles found two chervontsi in the bills and thinking, quite wisely, that you did not intend to give him such an amount took them to the rector, who, praising the unusual honesty of the poor man, brought these chervontsi to Father. I was there. The rector told me the story about the chervontsi and asked me to send them to you. I undertook this commission, but, unfortunately, before I found you I met a tempting occasion to try my luck. I put the money on a card and —I am in your debt."

"I am very glad! Who cares how much it was. But why did your father handle it so inhumanely. This money was to stay with him to whom Providence had assigned it. Well, I have philosophized enough. I might say something to you about what you did, but God be with you, there's no time for that now. I'll take braid and epaulettes from your pay. Goodbye!"

The scoundrel ran off, and I went for a walk. I always walk rapidly, and I am completely possessed by the meditations which attract me. Now I was thinking how beautiful nature was. How many joys for man in this world! I was thinking about how many unknowable paths lead us to this or that event in life, and that the best way to preserve spiritual peace is to submissively follow the Lord's Hand, which leads us in these paths, not seeking to know why this is done this way and not some other way. My thoughts were now important, now pious, now sad, now happy, and now extravagantly joyous. The happy proposition that I would have a beautiful house where I might put my old father, that I might decorate its rooms with all conveniences and magnificent luxury, that I would buy him a quiet riding horse, that he would have a carriage, musicians, and a marvelous cook! All this so enthralled me that I was jumping about like a wild goat. Now I see that Perrette* was not an invention. My active movements dispersed my dreams. Once again I saw myself as an uhlan officer, whose only silver was what he was wearing and who had none elsewhere, and for the fulfillment of whose dreams at least a miracle was needed and without that nothing would happen. Having become as before an uhlan lieutenant, I had in this capacity to hasten my return to the squadron in order not to be late for the time designated for the campaign. Sometimes one must answer severely for that!

*Perrette. In Lafontaine's fable the milkmaid Perrette, while speculating on the money she would earn from the milk, lets the pail fall.

1815

There is nothing special about our campaign except the reason for it:
Napoleon somehow disappeared from the island on which the allied
sovereigns had earlier decided to put him with all his plans, plots, dreams,
military abilities and broad genius. Now all this has again broken forth,
and thus again activity all over Europe! Troops are moving, again our
banners wave in the air, the lances gleam, the fine horses leap about. There
the bayonets glisten, there the drum resounds. The threatening sound of the
cavalry trumpets triumphantly arouses the still sleepy dawn. Everywhere
life is bubbling, everywhere there is incessant movement. Here a line of
cuirassiers moves forward proudly, here hussars stream past, there the
uhlans fly by, and there marches our beautiful, orderly, terrible infantry,
the chief defense, the strong bulwark of the fatherland, the invincible
musketeers. Although I love the cavalry intensely, although from the cradle
I am a cavalryman, still every time I see the infantry marching with its
determined and firm step, with fixed bayonets, with the threatening beat of
drums, I feel a kind of awe, of fear, something resembling both of these
feelings which I can't explain. At the sight of a flying formation of hussars
or uhlans the only thing that comes to mind is what fine fellows they are,
what excellent horsemen, how cleverly they slash, woe to the enemy, and
this woe usually consists in more or less dangerous wounds, in captivity,
and that's that. But when columns of infantry with their quick, even and
orderly movement stream against the enemy, here there are no longer any
fine fellows, here it's something else. These are heroes carrying inevitable
death, or going to inevitable death—there is no compromise. The
cavalryman attacks, withdraws, wounds, goes forward, again returns,
sometimes kills, but in all his movements shines some sort of mercy for the
enemy: these are only precursors to death. But a formation of infantry is
death, terrible, inescapable death!

Kovno

We arrived at the border without further adventures and established
our quarters in the areas around this village. Sometimes it is possible to fall
into a deadly situation quite unexpectedly. Yesterday the most amusing
misfortune overtook me. My brother and I dined at the home of a
landowner from Kovno, Pan St—la, a hospitable Pole of the old school.
Despite his sixty years, St—la was still a handsome young man, one of
those few people who live a long time and who age only a day before they
die. He seemed no older than forty. His sister lived with him, along with a
relative, a young lady of about eighteen of unremarkable appearance.
Apparently my brother and I pleased Mr. St—la very much, for he spared

nothing in making it pleasant for us to be with him. After a sumptuous table, all sorts of delicacies, coffee, ices, in a word everything that he might satiate us with, he decided to top off his hospitality with the most magnificent of pleasures, or so he supposed, the singing of his relative: *Zaśpiewajze moja kochana dla tych walecznych żolnierżów* [Sing, my dear, for these gallant soldiers]. The poor girl unsuccessfully insisted that she could not sing because she had caught cold, had a stuffy head and a sore throat. Her despot uncle paid no attention and insistently demanded that she sing this minute. She had to submit and sing before the two young uhlans. She started to sing. It is impossible to forget such a voice. I can't find it within me to describe it or to make any comparison. The young lady was right in trying with all her might to avoid this fatal singing. Hearing the first sounds of her voice, I felt a tremor run through my entire body. I wanted to sink through the floor or to be a hundred versts away from this songstress, but... I was on the couch directly opposite her. Unfortunately the evil one made me look at my brother. He didn't dare raise his eyes and was glowing red. I didn't know where to turn, or what to do to avoid bursting out laughing. Finally seeing the futility of all my efforts, I stopped resisting. As they say, I died laughing. The songstress fell silent. And I, had made myself a fool in her eyes, a total fool. I sought but couldn't find a way to excuse that damned laughter. Fortunately she was singing a Russian song in which mention is made of a butterfly, and the young lady, being Polish, could not pronounce it right and called it *grandmother*. I put the blame on this word and everyone gave the appearance of believing me. No one asked that the singing continue. Having paid so dearly for the hospitality and attentions of Pan St—la, we returned to Vilno, where our headquarters were located and where we shall stay until orders are received.

Squadron K*** is billeted on the estate of Prince Bishop G***. His sister lives here, the last person on earth to resemble what she is, that is Princess G***.

Yesterday I saw our major's young wife for the first time since her marriage. She has become unrecognizable: she has become big and fat. Seeing her, I could not believe my eyes. How in such a short time could she become a real Champion Dobrynya.* I have called her that because K***, who is ecstatic about her size and rotundity, says to everyone who will listen, "My little Sashenka has gotten plump."**

---

*A hero of Kievan times, *trans.*
**The word *to get plump, razdobret'*, suggests Dobrynya, *trans.*

Today at midnight while returning from headquarters I was passing by a field of oats and I saw something white twisting among the ears of grain. I directed my horse there, asking "Who's there?" At this question the white object straightened up and answered loudly, "I am, your honor, an uhlan from the fourth platoon."

"What are you doing here?"

"Laboring, your honor!"

I ordered him to his quarters and to labor no more. These brigands have chosen an amusing way to feed their horses. They take the nosebags into the oats and shake the oats all night. In their language this is called *laboring*.

It has rained incessantly for three days, and only today has the sun peeked out. I led my platoon to a green meadow and flew with them for two hours, that is, we were engaged in platoon training. Following that I let them go home and went for a ride. I dropped in on V***, saw his *divinité*, who is now wearing a woman's skirt and who looks surprisingly like a top. From there I returned to our village. Proceeding to my quarters, I thought I heard some sort of beating, and finally I heard a voice pleading for mercy. Oh, my God! Someone is being beaten at my place. Who dares do this? I set off at a gallop, and when I reached the courtyard, at that moment K*** gave the order to stop, and came up to greet me. "Excuse me, Alexandrov, I am playing the role of master here. Your uhlans stole some five liters of vodka from a Jew and hid it in the hay in your stable. They wouldn't let the Jew come to you, so he came to me, and I found out everything and have done the punishing. Don't be angry, brother, it had to be done this way."

"Why should I be angry? On the contrary, I am very obliged to you." But anger was boiling in my soul. What a damned group these uhlans are! Why should I want to be their superior, if I have to see them beaten before my very eyes?

All our life here abroad consists of smoking tobacco, playing cards, shooting at a target, exercising horses, jumping ditches or over hurdles. But what is the most amusing for me are our evening gatherings at this or that officer's. Of course, there are no ladies at these gatherings. Nonetheless, music resounds, and we dance alone, and everyone, young and old, dances the mazurka, quadrille, écossaise. This greatly amuses me. What pleasure they find in dancing without ladies, particularly the older ones! I always dance the part of the woman.

We are returning to Russia by way of Vilno. The days follow one another uniformly, monotonously. What happened yesterday, will happen tomorrow. It dawns. They play a march, saddle up, lead the horses out, mount, and we are off. And then step by step forward until evening in quarters. Nothing disturbs the tranquillity of our peaceful marches, not only no events but not even rain, wind, storm, nothing wants to awaken our sleepy campaign. We go, we go, we go, and we arrive. That is all.

This morning I was overjoyed. I should be ashamed to feel so and to write about it, but I really was overjoyed hearing someone's tearful wail near the major's quarters. At least there was some reason to spur my horse, to gallop up, to enquire sympathetically, to investigate. I flew at full gallop to K***'s quarters, and catching sight of a scene both funny and pitiful, I hastened to dismount to put a stop to this tragi-comedy. The major was punishing uhlan Bozier (the soldiers call him Bozya). With the first blow of the stick the poor fellow cried out piteously, extending his hands toward heaven. "O mon Dieu! mon Dieu!"

"I'll give it to you, you rascal, m'dieu, m'dieu!" said K***, trying to maintain an angry look, for which, however, his comic face was not suited. However, he was indeed very angry, and the poor Frenchman would have had to cry out ten more times "O mon Dieu! mon Dieu!" and Mr. K*** would have had to repeat the same number of his "I'll give it to you, m'dieu! m'dieu!" had I not requested him to stop.

"Well, you lazybones, thanks to this officer you get three whacks instead of thirty."

"What did he do, Major?"

"He won't obey anyone, my friend. The sergeant ordered him to clean his saddle, his ammunition, and to prepare to take reports to the colonel, but he didn't do any of it."

"But did he understand the sergeant's order?"

"That's a fine thing! Did he understand? He has to understand!"

It would have been useless to explain to K***. I simply asked that he transfer poor Bozier to my platoon, to which he willingly agreed, saying, "Take him, take him, my friend, I am sick to death of this German!"

Velikie Luki

We have arrived! We are here! These are our quarters, and it's all finished. The charming scenes of foreign lands and foreign ways have vanished. We shall no longer hear the greetings of the affable honest Germans. There will be no entrancing, charming Polish evening parties. Here everything is so pompous, so cold. Try to ask a peasant for a glass of water. For a whole minute he stands still, then starts out lazily, hardly moving, and finally he gives you the water, and as soon as you have drunk it, "Two kopecks for the trouble, master!" They are totally spoiled.

Our squadron is billeted in some sort of *Vyazovshchina*. What a harmonious name. One can pick out a rhyme right off, and a very suitable one. It is true that from boring quarters, smoky huts, mud, rain, and the cold autumn I have become so bad tempered I am irritated by everything. By the dirty peasants; why are they dirty? By the peasant women; why are they ugly? Why do they dress so repulsively? And they speak even more repulsively. For example, *svetsa, na petse, sotsyla*. Damn it. Who would think "*sotsyla*" for having done something. Nothing of the sort happened. The word is *iskala*.

A deathless death exists in this *Vyazovshchina,* without books, without society, lying all day on bunks under clouds of acrid smoke listening to fine autumn rain striking the little windows, which are glazed with mica or, what is even more nasty, with bladders. Oh the height of vileness! No, God be with them, with all the niceties of such billeting. I am going to headquarters.

Velikie Luki

Here, in any case, the smoke doesn't eat my eyes and I can look at God's world through clean glass! Every day G*** comes to me to recall the happy time spent in Hamburg and for the hundredth time to talk about his unforgettable Josephine, about the charming evening in which she, having accepted as a gift from him the thousand louis d'or which he had won, found him quite charming the whole week. But later her doors were always already locked before he came, and he, like an enamored Spaniard, came with a guitar in front of the house where this *jewel* lived. After several romances, sighs and similar stupidities, he stretched forth his hands to the silent stone mass and cried out just like Abelard, "refuge of God fearing, honest virgins!" And he related all this to me quite seriously, and with heavy sighs and brimming tears... O mad, mad G***!

Two Weeks Leave, 1816

"Otto Ottovich! Let me go to Peterburg for two weeks." Shtakelberg answered that this was impossible at present. "The time for leaves has passed and moreover the Emperor Himself is in Peterburg. However, you may go on a mission," he said, having thought a minute.

"What kind, Colonel? If it is not beyond my capacity, then do me the favor, give it to me."

"The regiment hasn't yet received from the Commissariat canvas, boots, armor, certain arms, harness, and thirty thousand in money. If you want to undertake to get all this and bring it to the regiment, then go, I'll give you a pass."

"Can I manage this mission, Colonel? I don't understand any of this."

"What's to understand? I will give you an experienced sergeant and some soldiers and they will do everything, and you will only have to take the thirty thousand from the Provision depot. Well, and in case there might be problems, consult with Burogo, he's the treasurer, and this is in his area."

"Very well, Colonel, I shall immediately go to Burogo and ask him, and if this mission is not beyond my capacity, then tomorrow, if you permit, I'll set off to Petersburg."

I couldn't get any sense out of Burogo. To my question about what I should do if I were detached to get supplies, he answered "Observe strict *honesty!*"

"How? Explain to me."

"No explanation is necessary. Be honest! That's all there is to it. I cannot give you different advice and admonitions, and there is no need for them."

"I don't need this. To be honest, I don't need either advice or your admonitions."

"Don't be too cocky, my friend. You are still young. All your chances in life have not passed you by. I know what I am saying. Be honest!"

Burogo is stubborn. I knew that if he was already harping on "Be honest, be honest" that he wouldn't say anything more. God be with him. Well, Shtakelberg did say that he would send me an experienced sergeant. I'll chance it and go.

Peterburg

I went straight to my uncle's apartment. He is still in the same place and still quite happy with it. My dear uncle has funny tastes! His apartment is on the Hay Market, and he says that he always has before him the most lively and diverse picture. Yesterday he led me up to the window. "Look, Alexander, isn't this a picturesque sight?" Thank God uncle had not said it was pretty. Then, without lying, I could not have agreed. But now my conscience is at peace.

I answered, "Yes, the view is picturesque!" adding mentally, "Only it is a scene from the Flemish School." I don't understand how it is possible to find something good in something unpleasant to the eyes. What is attractive in looking at a crowd of peasants, clumsy, coarse, badly dressed, surrounded by carts, tar, matting, and similar nastiness. That is the living picture on which my uncle has feasted his eyes for nine years in a row.

Today a concert is being given in the Philharmonic Hall. I will definitely go there. I think this will be something charming. They say that the orchestra consists of excellent musicians. True, I don't understand anything about music, but I love it more than anything. It acts upon me inexpressibly. There is no virtue, no great deed of which I could not feel capable when hearing sounds whose power I cannot explain nor understand.

I was sitting at the wall, below the orchestra, facing the audience. Next to me was sitting some person in a black frock coat, middle aged, with an important and noble appearance.

The hall was filled with women. They all seemed to me beautiful and beautifully dressed. I always like to look at women's fashions, although not for a fortune would I wear them. Although their cambric, satin, velvet, flowers, feathers and diamonds are seductively beautiful, my uhlan's cavalry jacket is better! In any case it suits me better, and surely it is said that the best taste is to dress as best suits each person.

Ladies continually arrived, and the rows of chairs were moved closer to ours—to mine and my neighbor's. "Look how close they are," I said, "Will we really have to give up our place to them?"

"I don't think so," he answered, laughing, "Our place isn't suitable for them."

"Well another row of seats has been added. One more and they will be at our knees!"

"And what's wrong with that?"

I fell silent and began to look again at the attire of the newly arrived ladies. Directly opposite me was sitting one with a pink beret and dress, gaunt, swarthy, but with a pleasant face and an intelligent physiognomy.

She seemed to be about thirty years old. Standing next to her chair was General Khrapovitsky.

Is that his wife? I looked at her steadily. There was something unusual in her appearance. Finally I turned to my neighbor. "May I ask who that lady in pink is directly across from us?"

"Mme. Khrapovitsky, the wife of the general who is standing next to her chair."

"I heard something...."

My neighbor didn't let me finish. "Yes, yes, we have few such heroines."

This testimonial assaulted my self-esteem. "It seems there was one other..."

Again I was interrupted. "Yes, there was, but that one is no longer alive. She died, she couldn't bear..."

Well that's news! Many times had I the occasion to hear my own life story, with all additions and changes, often inappropriate, but never yet had someone said directly to me that I had died! Where had this come from? How was it possible that word was flying around about my death when I was alive, personally known to the Tsar. However, let them think it is so. Maybe this is for the best. While these thoughts were flying about my head, I looked at my companion, and it seemed that he read my thought in my eyes.

"You don't believe it? I heard this from people who were related to her."

I didn't answer. Such graveyard conversation frightened me, and most of all I was afraid that he would notice how closely this concerned me. I didn't say another word to him until the concert ended.

As of today a week has passed since I arrived in Peterburg, and today I must begin my business. I went to present myself to the colonel on duty, Dobrov. This name suits him. He has such a kind face.

"When did you arrive?" he asked, as soon as I had finished the usual formal sound-off, by which we inform our superiors who we are, where we are from, and why. I answered that I had been in Peterburg more than a week.

"And you are reporting in only now! For this your head should be properly washed. Have you reported to the Prince?"

"Not yet."

"How is this possible! Come to me at eight in the morning, and I myself will go with you to the Prince."

From Dobrov I went to the Commissariat. Dolinsky, who was in charge, thought that I was a cadet just released from the corps, and was very surprised when I said that I already had ten years in the service.

My uhlans are masterful thieves, and I don't exaggerate. Every day they say to me, "Today we got so much of this and today we got so much of that, Your Honor, by economy." At first I didn't understand, but now I do: they accept canvas to be measured and immediately steal it. Burogo is a crank! Did he have this in mind when he insisted "Be honest!" That's funny. What can I do? Can one preach honesty to people who, like the Spartans, consider a clever theft a display of courage? We tell the uhlan: "Take care that your horse is well fed!" He reinterprets this order in his own way and takes care to steal oats in the fields. No, no, I am not going to fuss about this nonsense—let them steal! Who ordered Shtakelberg to give me this mission, which I don't understand? He said he would give me an experienced sergeant. Good luck! The thievery went even better when the experienced sergeant arrived. Now they say they'll get canvas for the whole infirmary by economy. I heard this while passing by the bales as they were tying them up. They disappeared totally, with the canvas and with the bales. My head ached from such unaccustomed exercises: to stand, to look, to count, and keep account.

Today I went at eleven to my boring duty, and, not finding any great need to stand where the goods were being received, I strolled along the passageways, stopping sometimes and leaning on the railing, letting my thoughts carry me away to places having no resemblance whatsoever to the Commissariat. On one of these pauses, a commanding shout resounded next to me: "Mr. officer!" I looked around. Behind me was standing some official in a uniform with braid on his collar, dry, tall, with a German face. "What do you wish?" I asked.

"From what regiment are you?" I told him. "You are here to receive goods?"

"Yes."

"How do you dare to begin taking them without letting me know? How do you dare not report to me?" Surprised by such a question from a person who, it seemed to me, was in the civil service, I answered that I was obliged to report only to my military superior.

"I am your superior now! Be so kind as to report to me, Sir! I order this in the name of the prince. And why do you not report to me about the progress of your receipt of goods? From you alone I know nothing, I receive nothing! And you alone I don't understand at all. How, how do you dare to speak to me so? I shall report you to the prince."

"I'll say the same thing in the prince's presence. I don't understand you, I don't know who you are, what right you have to demand reports from me, accounts, and why I must report to you." He fell silent.

"I am Counsellor P***! The prince instructed me to see that the gentlemen receiving goods should not waste their time and that the transfer proceed without delay. For this you must inform me every evening how much of what has been received. Now do you understand me, Mr. officer?"

"I understand."

"And so tomorrow deign to report to me for orders! I demand this in the name of the prince!"

"That is impossible. Tomorrow I must be at Colonel Dobrov's, and I'll go with him to the prince."

"No! You must go with me. I'll present you to the prince."

"Pardon me! Why should you present me? This must be done by my real superior, the military one." At these words P*** almost flew apart. He yelled, and in the prince's name ordered something else. But I no longer listened and left him to join my own people. Seeing that they would finish today, I returned to my uncle, to whom I related the amusing encounter in the passageway.

Next day I went to Dobrov, and from there with him to the prince. Our corps superior received me like anyone else: he heard who I was, why, and from where. When I had finished, he nodded his head slightly, and, not paying any more attention to me, left me free to do what I wished, to stand, to sit, to walk, to stay with him for a couple of hours, or to leave at once. I chose the latter and went to the Commissariat. There I found my people already at work. They again were receiving, measuring, and cheating. I didn't consider myself obligated to be a judge of this. Why do they give such a commission to a combat officer? I am not a treasurer, nor a quartermaster. If I take something incorrectly, let them complain about me.

Justifying myself in this manner, I went to Count Arakcheyev. While the duty officer went in to announce me, some staff officer entered. Seeing my free and easy gait in the count's vestibule, he became visibily upset, puffed himself up, and began to inspect me, measuring me with his eyes from head to toe. I paid no attention to this for about five minutes, but having approached the table to look at the book which was open there, I accidentally looked at him. He could not endure this disrespect. Injured pride was expressed on his face. How can a simple officer dare to walk about, dare to pick up a book, in one word, dare to move in the presence of a staff officer! Or dare not even to notice him when he should have stood in one place in a respectful posture without taking his eyes off his superior. All these words were printed on the face of the staff officer when he, with a contemptuous look asked me, "Who are you? And what are you?"

Ascribing his strange question to his inability to ask in a better way, I answered simply, "An officer of the Lithuanian Regiment." At that moment I was summoned to the count.

It is said that the count is very strict. No, he seemed to me to be very courteous and even affable. He came up to me, took me by the hand, and said that he was very pleased to meet me personally, that he was obliged to remind me that in accordance with my letters he had done everything without delay and with pleasure. I answered that I considered it my obligation to come to reiterate personally my gratitude for his kind attention. The count parted with me, assuring me of his willingness to do anything I might wish. Such politeness seemed quite at odds with the ubiquitous reports about his moroseness and unapproachability, as others say. The count, maybe, is only angry sometimes, and in that there is no great harm.

From the count I went to the family of N. N***, which loved me like one of their own. They were preparing to go to the theater. "Don't you want to go with us? Today they are presenting *Fingal*. You like tragedy, don't you?" I accepted this proposition with pleasure. At six the two sisters D*** arrived, gaunt old spinsters. "Oh, you are really going to the theater?"

"Yes. Do you want to go with us?"

"That won't inconvenience you?"

"Not at all."

At seven they announced that the cart was ready, and we left. I might have said that we poured onto the porch, for there were eight of us. The cart was a two seater. "How can we find enough room?" I asked with surprise.

"I'll arrange it," N.N.*** said, quickly seating me in the cart. "Sit tightly in the corner." This advice seemed unnecessary, since the remaining seven people pressed me tightly into this corner more than I cared to be, and unfortunately I had taken my cloak with me. I don't know by what unknown means N.N.*** seated us all so that we were able to sit quietly, did not muss our clothes, and did not suffocate, although we all were of proper height and size, that is, there were no dwarves among us nor any skeletons. "Your tactics are praiseworthy, honorable N.N.***," I thought.

Two guards officers arrived at the theater entrance at the same time as we did. One of the ladies in our party was a beauty, and unfortunately she had to get out of the carriage first. This circumstance put us in a critical situation. Seeing the beautiful woman, the guards stopped to look at her, and they were witnesses to a comic spectacle as an unending procession came forth from the two-seater cart, finally ending with an uhlan wrapped in a wide cloak.

The evening began comically and ended comically. *Fingal* is an excellent tragedy, but this day towards the end of one act an unexpected event suddenly turned it into a comedy. The tragedian, who usually played Fingal, was ill, and they gave his part to someone to whom the role was still new. He played it stiffly and hurriedly. But the person representing Starn was a real Starn. His acting aroused pity and surprise at the same time. It seemed to everyone that they were not watching an actor but the Tsar himself and the offended father. Apparently the excellence of his acting perplexed poor Fingal. He became confused. At the very moment when Moina must run onto the scene, the confused Fingal, hastening to seize

Oskar's sword, ran into Starn so clumsily that he tore off his beard! In a second the violent anger of the Tsar was stilled. The stalls burst out laughing. Moina, having run on stage, froze like a statue, and the curtain fell.

In the evening Dolinsky told me that P*** had complained to the prince. "Why?" I asked.

"In the first place you did not report to him, and secondly instead of reports you write simply notes about how much has been received."

"What about the prince?"

"Nothing. He kept quiet."

It couldn't be otherwise. P*** is complaining stupidly. Receipts of goods are never acknowledged by reports. And what a strange person. How is it that he can't understand it is wrong to expect this from a military officer.

I have been ordered to report tomorrow at the *Ordonans-gauz* at five in the morning. I'll enjoy going at night without knowing the way or whom to ask. At that hour it is the dead of night.

I was awakened at four o'clock. I dressed. "What should I do, Uncle? How can I find the *Ordonans-gauz?* Can you tell me?"

"I certainly can, now listen." Uncle began to relate in great detail and at length, and he made such an effort to give me a clear idea of my way that I understood nothing. Thanking uncle for his effort, I went at random. Passing Gostinny Dvor, I thought to pass closer to the shops under the roof. I was just about to cross the rope stretched along the shops when the frightful snarling of a dog stopped me and forced me to jump into the middle of he street. My journey at four in the morning along the empty streets of Peterburg to a destination I didn't know how to reach would have been very interesting for me had I not been upset by fear of being late or not arriving at the designated time at all. From uncle's lengthy account I remembered only that I had to go past Gostinny Dvor. But surely Gostinny Dvor would come to an end, and then where? I approached the last shop and was about to turn my path directly toward the palace, assuming that such a place as *Ordonans-gauz* would surely be located close by. Well, I can find out from a guard. The sound of a drozhky forced me to abandon all my plans. This was a conveyance driven by a coachman. I stopped it and the coachman, not awaiting my question, himself asked, "Are you going to the *Ordonans-gauz,* master?"

"Yes."

"Deign to be seated. I just now took an officer there."

"Move on as fast as possible." And that is all that was romantic about my voyage in the deep December night along the deserted streets of the vast town, armed to the teeth, intending to find a building to which I did not know the way. And all this instantly vanished, and now I am a typical officer riding quickly in a drozhky to the *Ordonans-gauz,* the least romantic place in the world and where I will receive some order delivered in a dry and commanding tone.

"Go on, please, faster. Is it still far?"

"It's right here," said the driver, stopping the horse at the entrance to a huge building over whose doors was a dark sign with the inscription *Ordonans-gauz.* I ran up the stairs and entered the hall. Here was a congregation of infantry and cavalry officers. An adjutant was sitting behind a table writing something. A fire was burning on the hearth, and I sat down beside it to await what was next. None of the officers was speaking to the others, and all of them silently walked about the hall or were standing at the hearth looking pensively at the fire, when suddenly this sleepy scene became animated. Zakrevsky entered. "Gentlemen!" At this word all the officers stood in a row. "Cavalry, forward, to the right!" And then we, four of us, a cuirassier, two dragoons, and one uhlan stood on the right side, directly in front of Zakrevsky. He looked at me very attentively twice while giving us our orders. "Report to Arsenyev, the commander of the Horse Guard Regiment." Finally they announced to us in detail that at the Horse Guards our soldiers would be given modified uniforms. We heard this out and dispersed. The cavalrymen went home, and the obedient infantry were sent directly to Arsenyev. I found this out, because at the entry they were making arrangements to go there, and they asked us, "And you, gentlemen, are you going with us?"

"I don't have time to do so," I answered.

I sent Rachinsky to the Horse Guard chancery to be measured for a new uniform. On returning he said to me, "Your Honor is ordered to report in person there."

"Where?"

"To Major Shaganov at the sewing shop." These trifles bored me. With difficulty I got rid of them. I went to Arsenyev's only once, and I told Shaganov that I would send an uhlan to him, that I had no need to be present during this, and that I had a quite different commission from my regiment. Having said this, I left.

Tomorrow I set off for the regiment. Two weeks of leave had passed. I spent them tediously. From morning to night in uniform, importuned, standing at attention, receiving directions, report there, report here! Never again will I go on such a leave.

A Trip to the Izhev Armament Factory

I didn't know how to use my four months' leave. In district towns there are few ways to spend it pleasantly, especially during the winter: boston, whist, whist, boston, pie, tasties, tasties, pie, those are the ways to free oneself from the superfluous hour which almost all of us have. For me not one of these ways was suitable. I don't like cards, and pie and tasties are good only for half an hour. I passed a month without being bored, however. Now I would talk with my father, my brother, my sisters, now I would walk in the forest, follow paths, make my way to the tops of mountains, now descend into ravines. Finally, having become acquainted with all places within twenty versts, having repeated everything both amusing and terrible and important and comic, and even having reread all of Radcliffe's horrors, I say that not only was I alone but that even my timepiece was *superfluous*. And two months of leave still remained, and to depart early would seem strange and somewhat out of the ordinary. So I decided to ask Papa if he would let me go somewhere for a couple of weeks. From my first words my solicitous father agreed: "That's a good idea, my friend," Papa said, "the arms factory is in our neighborhood, so go there. The man in charge, General Gren, is a good friend of mine, there is excellent company there consisting of the most educated, well-bred people. They have their own theater, music, many have choice libraries. So Godspeed, and I shall let you stay there over Christmas and New Years. When do you want to leave?"

"Tomorrow, if you permit me to do so."

"Well, aren't you in a bit of a hurry? We have to get a cart, because I don't have one for trips."

"Kazantsov has one ready, which was recently made. I'll buy it."

"What does he want for it?"

"Three hundred rubles."

"Tell them to bring it around. We'll have to look at it."

I sent for the cart, and both Papa and I thought that it was worth far more than the money which Kazantsov was asking, and I immediately gave him the money. The next day after breakfast I embraced and kissed all my family one after another, pressed to my heart the hands of the kindest of all fathers, kissed both of them, and biding them all goodbye again, threw myself into the conveyance. The troika, which had been shaking from the cold and impatience for some time, reared up and tore off at once, the runners squeaked, and the cart flew like the wind along the road which was smooth and hardened by a frost of thirty degrees.

At eleven o'clock I arrived at Colonel Tseddelman's gates. He was my father's old acquaintance. My inquiry as to whether I might stay with them was met with joyous cries of his two sisters-in-law, young maidens, whom I loved to distraction. They both sprang onto the porch, grabbed the cloak from my shoulders, threw it into the hands of a servant, and carried me off into the house. A quarter of an hour passed before Tseddelman finished embracing me, asking about my father's health, and offering his pleasant hospitality. Natalya and Maria did not let me out of their hands. They, that is both together, would suddenly start talking, one would interrupt the other, so that I didn't know whom to listen to.

"Stop it! You'll drive him crazy," Tseddelman said, laughing and trying to free me from their grasp. Finally the joyous rapture of my friends quieted down somewhat, and as they had already sat down to eat when I arrived, they invited me to have supper and again sat down. In the course of supper they related to me in succession the entire mode of the various diversions at the factory, the chief of which was the theater.

"Who are the actors?" I asked.

"The general's son and many other officials."

"And do the ladies act?"

"Not one of them."

"And who plays the feminine roles?"

"Well, however it turns out. The male roles are excellently performed, because young Gren, Smirnov, and Davydov are actors such as you seldom see on the stage, even in the capital."

"What sort of plays do you prefer to present?"

"Comedies and opera."

"Opera?"

"Yes, and what operas, what voices, what music!"

"Well, this will surely be interesting to see. I am delighted that I thought to come here. Do you have performances often?"

"Twice a week."

"Is young Gren married?"

"He's married to a beauty." After dinner Natalya and her friend wanted to tell me more about various happenings in their small kingdom, but Tseddelman led them both away, saying "Until tomorrow, until tomorrow! Not everything at once. Let him see something for himself. I hope you will be our guest."

"Until you become bored with me."

"In that case you will stay with us for your whole life. Here is your room. I wish you a peaceful sleep."

I remained at the door while Tseddelman and both maidens, having crossed the hall, disappeared into the opposite room. Then, opening the door to my room, I expected to find heat and light in it, and I was very surprised to find neither. From the opening of the door the cold of

Greenland wafted on me, and in the darkness only the windows showed white, frozen more than an inch thick. My confusion was interrupted at that moment by the arrival of my servant with a candle in one hand and a brazier in the other.

"Aren't there any rooms warmer than this? This is just the same as outside."

"What's to be done, sir. It is impossible to heat this room. They always give it to guests, not because they want to freeze them but because it is the most suitable for them: it is separated from the owners, is adjacent to the hall, it has the best bed and its own entrance. Its only fault is that it is as cold as a dog house on a winter night."

Listening to my servant's nonsense, I entered the room. The bed was made up with wolf and bear skins. The servant set down the brazier and put a small basin with alcohol on it, which he immediately lit. "There, sir, this minute you will be warm for a whole half hour. That's long enough to undress and get into bed, and you'll be warm among such a multitude of furs." I went to the bed desiring to look at this couch of animal skins. Raising the top fur, I was surprised and pleased to see in the middle of the wolf skin a charming puppy six weeks old. He was sleeping, rolled up in a ball.

Turning to the servant to ask where this beautiful little animal had come from, I noted some sort of stupid-triumphant look on his face, from which I immediately guessed that it was he who had done me this unexpected favor. "Where did you get it?" I asked.

"On the street. Some boys were tormenting it and they abandoned it. He began to freeze and could hardly crawl when I found him and picked him up at once. If this doesn't suit you, then permit me to keep him myself."

"No, let him stay with me." I sent the servant off, undressed, and lay down to sleep, having first taken into my arms the dear little creature, tiny, defenseless, and gifted from nature with such a capacity for love which people never achieve, notwithstanding whatever refinement of sensibilities.

My servant was right when he said that the furs would make me hot. I slept not more than an hour and a half and awakened from the whine of the dear little pup. It had fallen off the bed. Picking it up, I again put it next to myself under the fur cloak. But for him and for me it became unbearably hot. He climbed out on top, stretched out on the skins, breathing heavily, although in the chamber it was extremely cold. Clearly he wanted to drink, and therefore the heat of his natural fur and the heat of the skins made him unbearably hot. He kept darting around the bed, falling off it, walking around the floor and whining. Each time I got up and groped for him under the bed, lay down again. Finally I became quite unhappy with my acquisition. Come morning, I shiveringly dressed in my Lappland and hastened as never before. Finishing my toilette in five minutes, I grabbed my little comrade in my arms and went to Tseddelman's family. They were already at the tea table.

"What is this delight?" both maidens cried out as soon as they saw my pup. "Where did you get it? Did you bring it with you? Why didn't you tell us yesterday? Where was it?"

"This homeless orphan was condemned to death yesterday by your street scamps, but fate thought otherwise and so it found itself in my bed in the middle of the half dozen furs which formed it."

"Yes, as to furs, were you warm?"

"It goes without saying that lying there in the middle of furs was not only warm but even stuffy, but there are no words to express what it was like when I had to get up and dress. You must experience it yourselves."

"How is that? Certainly we gave orders to heat your room with spirits while you were still in bed."

"Well, obviously I didn't give anyone time to fulfill your order. I never lie in bed once I have awakened. I immediately get up and dress."

Tseddelman interrupted our pointless conversation by asking me if I didn't want to go with him to the general.

"With pleasure, dear Colonel, let us go!"

"And meanwhile I shall take your little beauty in my care," said Maria, and took the pup from my hands. "She must be washed," she said, carrying her off.

A sleigh was provided, which here is called *poshevni*. It is a rather poor vehicle and ugly, at least to my eyes. A Tatar with an angry expression was sitting on the driver's seat. He looked at both of us with an expression of hatred. We got in.

"Why is your coachman so gloomy? Is he ill?"

"Oh, no. That's his usual expression. He only looks that way, but in fact he is a very fine fellow. I love these people! In many respects the Tatars are better than our own people...." Tseddelman was riding his hobby horse: he had some kind of funny attraction to Tatars, and, having begun to praise them, he did not quickly conclude his panegyric. Meanwhile we traveled at a very quiet trot.

"Be that as it may, honorable Colonel, but why are we going almost at a walk? Its twenty-five degrees of frost, so instead of this parade pace can't you order us to fly like the wind?"

"What's the matter with you? God forbid. Sharyn will be in despair and will simply not obey. He loves horses more than anything man can love."

I said nothing. It was still far to the general's place, and the frost was insupportable. I decided that without the acquiescence of Sharyn or Tseddelman, I would make the horses run, and I began to make clicking noises and cluck as one does to make the horses more lively. This proved successful. The horses set up a good trot. The side horse began to shake the yoke and jump about.

"What's happening? What's this, hold them back, Sharyn! Hold them back, brother."

I stopped, but when Sharyn checked the horses, then I started my actions again, and with the same result.

"I don't understand what's the problem with my horses today. Why are they running," Tseddelman said. Sharyn became angry and grumbled something mentioning the *devil.* He didn't suspect that I was the devil. Neither Sharyn nor Tseddelman were able to hear the encouragement I was giving the horses. The former was deaf, and the latter too muffled up. Finally clicking and clucking, admonishing and being astonished, jumping and weaving, we flew to the general's doorway.

Old Gren received me very kindly. He was one of those straightforward, solicitous and at the same time strict persons whose service is so useful to our government in all circumstances. They usually fulfill their duties diligently and exactly, have a good understanding of their duty because they methodically learn what it's all about. They are loved by their subordinates, because they correct them, punish them, and reward them in a fatherly way. They are respected by the Government, because they serve as a strong support to all its decisions. Such was old Gren, and to these virtues he added the qualities of cordial hospitality.

"Oh, hello, hello, my exceptional guest," he said, embracing me. "Is your father well? Are you not ashamed for having been absent so long?" "Petya! Petya," he cried to his son, "What is our theater doing tomorrow?"

"Opera," young Gren answered.

"Which?"

"The Miller."

"Are all the roles assigned?"

"All of them."

"What a pity. And I wanted you to become part of our troupe," Gren said, turning to me with a smile. I answered that I would willingly take a part in some comedy.

"Well, that's marvelous! What play is for Sunday?" His son answered that they would pay *The Young Hopeful.** "Oh, there are lots of parts. You may choose one of them."

Young Gren very politely proposed to me to chose any role for myself. "I will order a copy for you, because you need to learn it by heart for the rehearsal."

I asked what role he himself usually played.

"Kuteykin."

I couldn't help but laugh imagining this handsome and well built young officer in a clerk's smock with a wisp of hair on the nape of his neck.

"Well, I'll take Pravdin." Gren began to laugh as well.

Returning to Tseddelman's, my first concern was to find out about my foundling. I didn't recognize him, as he has become so charming after his bath. His fur was long, soft, gleaming white like snow, except for his ears,

*A satire by Fonvizin, *trans.*

which were dark brown. His little muzzle was pointed, big eyes, black, and, in addition, an unexpected charm, black eyebrows. At this moment he had just come out from under the cloak where he had been sleeping all cuddled up, and as it was hot, in order to breathe more freely, he opened his little mouth and the rosy little tongue, which, along with his black eyes, brows and little nose, made him such a charming creature that I could not feast my eyes on him enough, I couldn't love him enough, and all day I carried him in my arms.

"What name are you going to give him?" both of the maidens asked.

"Amour, obviously. Could such a beauty be called anything else?"

I spent three weeks with Tseddelman, and for all of this time I was his most diligent stoker. I always slept in that same chamber, which because of the impossibility of making it warm they stopped heating at all. Naturally after getting up and dressing in such cold, I couldn't get warm all day, and so all day I worried that the stoves were well stoked and dampered hot. This latter was strictly forbidden by Tseddelman. It always seemed too warm for him, although his house was the coldest, and he even prided himself on this among all the other houses. As proof of this was the fact that his wife and both sisters from morning to night went about in warm dressing gowns. It was amusing to see Tseddelman going from one stove to another, putting his hand on the dampers, and exclaiming, "Oh, my God, how hot they are!" and quickly closing them. And I followed him and quickly opened them. Every evening he instructed the worker, "Less fuel," and every morning this worker received a tip from me to put in "more fuel," and it goes without saying that the request and the money won out over the threats and orders. Tseddelman said that he didn't know where to escape from the heat, and that he just couldn't understand what imp had possessed his workers, who despite all prohibitions stoked his stoves past all endurance.

In the course of these three weeks my pup grew a bit and became even prettier. Needless to say he was inseparable from me, except when I went to the theater or to the general's, when I would give him into the care of one of Tseddelman's women, asking her not to pet him and not to feed him when I was not there. I didn't want anyone to have a right to my Amour's love, so all this love would be mine alone.

However, I took measures that my dog would not lack solicitude. Before leaving the yard, I fed him until he was full, played with him, fondled him, and finally put him on the bed, and, when he had fallen asleep, I would leave him in Anisya's care.

Along with the end of the holidays, Christmas games, dances, rehearsals and performances, the time arrived to return home. Setting the day of departure for the next day, I went to the general's to pass the entire day with him. "Why do you want to leave so soon?" the kind Gren asked.

"It will be dull for father without seeing me for so long."

"Well, then go with God! I can't argue with that." Parting with me, the general mentioned that he wanted to give me something he knew would be very dear to me. At his order his servant brought me a little steel hammer of excellent craftsmanship. "There, Alexandrov," the general said giving it to me, "I give you this little hammer. You will agree that I couldn't give you anything more valuable when I tell you that it was made for Emperor Alexander." I didn't let him finish, seized the little hammer, kissed it and pressed it to my breast.

"There are no words to express my gratitude, General, for such a gift."

"Don't you want to know how it chanced that this didn't serve the purpose for which it was designated, and having been made for a powerful Monarch is now conveyed to his protégé?"

"Be so kind, explain! General, you are kind to me beyond all due."

"Well, then listen. The Sovereign Emperor was disposed to inspect our factories Himself. In such cases the Great Visitor is usually shown all the work in whose manufacture He takes interest. That is why this little hammer was made, so that the Sovereign might pound several times with it on a strip of red hot iron. After that they would put a stamp on the hammer with indication of the time of this occurrence and preserve it for all time in memory of the visit and labor of the Most August Father of Russia. But as this hammer came out not quite so good as it should have, I gave orders to make another and kept this with me, and it has been kept here until it reached the hands of the person who is loved by the Tsar Father incomparably more than anyone else."

Having thanked the general again for the gift, for the anecdote, the wonderful reception, and his fatherly love, I said goodbye to him, probably for ever.

I found Papa occupied with the dispatch of mail, and although I knew that he did not like to be disturbed at this time, I could not restrain myself from putting the little hammer in front of him. Father was startled, and was about to become angry, but, seeing that it was I, he satisfied himself by saying only, "Oh, uhlan, when will you learn better. Is it proper to frighten your old father?"

"I had no such intention, dear Papa. On the contrary, I wanted to make you happy. Do you know what this hammer is?"

"Tell me later. I don't have time to listen. Go to your sister." I was about to leave. "Take the hammer."

"No, Papa, let it lie in front of you! This is a precious object! You will learn later." Father waved his hand, and I ran to my sister with my Amour, which I immediately put on her knee.

"Oh, what a delight. What a beautiful pup. Is it not a present for me?" Cleopatra said, caressing the entranced Amour.

"No, little sister, excuse me. I wouldn't give him to anyone for anything. He is going with me to the regiment."

"How is that possible."

"I will, without fail."

"Well, then take him from me. There's no reason to pet him if he isn't to be mine."

"Yes, I don't advise it. I shall be jealous."

"That's nothing new for you. You always want exclusive affection."

"And who doesn't want that?" My sister fell silent and sulked a bit. I took my little dog and went to my own room to wait until Papa finished his business.

Hearing the story of the hammer, my father took it and said that this was too valuable for him to permit me to carry it everywhere with me and that is should remain with him. There was nothing to do but acquiesce. I looked again at the gleaming, smoothly polished handle whose destiny had at first been so great and gave it to my father, saying that I was very pleased to see him the possessor of this thing.

With every day I become more attached to my Amour. How could one not love him? Meekness has an invincible power over our hearts, even in an ugly animal, but what if the best, the truest, and the finest of all looks into your eyes with meek submission, follows all your movements, lives only for you, and can't for a minute be parted from you, which would give its life for you. Be unjust to it, beat it for nothing, terribly, even inhumanly, and it will lie at your feet, lick them, and, not at all angry at your cruelty, will await only a single caressing look in order to jump into your arms, embrace you with its paws, lick you and spring about. Oh, the best and most unhappy of animals. You alone love as we have been commanded to love, and you alone suffer more from the crying injustice of man. If someone suspects that poison has been put into his food, he will give it to a dog in order to make certain. If a dog becomes old in his master's house, serving him as nature intended, he will replace it with a young one. And what does the person do who is replacing it? He kills it for the skin! If a borzoi hunts poorly, hang it! Why is this so, why?

The miserable fate of the dog has even become proverbial, although of all animals it alone loves man. A horse, which is a noble beast, will indifferently smash its rider's head. A cat will scratch out someone's eyes. Given a chance, a bull will gore you no matter how well you have fed it or petted it. Only the unmatched friend of man, the dog, for a stale piece of bread remains true and devoted until death. Sometimes I thoughtlessly punish my meek, unprovokable Amour. The poor little darling. How he curled himself around my legs, lay down, crawled, and finally sat up, looking at me with his beautiful black eyes with such an expression of meekness and sadness that, almost in tears, I would reproach myself for my injustice. I would take him on my knees, pet him, kiss him, and he instantly would begin to play again. Not for one minute did my Amour leave me. Wherever I was, he was always lying next to me on the floor, or sitting at the window, on the chair, on the couch. But without exception next to me, and without exception on something that belonged to me, for example, on a kerchief, gloves, or my cloak. Without this he was not content.

Once at dawn I let him out of my chamber and waited until he would ask to come into the room, but a quarter of an hour passed and he did not return. I became very disturbed and went to look for him in the courtyard. He was nowhere. I called. Nothing! Deathly afraid, I sent my servant to look for him in the streets. A whole hour passed in tormenting expectations and vain searching. Finally my dog arrived and sat down outside the gates. Hearing his bark, I looked out the window and couldn't help but laugh, seeing him lift up his muzzle and howl like a grown animal. But I paid dearly for this laughter! My heart even now constricts at the memory of this howl! This was a premonition. I took my runaway into my chamber, and, seeing that he was all wet from the dew, I put him on a pillow and covered him with a laprobe. He went right to sleep, but alas! His evil fate was not asleep. In an hour I dressed and as usual decided to take a walk. Something told me that I would walk alone. But when do we listen to secret premonitions, they are so quiet, so modest. I took the robe off the sleeping dog. "Let's go for a walk, Amour!" Amour jumped up and sprang about. We went. He ran in front of me.

Within an hour I was carrying him in my arms, pale, trembling in all my limbs. He was still breathing. But how? His breath passed through two huge wounds made by the teeth of a monster dog. Amour died in my arms. From that time it often happened that I danced all night and laughed a great deal, but true joy was never in my soul. It lay in the grave of my Amour. Many will find this strange, perhaps worse than strange. Be that as it may, but the death of my little friend brings involuntary tears to my eyes amidst the happiest gatherings. I cannot forget him!

I am leaving today. Father, parting with me, said, "It is not the time to leave me. I am old. I need peace and someone to take over management of affairs. Think about this." I was frightened with such a proposition. It had seemed to me that I would never have to put aside the sword, and particularly at my age. What was I to do at home? To condemn myself so early to the monotonous cares of management. But Father desires this. His old age. Oh, there is nothing for it. I have to say goodbye to everything, my shining sword, my good horse, friends, a happy life, drills, parades, cavalry formations, galloping, slashing, to all, to all an end. All will become silent as if it never had been, and only unforgettable memories will accompany me to the wild shores of the Kama river, to those places where my childhood flowered, where I conceived my unusual plan!!

Past happiness! fame! danger! noise! glitter! my life of seething activity! *Goodbye!*